THE WOODWORKER
BOOK OF JOINERY

THE WOODWORKER
BOOK OF JOINERY

ARGUS BOOKS

**Argus Books
Argus House
Boundary Way
Hemel Hempstead
Hertfordshire HP2 7ST
England**

First published by Argus Books, 1990

© in this collection, Argus Books, 1990

ISBN 1 85486 043 7

Phototypesetting by Croxsons of Chesham, Buckinghamshire.
Printed and bound in Great Britain by Dotesios Printers Ltd, Trowbridge, Wiltshire.

CONTENTS

Introduction

The first issue of *Woodworker* magazine appeared in 1901. Since then the magazine has grown in quality and stature, such that it is now regarded as one of the world's leading woodworking magazines. With its lively and informative mix of features, articles, projects and advice, it is regular and essential reading for woodworkers worldwide.

Now for the first time, our sister company, Argus Books, has gathered together in one series the best of *Woodworker*. The selection has been made mainly from more recent issues of *Woodworker* in order to provide the reader with a comprehensive and up-to-date overview of each particular subject. Thematically arranged, with the first two titles on *Turning* and *Joinery*, the books cover a wide range, from the practical to the more whimsical, and will be of interest to all engaged in this fascinating craft of ours.

I am pleased to commend this selection and am sure that, like the magazine itself, the books will be an indispensable addition to your woodworking library.

Nick Gibbs
Editor *Woodworker*

Wooden Wonder

' . . . I turn green and yellow with envy when I see the Mosquito. The British knock together a beautiful wooden aircraft that every piano factory over there is building . . . There is nothing the British do not have.'

Reichsmarshall Hermann Goering

Truly classic aircraft have often been produced in the face of official policy. As a nation we are fortunate to have had individuals and companies who have put private money and resources into a project they believed in; one such was Geoffrey de Havilland, whose foresight and determination brought us the Mosquito, so aptly nicknamed the 'Wooden wonder'.

Before WW2, the concept of an unarmed bomber was considered by officialdom as unthinkable. De Havilland's design was not only unarmed, but also made of wood, which was considered an equally retrograde step. All aircraft at that time were metal.

Design work on the Mosquito started in late 1938. The design team moved a few miles away from de Havilland headquarters, with the idea of working unhindered by officialdom and away from the main (bomb-threatened) factory. Thanks mainly to Sir Wilfred Freeman, Air Member for Development and Production at the Air Ministry (at the time virtually de Havilland's only ally in the government), a contract for 50 Mosquitoes was awarded to de Havilland on 1 March 1940 — even though construction of the aircraft hadn't started.

Why was it made of wood? Not only was there a saving in weight, but it could also be built by the semi-skilled labour employed by furniture manufacturers and coachbuilders all over the country. This left the aircraft industry's own workforce to get on with vital Spitfires and Lancasters, and it also saved valuable metal. Other advantages of using wood were that the initial design stages could be cut down and the prototype built quickly, so it went into production very quickly — less than two years from the start of design work to the aircraft entering service.

The Mosquito design had many special features, including the plywood and balsa-wood sandwich of the fuselage, a simple construction for a monocoque (where frame and skin share the stresses). The fuselage was built in two halves (which simplified equipment installation), each half formed over a concrete or mahogany mould shaped to the interior. First the structural members were located in recesses in the mould to form the internal stiffening or bulkheads of the fuselage, then the inner three-ply birch skin, 1.5 and 2mm thick, was applied. Broad flexible steel bands were used to cramp the skin down over the mould.

The fuselage skin was made of a number of plywood panels scarfed and glued together, getting narrower towards the nose with its sharper double curvatures. Balsa strips were laid over the inner skin and then glued, and the steel bands applied again, after which the balsa was smoothed to the contours; the outer plywood skin was attached, and after the glue had set and the equipment was assembled in them, the two halves were bonded together on special jigs with wooden cramps.

The Mosquito wing was made in one piece with a front and rear spar and stressed skin covering. The top surface was of two birch plywood skins, interspaced by square-section stringers which ran the length of the wing. On the undersurface, the outboard panels were of only one ply skin, while the centre section of the wing (which housed the fuel tanks) was made of stressed balsa-plywood panels which formed the tank doors. Both main spars were box construction, separated by interspar ribs made of spruce laminations.

The tailplane had two spars separated by inter-spar ribs and covered with plywood, while the flaps consisted of a nose section formed by the leading edge end spar, connected by ribs to the trailing edge. The fin was also of two-spar construction with inter-spar ribs. All the surfaces were given a covering of Madapolam (fabric) using red dope, and then the camouflage was painted.

By November 1940, the hastily-constructed prototype was ready and made its maiden flight on 25 November, piloted by Geoffrey de Havilland Jnr. Three more Mosquitoes were constructed before production moved to the main factory at Hatfield.

Once the Mosquito had proved its worth, Hatfield couldn't cope with the demand, so de Havilland's factory at Leavesden, near Watford, went over to Mosquito production, followed by Standard Motors at Coventry, Percival Aircraft at Luton and Airspeed at Portsmouth; after the war another line was set up at Chester.

Before the end of 1942, a production line had been set up in de Havilland's Toronto factory, and in 1944 one started in Australia, in the company's Sydney works.

Wooden Wonder

A total of 7,781 of all models of Mosquito were built before 1950, when production finished.

There were nearly 50 different models of Mosquito, used in every role imaginable. 'Multi-role combat' is a modern military term, but the Mosquito's flexibility pre-dated it by 40 years. As a bomber with just two crew, the plane could carry as great a bomb load faster, farther and higher than some of the four-engined bombers with crews of up to 11. It was equally successful as a 'pathfinder', and the night-fighter version protected Britain by night, virtually stopping enemy activity. It was also successful against the V-1 flying bomb. Our heavy bombers on their raids over Europe were protected by the Mosquito day and night, and by November 1944 Mosquitoes had claimed 659 enemy aircraft and over 500 flying bombs. Fighter bombers, land-based marine combat aircraft, photo reconnaissance planes, even mail planes, training and torpedo bombers — the Mosquito played all the roles. They went to many post-war foreign air forces, and even the Russians got at least one!

It wasn't until 1953 that the weary planes were phased out of front-line service; however, they still operated in secondary roles and a number were towing targets as late as 1963.

In the 1940s and 50s many surplus Mosquitoes were bought up by civilian operators for survey and experimental work, where they ranged the world carrying out their tasks. Indeed, there were cases of civilian Mosquitoes carrying out clandestine work for the CIA over South-East Asia in the early 1950s!

Thanks to its wooden construction, some 28 examples of the Mosquito still exist today — a healthy number, when you think that not one example of many other famous designs now exist. It's partly due, of course, to the fact that a wooden airframe was no use to the scrap metal man.

Today, many of these 28 are now being rebuilt, and currently two are airworthy, while a third is due to fly in Canada in the very near future. On 15 May, 1959, the unofficially preserved prototype was officially enshrined in its own little hangar at Salisbury Hall, its original Hertfordshire birthplace, as a memorial to all those that had built, flown and maintained it. It now forms the centrepiece of the Mosquito Aircraft Museum.

The Mosquito rebuild

I recovered the fuselage of a Mosquito FB.VI (the widely-used fighter-bomber version) from Delft Technical University in Holland in 1978. This particular plane served with nos. 605 and 4 Squadrons, entering service in 1945 and seeing at least one operational mission before the war ended. Although some components were missing, and some parts carefully sectioned out of the fuselage to show construction, the fuselage was in very good condition. I

● *After 20 years in Israel, the wing is resurrected. A bit of work to do!*

● *The wing comes to the Mosquito Aircraft Museum. Some of the fuselage still remains*

decided to try and make up a complete plane — its serial number was TA122 — but with components now like gold dust, this was clearly going to be no easy task!

The biggest missing component was the one-piece wing, which I found in Israel, and which was generously flown back to England free by El Al in July 1980. It remained in the Museum's workshops while we concentrated on our second Mosquito, but in spring 1985 work began on rebuilding the wing under the direction of Colin Ewer, who had helped build Mosquitoes after the war at Hatfield. This rebuild is probably the most ambitious restoration task undertaken by a private,

voluntary aviation museum in the UK.

Colin's task isn't an easy one. All the plywood skins have rotted away, as have all the trailing and leading edges. The spars also need repairs in several places and almost all of the 32 ribs will either need repair or replacement. Several feet of the starboard wing and the port wing-tip are missing altogether, while all four of the underwing tank doors require major repair work. The spruce stringers, which run outwards, dividing the two top wing-skins, had become exposed when the skins rotted away, but are still attached to the ribs and most of them are good enough to be used again.

The first task was to remove the old plywood facings on both spars, which were in good condition. Colin decided to start rebuilding the centre section, and then work his way out on both sides, the best way to retain the shape of the wing. First of all, the stringers were removed and both rib no. 1s, which were in poor shape, were taken out. The front and rear spars were then repaired as far as 'rib no. 2' on either side, and new plywood facings were attached to the inside and outside of both spars. Two unused rib 1s, which had been donated to the Museum many years ago, were then fitted in place of the damaged ones, and at the time of writing both rib 2s were almost repaired. The metal undercarriage brackets have all been refurbished and re-attached to the wing.

The material being used in the rebuild follows the original specifications laid down by de Havilland. The most expensive part of the project is the aero-grade Canadian birch plywood, a top-quality 8x4ft sheet of which costs about £300! Finnish birch to a similar specification isn't quite so expensive. It's estimated that the wing rebuild will need some 60 sheets of birch plywood of various thicknesses, so we were grateful when British Plywood Manufacturers Ltd of Enfield, Middlesex (suppliers of the original plywood) generously offered us a substantial discount. We are also indebted to Humbrol Ltd for the Cascamite glue, much of which will be needed before the project is completed!

And of course we need help. Please get in touch if you want to be involved in the rebuild of one of the classic aeroplanes of all time!

Making Mosquitoes

Ken Taylor writes: When I joined F. Wrighton & Sons as a 16 year-old apprentice in 1942, production of the Mosquito fuselage was already well established and was followed a few months later by the wing. Considering the all-wood construction of the aircraft, the mill was quite small and the machinery very basic — a hand-fed rip saw, a surfacer, a thicknesser, two small dimension benches, a bandsaw, a spindle, a router and two bobbin sanders.

The spruce, balsa and ply were inspected and check-weighed on delivery to determine moisture content and any material not up to spec would be rejected. The spruce was of superb quality and was a pleasure to cut, but as there wasn't dust extraction on the saw the machinist soon began to look like a snowman. Because of the sharp taper of the wing, every wing rib was a different size, so many settings were required on the dimension bench to produce a batch of components. Each batch was inspected, and if it was within the specified tolerances, it was given the AID (Aircraft Inspection Department) stamp and sent for assembly.

The ply for the skins was cut oversize on the bandsaw and then brought to size on the router using very accurate jigs supplied by

● *The fuselage of TA122 is offloaded at the MAM, February 1978*

● *The inner skin and between-skin structural members being fitted; in the former behind, numbered steel bands are set on for bonding*

British Aerospace

de Havillands. There were no tungsten-tipped cutters in those days, so frequent regrinding was necessary because the ply was bonded with resin glue. The edges of the skins were then scarfed on the bobbin sander, marked with a serial number and identified with the fuselage assembly position.

The balsa was machined into planks ⅜in thick, but left quite random in width and length — generally they were 3-4in wide and from 2-5ft in length.

The next shop contained the jigs for the fuselage shells. They were made of mahogany, and well polished to prevent the ply or balsa sticking to the jig. The turn-buckles which secured the band clamps were attached to the jig supports and were placed edge-to-edge across the shell, running the whole length of the fuselage. The bands had holes punched over their entire length to let out surplus glue when

the balsa planking was being clamped down on the shell. Large bradawls were pushed through the holes into the balsa so the excess glue could squeeze out and be washed off. The bands were applied three times; first when the inner skin was being fixed to the formers and longerons (which fitted into slots in the jig); second when the balsa planking was being glued down, and third when fixing the outer skin. The completed shell would be lifted off the jig bodily by the jig crew, and the two half-shells would then be joined temporarily with special clamps so no misalignment or twisting could occur. They were then taken to de Havilland's for finishing and fitting out into finished aircraft.

The one-piece wings were assembled in vertical steel jigs with the trailing edge upwards. The main spars were delivered pre-fabricated, and the ribs were attached by gluing and screwing plus hundreds of

Wooden Wonder

hand-cramps. The ply skins (the upper one was reinforced by douglas-fir strips) were then glued and screwed to the ribs and spars with brass screws. The screws were close together and it was all hands to the 'Yankee' pump screwdrivers — no electric or air-operated drivers then! After our work on them, the wings were taken to the finishing department for covering in Madapolam (a fine linen-type fabric) which was stuck in place with red cellulose dope applied by brush.

Special mention should be made of the adhesive, which was known as 'Beetle Cement', a type of urea formaldehyde manufactured by B.I.P. Ltd. This adhesive was used in the furniture trade just before the war. Two types of Beetle cement were used; type 'W' for bonding the plywood laminations and type 'A' for gluing the balsa to plywood and for general assembly work. Cement 'W' used a special hot hardener so the glue-line could stand the three-hour boil test which was required for aircraft use. Cement 'A' was a special gap-filling type where joints might not be in close contact while the glue cured. As heat could not be applied, it had to set properly at normal shop temperature.

As far as I know, things went as the designers intended; large numbers of inspectors made sure they did! At the end of the war, F. Wrighton's went back to making furniture. ∎

British Aerospace

● **Above:** *The two-halved construction of the Mosquito fuselage;* **left:** *fitting out FB.V1s at Hatfield*

Trouble-free curving

For those amongst us daunted and defeated by sophisticated geometry, Stan Thomas has no-sweat solutions to curved stairbuilding and handrailing

There seems to be a traditional antipathy to the word 'curved' in connection with stairbuilding. Call it a 'geometrical' stair if you will, but they certainly weren't geometrical in the workshops of my apprenticeship days; the men I worked with didn't know of the *existence* of geometry. But I and my peers sweated blood over it, for even though no full-sized curved stair was ever made by geometry in the bread-and-butter workshops, it was a regular City & Guilds subject, and if you wanted your 'Final', you just had to get down to it.

The non-geometrical stair

Back in the sixties I had a shop to fit out, including a stair up to the first floor. It was an ideal situation for a curved stair, but the economics wouldn't go to that, so I figured out a compromise; an open-tread curved stair on straight strings (!),and very nice it looked too. It was quite non-technical to construct.

The first move was to mark the area of the first-floor landing out on the ground floor (fig. 1). From this, at points corresponding to the width of the stairs (36in), I struck two arcs of radius 12 and 15ft respectively. The total rise was divided into 14, which gave a riser height of 7¾in, and applying the 2R + T = 24in (twice riser height plus tread width should always equal 24in) formula at the walking line, I got the requisite tread width; 13 at 8½in.

Next, lines were struck from the 'focal' point, intersecting on the tread points of the walking-line arc, and terminating on the outer arc. This determined the outline of each tread. Then the strings were marked in, the outer one with the outer faces of its extreme ends intersecting the arc on nosing 1 and the back edge of tread 13, forming a chord. The inner string was drawn parallel to this with the centre of its length on the inner face touching the inner arc, forming a tangent.

For geometrical reasons — note the tread cuts vary for each step — the strings couldn't be set out with a pitch-board. Each string was given its top and bottom cut, and placed in its 'working' position; the rise cuts were then picked up by plumb-bob off the floor plan (fig. 2). It will be seen from fig. 1

that treads 1 and 13 overhang the inner string by about 10in, and that this measurement decreases as the centre of stairs is reached to about 2in. The reverse occurs on the outer string. It may also be seen that the vertical cuts — 'riser' cuts — of the strings are, at rise 7, square to the face of the timber, and that this angle of 90° varies as you go down and up from obtuse to acute. With the full-size setting-out, there is of course no problem in finding these angles. And since there was so much of the string cut away — they were 11x2in — 1½x¼in mild steel reinforcing strips were screwed to the bottom edge of each string.

The handrailing for a stair of such a 'slow' curve was quite simple. In this stair they terminated as shown in fig. 3. They could have run into an ordinary newel, of course.

So there is an attractive, bona fide, curved stair of simple non-geometrical construction, ideal, I would say, for any domestic situation. DIY 'Geometrical stairbuilding' if you like!

Non-geometrical handrailing

What makes handrailing so difficult is the fact that besides having to be curved, it has to be twisted, so its top surface anywhere is horizontal along any radius line of the curve in section (fig. 4). This is the basis of handrailing by 'normal sections'. However, a simple way of surmounting this little problem is to make the handrail circular in section — 'mopstick'. Such a rail can look very attractive, and we are not now bothered by this tiresome 'twist', or 'twist

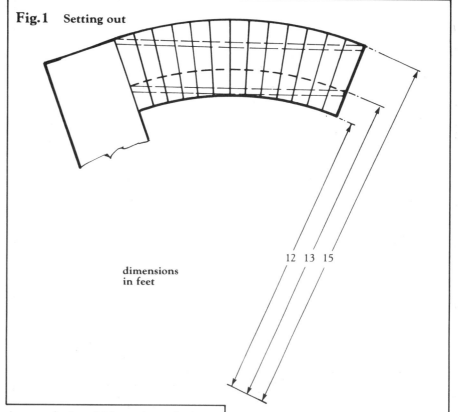

Fig.1 Setting out

dimensions in feet

12 13 15

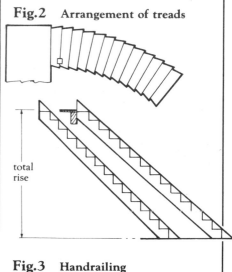

Fig.2 Arrangement of treads

total rise

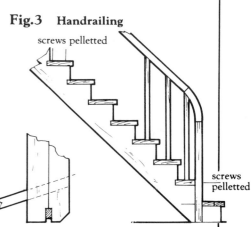

Fig.3 Handrailing

screws pelletted

screws pelletted

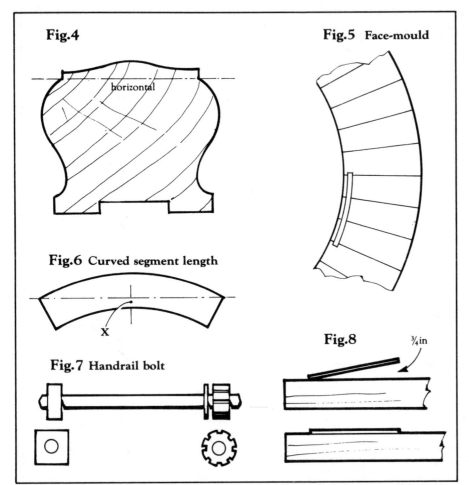

Fig.4

horizontal

Fig.6 Curved segment length

X

Fig.7 Handrail bolt

Fig.5 Face-mould

Fig.8

¾in

bevels'. All we now need is a 'face-mould', and this is produced by the simple process of cutting a segment of ply or hardboard to rest upon the nosings; in the case of a closed-string stair, this template can be fitted to the top edge of the string (fig. 5). Say now that the rail has to be 2in section; our face-mould should be 2⅛in wide, and the required number of segments cut out of 2⅛in material — the ⅛in being 'working allowance'. These segments can now be rounded off to approximately the finished section. Their lengths will depend on the radius of the curve; as a guide to length of segment, see fig. 6. Let measurement **X** be about a third of segment width, so only about half the short grain 'runs out' inside the curve. For a stair of, say, 12ft radius in plan, the segments would be about 4-6in long; but as this would require 7in-wide material, they can be shortened if preferred, and to advantage.

The classic method of jointing up is by handrail bolt, and this rail would need to be fixed with handrail brackets. But it would be a most difficult job to locate and tighten the live nuts, working underneath the assembled rail with the rail lying on its brackets. So turn the segments upside down, lay it on the stair nosings vertically beneath the rail's finished location, assemble, glue, and tighten the live nuts (fig. 7). The rail can now be fitted and finished with glasspaper.

So much for the simple 'mop-stick' rail, which depends on side walls and brackets for its fixing. But for a stair that has no side walls, the rail has to be supported on balusters ('sticks'), and for this a flat under-surface is required — which will have to be helical (twisted) Here come those dreadful 'twist bevels'; in handrailing geometry, they are applied to each end of the rail section, but we aren't using geometry.

So we start as before with cutting face-moulds of ply, as in fig. 5. The mould should be of rail width, say 3in, and of segment length as mentioned. Now if this face-mould or pattern is rested on the stair nosings directly beneath the finished location of the rail, it will be seen that while at one end — say the bottom — it will lie flat on the nosing, its upper end will be inclined. Being thin material, it can be pressed down so it lies flat at top and bottom, which gives our helical surface to which the rail has to be shaped. but it wouldn't be possible to press our rail segments into shape, so in cutting out our segments this time, unlike the mop-stick, allowance must be made for 'twist'.

Let's assume that with our pattern laid on the nosings, its top end 'kicks up' ¾in (fig. 8). Our rail is to be 3x1in section, so our 'thickness of plank' will be 2in plus *half* the kick-up, ie 2⅜in. Half because the pattern can be tilted to give equal tilt top and bottom — ⅜in (fig. 9). Now it can be seen

from fig. 9 that if we cut our material to finished rail width (3in), we aren't going to have enough width for twist, so our segments will have to be 3in wide plus measurement **Y** — say ¼in (fig. 9). Half this measurement is added to each side of our pattern. So we need segments of 3¼x2⅜in section, plus again, a little working allowance. Technically on the centre of their length, the segments could be 3x2in dead, for the twist (half top and bottom) neutralises here, the template lying flat on the nosing. But the work is simplified by ignoring this, and cutting the segments parallel in width and thickness. Having done this, each sement must now be spoke-shaved on its underside to fit on the plane of the nosings; we have now achieved on our rail what we had by pressing down on our pattern. It's now a relatively simple job to square along the edges off this bottom face (fig. 10), and similarly with the top face, then finish up with a calipers to get even width and thickness. We now have the rail

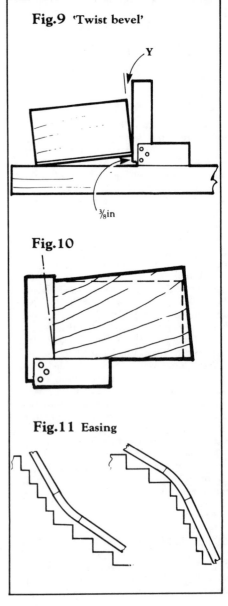

Fig.9 'Twist bevel'

Y

⅜in

Fig.10

Fig.11 Easing

Trouble-free curving

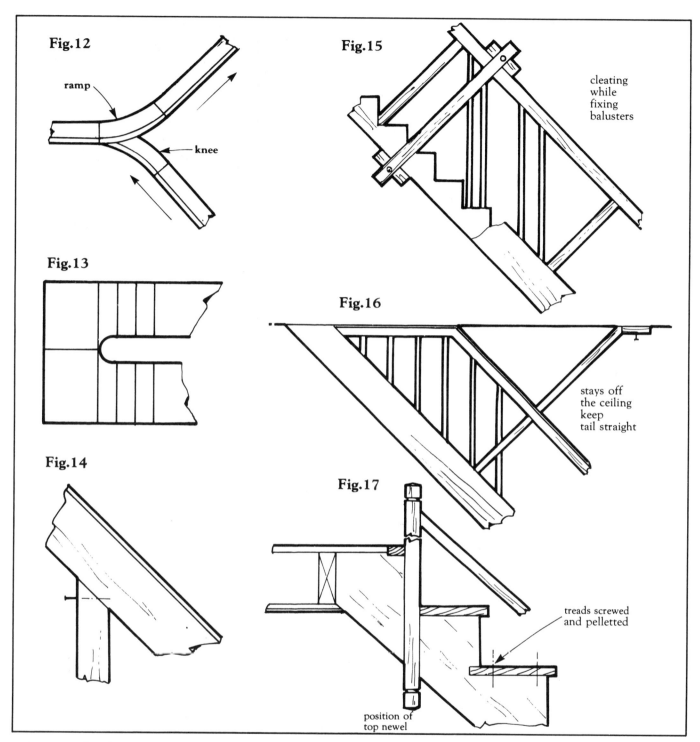

Fig.12

ramp

knee

Fig.13

Fig.14

Fig.15

cleating
while
fixing
balusters

Fig.16

stays off
the ceiling
keep
tail straight

Fig.17

treads screwed
and pelletted

position of
top newel

in the square; from here on it's just a matter of moulding to the required section.

This is the principle of *practical* handrailing. The same methods apply to a small-diameter wreath, but here of course the twist may be far more pronounced, according to whether we have a landing or winders. If in any doubt, it's a good plan to make a mock-up of softwood — no need to mould, just up to 'in the square'.

A kink in any part of the rail is unacceptable, so it's necessary to connect any two varying pitches with an 'easing' (fig. 11). And if the rail runs on to a half-landing, the wreath here should be in a flat plane, connected by a ramp and a knee (fig. 12). But should there be a single riser, making two quarter-landings as in fig. 13, the rail should rise continuously.

The balusters can be dowelled or dovetailed at their bottom ends, according to location. In the 'cut and mitred/bracketed' stairs, they were dovetailed into the tread ends, and this jointing was then concealed by the return nosings. But for 'open plan', the newels have to be kept rather too far from the tread ends for this, so they can be fixed with dowels. Don't be tempted to screw up through the treads; screws are useless in endgrain. The tops are usually fixed with a pin (fig. 14). But the tapping of each pin will tend to bend the rail upwards, so your balusters will get too short and the rail will look like a banana. Guard against this by cleating as in fig. 15, or by stays off the ceiling (fig. 16). With straight-string stairs, the rails, instead of terminating into the usual newel or scroll, can run right down to the floor (figs 17 and 3). ■

● **Note:** In any stair work, be sure to check up on current rules and regulations regarding pitch, clearances, etc.

The craft of cabinetmaking

Hand veneering: this month and next, David Savage explains how to tackle it and enjoy it. First, the gear you need

Photos John Gollop

S ome are born teachers, some aspire to the mantle of guru and some, like myself, have teaching thrust upon them. Jim and Malcolm now share my workshop. They started off on a one-year course in cabinetmaking at another teaching workshop nearby. It closed because of the illness of the principal, and they cast around for a place to spend their remaining six months. Their presence, besides aiding the exchequer, gives me the chance to show off. And veneering is one of the techniques better demonstrated than described.

There is a common misconception, frequently extending even to woodworkers, that veneer is a cheap substitute for solid wood. Dickens named Mr Veneering as a character to represent the superficial, the misleading and deceitful dazzler. However, in the correct place veneering is a wholesome and thoroughly good technique. How else can we economically use rare, exotic and beautiful timbers? There are places, such as the working family dining-table, where veneer might perhaps be a poor choice, but it would be foolish to condemn veneering because it has been, and is being, used commercially to produce only the illusion of quality. Besides, contrary to popular belief, veneered work in a small workshop is usually more time-consuming and almost always more expensive than work in the solid.

Veneering basically takes two forms, distinguished by the equipment used. Caul-veneering requires a press (or, on a small scale, bearers and cramps) to exert pressure on an assembly of groundwork, glue and veneer. One day, one happy day, I shall have a monster veneer-press for everything from storing machined timber to cracking walnuts. Until then I shall lay leaves of veneer by hand using hot glue.

Hand-veneering is ideal for the small workshop, and you can do surprisingly large and complex jobs very quickly once the skill has been acquired. Its limitations really concern the complexity of the design that may be applied. If you have a press, a complex lay-up can be assembled dry, taped together and glued to the ground in one operation. Working by hand, the pieces are laid oversize, each overlapping its neighbour, before being cut and fitted together. This is done with the glue still moist; as it dries there is some danger of shrinkage away from the joints, especially with some species of timber.

F irst of all the glue — hot glue; nice, old-fashioned, stink-the-place-out, hide or rabbitskin or pearl or call-it-what-you-like

● *Animal glue sets as fast as it cools: that's why hand-veneering demands both co-ordination and speed*

glue. Wonderful. I don't use hide glue for a lot of jobs, but on occasions there is just nothing to touch it for speed, strength or flexibility. It comes either in a sheet, which you shatter with a mallet inside a plastic bag, or more conveniently in little dark- or light-brown balls or pearls. Now and again you may find hide glue in crystal form in art

shops; it costs about 10 times the usual price.

All these varieties are produced by boiling up animal bits of sundry sorts and species. The lighter-coloured pearls tend to be the most carefully made — House of Harbru are presently selling a well-made glue, the pearls of which are almost amber

The craft of cabinetmaking

● *Hubble, bubble . . . but don't boil!*

in colour. Do not pay a lot for dark-brown or black pearls: the glue is not so strong. Rabbitskin glue is traditionally the palest, and best reserved for light-coloured veneers. White pigment can also be added, which is handy for camouflaging dark glue-lines.

Soak the glue in cold water for a few hours. Make sure it's covered with water, and stir well and often for the first few minutes, or it will stick together and take too long to soak up the water. Keep it covered with water as it doubles or even trebles in volume. This will take at least two hours (except in the case of finely ground granules), and it is best to allow longer.

Pour off the excess water and use a double-boiler glue-pot. Very good aluminium pots are now made; if your pot is the old cast-iron type, be sure the receptacle is tanned to prevent the glue being discoloured by rust. If you have one of these thermostatically controlled electric glue-pots that heat the water to exactly the right temperature just short of boiling-point, you're quids in and half the fun of glue-making has been stolen from you. We ourselves have various ways of heating the glue-pot — the best, in winter, being the woodburning stove that keeps it bubbling away, gently and at some distance from the bench area. In summer months an ancient Primus stove did duty until very recently, when a Calor-gas ring was drafted in.

The problem with all heat sources is control. Too much heat, and the water in the lower pan boils and froths down the sides of the glue-pot — extinguishing the flame with a loud hiss. The Calor-gas system, which bears great visual similarity to a miniature nuclear reactor, performs this spectacle to a workshop chorus of 'Melt down!'. For strength never, never, never boil the glue. Adjust the consistency by adding water until it flows and brushes out well without being thin and weak. Nobody can explain this precisely, but there is an ideal consistency dependent on temperature and on water content. The expert will adjust it all the time throughout the day as the glue is being used.

This glue is best used so hot that a drop on the back of your hand is painful. Anyone new to it would do well to experience the way the stuff sets. Take hot glue between finger and thumb and rub together. For maybe a minute nothing will happen; maybe this glue is a bad batch? But then, as it chills, quite rapidly the stickiness comes. Continue rubbing and very soon the tack will be complete. At this stage no amount of pressure will get two separate glue surfaces to become one. All your pressure should occur just after the initial no-tack stage but before final chilling.

Once the joint is effected and the glue chilled, the second stage of hardening is by loss of moisture. In a day or two the joint is as hard as it ever will be.

Animal glue, to give it the correct name, is exceptionally strong, with a flexibility that suits timber well. It allows speedy assembly of joints without cramps if the craftsmanship is precise. For hand-veneering it is without equal. However, it has considerable disadvantages — the main one being a vulnerability to dampness and moisture. Your sticky fingers can easily be released by warm water. A hot cup or alcohol spill on a table top has been known to loosen a patch of veneer (though not on my tables, I hasten to add). There again, this capacity to be 'brought back' by heat or moisture can have considerable advantages for the furniture restorer. Indeed, animal glue is the only adhesive that should go anywhere near a prized antique.

Besides the gluing impedimenta, hand-veneering requires several tools that are used for little else. A veneer-hammer, knife and saw, a toothing tool and an electric iron form the basic kit, together with various sponges, cramps, straight-edges, newspapers and buckets of hot water.

The veneer-hammer can be bought — but it's better to make your own, for the tool is a simple one. Its blade is brass, from sheet material $\frac{3}{16}$in thick. Fit it well into the stock as it will have to withstand some pressure. The blade is rounded over and polished smooth. The handle can be made to any convenient length. The word 'hammer' is a slight misnomer, for nothing is struck with the veneer-hammer except perhaps the slumbering student.

The action involves applying pressure to the top of the stock and working the handle to and fro so that the hammer proceeds up the veneer like an indecisive crab. If this is done well, a wave of excess glue is squeezed out ahead of the hammer — leaving a thoroughly attached veneer in its wake.

The veneer-saw, as it comes from the maker, is a totally useless implement — but then, so are most other tools. I very rarely use the side of the saw which has a wide, square kerf. The useful side is the one where the teeth are sharpened by file across the saw in the usual way and then ground to a point down the length of the blade on both sides. This gives them needle-sharp points that will cut veneers easily, with a very narrow kerf. The saw looks an unlikely weapon for work on delicate veneers, but it does a surprisingly good job if properly sharpened.

The veneer knife is best made from a standard bench or chip-carving knife. Attack the blade with the disc-sander to re-model it. It should be thin, but not so thin that it loses its edge under pressure.

As for the toothing tool . . . In days of yore, there was none of your MDF nonsense. Veneer was laid up on a solid wood ground, usually pine or mahogany, and a toothing-plane both flattened the ground and prepared it for the veneer in one operation. Now we have board material that is dead flat; all that's needed is a tool to scratch the surface. Some I have heard argue that it is unnecessary to deface a perfectly good board, but I still do it. Even more than most man-made boards, MDF has a hard and almost glossy surface; by scratching it in two directions, at right-angles to each other, you form a mechanical key whereby the glue can attach itself more readily. A toothing tool can be made from broken hacksaw blades in a simple wedged handle.

Next month, having assembled the equipment, we might just get down to laying a few leaves of veneer!

● House of Harbru, 101 Crostons Rd, Elton, Bury, Lancs BL8 1AL, tel. 061-764 6769. ■

Peter Collenette writes: Last summer I spent a good and productive weekend in the light, airy fastness of David Savage's workshop in Bideford, Devon. I was learning (though vanity would rather I said 're-learning') how to cut dovetails.

David provides all the materials, some of the tools, the bench, the explanation, the encouragement and the atmosphere needed to make a nice little hardwood box with four dovetailed corners. His instructions are full and authoritative, and leave little to chance or the student's blind guesses. Yet perhaps the main benefit lies in setting aside two days of early starts, free from interruption, for nothing else but concentration and trying to get the job just right.

Even so, you still won't finish it, and a good two months elapsed before I glued up. Gaping mitres told their own sad story; but they didn't reflect on Dave, who is clear about his own methods and imparts them pleasantly yet thoroughly. He does one other weekend course, which deals with making and fitting drawers, and he also takes full-time students. By the time you've got to Bideford (an attractive place), stayed there, and paid Dave for his labours, you'll be lighter in the pocket by about the same amount you'll be heavier in the skills. Details from Dave at 21 Westcombe, Bideford, Devon EX39 3QJ, tel. Bideford (023 72) 79202.

The craft of cabinetmaking

Hand-veneering: the other half. David Savage turns his attention to the tools and techniques of the subtle art of cover-up

There's a popular prejudice against veneer — but show someone the care with which it really needs to be done, and they will see the art. Instead of superficiality and cheapness, veneering becomes a combination of aesthetic judgement, skill and dexterity.

Buying veneer is infinitely more pleasant than buying timber, as it's on show indoors and the surface figure is there to be seen rather than guessed at. Crispins in Shoreditch, one of the major London suppliers to the trade, have wonderful warren-like premises full of evocative smells and superb veneers. Don't get carried away; a few leaves of this and a bundle of that will probably set you back £50.

It's difficult stuff to store, however. It's very delicate, especially as single sheets or part-bundles that invariably get left over from a previous job. Always tape the end-grain and any splits with sellotape, not masking tape which dries on and has to be cut off after a few months. Store it in a cool and moist place — a basement is ideal.

Veneer is generally cut with a knife these days, rather than a saw. This actually tends to weaken it and create a series of minute cracks, more apparent on one side than the other; to discover which is which, bend the veneer across its width — the direction in which the bend is easier is the 'loose' side, with the cracks. With solid wood, it's common to 'book-match' boards, showing the figure like the pages of a book. With veneer it is usual to 'slip-match', or slide the veneer leaves sideways without turning them over. This allows you to keep the tight (crack-free) side upwards. In some veneers there is very little difference between tight and loose sides, but those timbers with good figure, especially a light-refracting one, do show the difference. They only disclose their secret at the very last moment when the finish is applied. Leaves that matched perfectly now look hopelessly unbalanced. Beware!

Veneers almost always need flattening before use, a process which makes the material a little more pliable. Damp the veneer with a sponge without getting it too wet, moistening it evenly on both sides. Store it in the correct order between sheets of chipboard with some heavy weights on top to aid the process. This is one of those few occasions where fire extinguishers are really useful. Try to leave the pile for several hours, but not too long because there's the possibility of mould growing after a day or two, especially on the top and bottom leaves. Mould will totally ruin a pale veneer, discolouring it irreparably.

Prepare the ground — the base — to be veneered, a purpose for which I think MDF

● *The tools of the trade: gluepot, brush, saw, and care. The edges need special attention*

is best. Lip the edges of the board with a solid form, using a good width to allow some edge decoration. Don't go too wide or the movement of the timber will transmit through the veneer. A tongue-and-groove is the safest method of attachment for quality work, although I'm certain that a plain butt-joint, well made, would suffice where price is a consideration.

Fit the lippings and plane them flush with the ground, then systematically tooth the entire surface. If this is a real top-class job, a counter-veneer of gaboon or Honduras mahogany is laid underneath the top leaves and at right-angles to them, before the edge-lipping. I've never been entirely convinced of the necessity to do this, but I admit I always do it for safety.

With the ground prepared and well brushed, you are ready to start. Place the glue-pot on the stove nearby, and get the glue to a good temperature and consistency. Put out a bucket of hot water, and put your veneer hammer, saw and knife in it, plus a small sponge. Have a clean dry cloth nearby. Cover the bench with lots of newspaper, and see how much glue is exuded onto it as a mark of your skill. A real expert works cleanly and neatly enough to change the paper only once or twice a day, turning out first-class work. Put the electric iron on at its coolest setting, but it should only be needed to bring back areas that haven't stuck the first time. The larger the job (desk-tops or boardroom tables) the more you would have to use the iron.

Laying leaves of veneer by hand is a matter of temperature, moisture, touch and timing, and to do it cleanly is a great skill. Beginners will get quick-setting animal glue on and in walls, hair and nostrils — everywhere except where it's wanted. The entire world takes on a sticky consistency, and things adhere to you that shouldn't.

This is the procedure for veneering:

1 Cut the veneer roughly 1in larger all round than the area to be covered. A good initial practice area is about 6x18in.
2 Identify which side of the leaf is tight, the face which should go upwards. Locate the position on the groundwork by marking both veneer and board with chalk, which tells you where and on which side of the veneer to glue.
3 Brush the ground free of dust.
4 Carry the glue-pot to the bench, check the consistency, and coat the groundwork quickly and smoothly.
5 Turn the leaf so the 'up' side is down and place it on the glued area. No, I'm not mad!
6 Coat the 'down' side of the veneer with glue.
7 Put the glue-pot back on the heat.
8 Turn the leaf right side up and place or slide it into position.
9 Lightly sponge the top with a little warm water — too much will encourage the veneer to shrink on drying. The water mixes with the glue that is stuck to the 'up' side and acts as a lubricant for the hammer.
10 Begin rubbing down from the middle outwards, lightly at first. Check the veneer's position again, as it can easily slide at this stage.
11 Begin working that hammer in earnest, squeezing out the glue ahead of it. Work the hammer slowly and systematically and pay particular attention to the edges.

It's not that easy, but basically that's all there is to it. It's not about slop and glue and mess, but a little moisture, nice strong hot glue, slightly moist flat veneers and pressure at the right time in the right place in the right direction.

● *Lifting the overlap after cutting with the veneer saw and straight-edge*

It should be possible to avoid using the hot iron by working calmly, methodically, and briskly. Never hurry. If you do have an area, or more likely a corner, that hasn't stuck, try a quick dash with the iron (set the temperature to very low or 'silk'). If this fails, try putting in some new glue if this is possible. If all else fails, go back to the iron and apply more heat and more moisture. Don't overdo it, for excessive local heat can dry out and shrink the veneer quicker than anything.

You will probably want to make a joint between two leaves of veneer, which with a veneer press is done dry, before application of glue, heat and pressure. With hand-work, each leaf is laid in turn. Your first leaf will now be laid, perhaps an inch oversize. If the leaf overlaps the edges of the job, cut these off straight away, because it will lay nice and flat for a few minutes, but if it's left dangling much longer it will curl and lift the glue from round the edges. Trimming is a simple business. Invert the job onto a clean cutting-board, and use the edges as guides for your knife or veneer saw. Be careful at the end of a crossgrain cut.

Lay the second leaf overlapping the first by as much as 2in — remember the first is already an inch oversize. Lay in exactly the same way, but be careful of the seam where they change from a single to a double thickness. It's very easy for a carelessly applied veneer hammer to tear the wood at this vulnerable point. Never use the veneer hammer except with extreme precision and purpose, for it's capable of the most delicate work. With the leaves in position, place a straight-edge down the joint, and take the precaution of clamping it if the cut is long. I have a rubber-backed heavy rule for this sort of work, but don't expect an ordinary metre rule to do the job of a proper straight-edge. A rule is a measuring instrument, not a guidance system.

Now the cut. A veneer knife should have a very sharp-pointed blade with a thin kerf, a combination which makes it less inclined to stray from the line when working with the grain. Don't lay the blade in the cut, just use the tip. The veneer saw does the job just as well. In my shop the saw has slightly more use than the knife, perhaps because it holds an edge slightly longer. If you lay veneers all day long, after a few days it will come naturally to make this cut with one pass. That is the aim, but I for one seldom hit the right consistent pressure down the entire length of the cut, severing two thicknesses of veneer but not damaging the ground. This is something that only comes with daily experience. The touch can be acquired towards the end of a long job, but it gets lost again without regular practice.

Having made the cut, lift the veneer and peel out the unwanted piece underneath the second leaf. If you've taken a tea-break between the two leaves, this piece will be well-chilled and well stuck — hard luck. For speedier workers, a crank-handled paring chisel will help ease it out of its hidey-hole. Apply a bit of hot glue and wait. Go away and cut up the veneer tape — 4in lengths every 4in across the joint and one length down the whole lot. By now the glue will be tacking; rub it down with a hammer, damp the veneer tape (or brown paper tape 1¼in wide) and rub it on. Wipe up any excess dampness, check for bubbles and blisters, then cover the whole surface with newspaper so that it will dry out slowly and evenly.

After a couple of days remove the tape with warm water and a scraper before either sanding or scraping to a fine finish. And there you have it — just don't go berserk with the belt sander! ∎

● **J. Crispin and Son,** Veneer Merchants, 94 Curtain Rd, London EC2, tel. 01-739 4857; **The Art Veneers Co. Ltd,** (Mail order specialists), Industrial Estate, Mildenhall, Suffolk IP28 7AY; **R. Aaronson (Veneers) Ltd,** 45 Redchurch St, London E2, tel. 01-739 3107.

The craft of cabinetmaking

Edge-jointing: David Savage continues his occasional series with a detailed look at making narrow boards wider

Next door to my workshop is a small joiners' workshop run by Dezzy and Ginger. They make windows, staircases or whatever is needed at ferocious speed and with great skill. Last week Dezzy had the top joints of two fingers removed by the planer, and the effect on me and the other members of the workshop was profound. Sympathy and concern are quickly followed by shock and worry . . . After all, Dezzy is no cowboy — he knows his business and is a careful machinist. If it happened to him . . .

However, just as happens when you drive past a serious accident on a motorway, the effect of this was salutary, but temporary. It's too easy to forget the uncomfortable truth. Writing about safety is an immediate turn-off for everyone, including myself, for nobody wishes to contemplate the truth of the situation for more than a moment. We all know machines are dangerous, and accidents happen despite our best efforts to prevent them. But who would wish to dwell upon the grizzly reality of maimed hands for more than a moment? Our hands are fantastically complex manipulative and sensory mechanisms; the antics of the CNC robot or the dense complexity of the micro chip are feeble and crude compared to the wiggly bits on the ends of our arms. Because we cannot consider mutilation of ourselves for more than a moment, we deny ourselves a valuable safety mechanism.

We can guard machines fully, and I am not for one moment arguing against this; but there are occasions when the guard isn't there to protect us. How does this happen? Why does it happen? I don't pretend to know — but human fallibility has a lot to do with it. For this reason, I believe it isn't enough to say that guarding a machine is the answer to the problem. For those occasions that, heaven forbid, the guard is not in place, there must also be a secondary protection for the operator — good technique.

Good technique is simply something by which you accomplish the task in hand, pressing the job against table or fence in the necessary way, but without putting your hands in danger. If a slip, either from the job or from loss of balance, could carry your wiggly bits into the meat grinder — that isn't good technique. If you can feel the breath of the table-saw on your hand, that's too close. Use any manner of shop-made devices to control the job over the cutters; push-sticks are found on almost all my machines, and I get very ratty if they aren't put back in the same place *every time*. If you

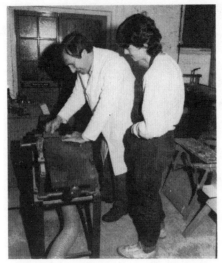

● *Above, Dave Gardiner of CoSIRA 'joints' new cutters to the same arc with a small slip-stone; **above right**, the safe way – pressure forward*

reach out for a push-stick, it should always be there.

Finger-boards are home-made pressure blocks. Easily made from scraps of plywood, they can clamp to the fence for downward pressure, or on to the machine table for sideways pressure. When you are making one, make two more; they are invaluable aids that only get used if they are close at hand.

The final thing is to examine the existing guarding systems on your equipment. From the manufacturer's point of view, a good guard isn't always the same thing as it is to you and me. I have two Startrite table-saws in my shop, a large dimension saw and a smaller 9in saw used for joints and fitting. Both machines' guards are attached to the riving-knife, and with the guard fitted, it's impossible to bring the fence nearer than 30mm to the blade. A better system is Luna's where the crown-guard is hung above the table, allowing it to be positioned very quickly and easily. A good guard is one that gets in the way of accidents without obstructing operations to the point of frustration.

It was edge-planing a board that took Dezzy's fingertips, and it is this operation I want to examine in the context of a basic cabinetmaking technique; edge-jointing.

The joint

Almost every piece of furniture we make in the solid has edge joints in it somewhere. Even if trees grew with faultless wide boards, it wouldn't generally be good practice to use them. So we joint narrow boards together to make wide panels and carcases. The maximum width of board without a joint is usually determined (apart from the grain factor) by the width of your planer or thicknesser, and if that doesn't stop you, the stuff you plane will. We have a 16in planer/thicknesser, which allows us to take advantage of good wide boards when they

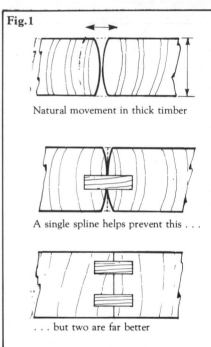

Fig.1

Natural movement in thick timber

A single spline helps prevent this . . .

. . . but two are far better

come up; a smaller 10in machine would do good work, but make edge-jointing a more regular job. An 18in-wide panel can be made quite simply by bookmatching a 9in board, so the creative limitations of the smaller machine are very slight.

To achieve a faultless invisible joint between two boards demands considerable care and attention to detail. Producing it quickly and effortlessly is the result of practice based on faultless technique. As in most general cabinetmaking skills, the attitude of mind, the method, the procedure, all determine the result.

There are three common types of edge joint; plain butt-joints, splined joints and dowelled joints. I must confess I have never used the slot-screwed joint. A plain butt-joint, well made, will suffice for most cabinet carcase work, because a glue joint long grain to long grain has great strength. Work like this would generally be in timber less than 25mm thick.

For thicker sections, the extra strength gained from splines is an advantage. A thick section of timber has more problems to concern us; being thick, it may not be dry right through, or it may have been kiln-dried too quickly, drying in stresses that usually relax with slow air-drying. Even a perfectly behaved board may distort across the joint enough to break the glue's adhesion and ruin your perfect work. For edge-jointing timber more than 25mm thick, I generally insist that at least one spline is used. Where there's room for two splines, this gives the best joint as strength gained from the increased glue area is positioned where it is needed, near the surface (fig. 1). A spline may be fitted to a narrow board to give a location if the boards were twisted.

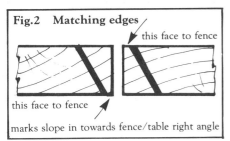

Fig.2 Matching edges

this face to fence

this face to fence

marks slope in towards fence/table right angle

Most of the splined work we do is in stopped grooves, which can be the very devil to cut. A spindle moulder with a variable grooving saw is the best solution, and a no.1299 Leitz grooving saw, which allows the width of groove to be dialled in, is a favourite but expensive toy. A router can do the job, with a jig to stabilise it on the edge of a board; a table-saw can also cut stopped grooves with a dado head fitted for the wide kerf. This is less satisfactory, as the guard and riving knife must be removed from the saw and the job dropped on to the cutter — illegal in a commercial shop. The biscuit jointer can cut a very clean groove, if like the router it can be stabilised on the narrow edge. The cutters are 4mm, so usually two passes are needed to cut the groove for a 6mm spline. (The splines themselves are best made of plywood, which takes advantage of long-grain gluing surface and cross-grain strength across the joint.) The only trouble is, the biscuit jointer is rather an unwieldy beast, which, rather than cutting perfect stopped grooves — doesn't. Stop, that is. It gallops off across the job instead, leaving a trail of toothmarks.

Dowelled edge joints are much less common than splined ones, because it's just a more complicated operation to align 20 or so dowels down the length of a board than fit two splines. Dowels do, however, have a valuable role to play in locating a board so it sits dead flush with its new neighbour. Splines do this as well, but they allow for lateral movement in the glue-up, and so if end dimensions have been determined before gluing, a dowel at each end will help to make sure everything bangs up nicely.

But the plain old, honest-to-good butt-joint, despite its simplicity, is still the most common edge joint in carcase work. Beginners often needlessly incorporate tongues and grooves, splines and dowels to overcome the butt-joint, for a good butt-joint takes a bit of skill.

The equipment

In years gone by, hairy-armed woodworkers wielded planes much longer than is common today — wooden jointers, sometimes 30in long, did the task of edge-jointing superbly. The length of the sole and the fineness of cut ensured a straight edge, and the skill of the craftsman kept it square to the job. A jointer plane was often only used for this task as it was too cumbersome for general work.

Today the name is given to the machine that does the same work. A 'jointer' is a planing machine set up for edge-jointing, which may just mean your general-purpose planer is fitted with a vertical fence and used as a jointer. We keep a separate machine for this work, with a shop-built fence permanently fitted. The main feature of a good jointer is the length of its tables, the longer the better. Many industrial jointers extend for 6 or 7ft — most of us have to be content with something less than this ideal. Edge-planing a long board on a short jointer demands the careful setting up of roll-on-roll-off tables before and beyond the machine; a large 2500mm walnut table we are currently making will need this fiddling about to ensure a perfect straight edge along its length.

The jointer needs careful setting up if it's to function correctly. Spend some time with a bright light and a *real* straight-edge, checking the tables don't twist or droop in relation to each other. The outfeed table is the important one — this should be set at a height fractionally below the top of the cutter arch, but *only fractionally.* The cutters must be set to exactly the same cutting circle, because if only one cutter is doing the work the finish will be poor. If any of these factors are ignored, indeed, the chances of getting good results are very poor.

The next task is to set up a fence at right angles to the cutter. Most jointers have adjustable fences allowing them to cant over to plane chamfers; wonderful, the chance of holding a constant 90° immediately shoots straight out of the window. Other jointer fences I have seen twist the job as it's fed across the cutters or better still, were permanently bent into a banana shape at birth. I have given up with jointer fences and made my own, but even this isn't trusted implicitly, for wood chips can get under it. Always check the fence with a square as the job proceeds.

Using the jointer accurately and safely demands a fairly high degree of co-ordination. The first thing is the length and straightness of your workpiece; if you have a fair way to go before you get a very fine and straight edge, you can set the cut quite deep, then finer. Passing the work over the

● *Apprentice Neil keeps the valuable fingers well away from the cutters*

cutters, the golden rule is *no hand should be on the work immediately over the cutter-block.* You stand with the machine to your right, your left (forward) hand pushing the work in to the fence and down to the table; push it forward, keeping your forward hand behind the cutters and feeding with your right (back) hand too, and as soon as there is a good hand-hold length on the outfeed table, transfer the pressure of your forward hand smoothly to the outfeed side. Keep the work moving all the time, but *don't let your forward hand travel on the work over the cutters.* Once the left hand is on the outfeed table side of the work, that is your reference; keep pushing in and down and forward with it, and assist with very light feed pressure from your 'infeed' hand — but don't press down on the table or fence on the infeed side, because it's the outfeed surfaces that you must work to.

The surface held against the out table will be sufficient to maintain the perfect straight right angle, and during the entire process your precious fingers will have been nowhere near the cutters. Fences are set up so the minimum of cutter is exposed and guards are there to prevent accidents, *but* the technique used by you, the operator, would have saved you had they not been there. Heaven preserve us from people who leave off guards, but wiggly bits are still being turned into dogmeat every day. Legislation prevents employers like myself from risking the very precious digits of my staff, but the home workshop has no such protection. You must tend your own meat grinder and guard your own digits; 'nuff said.

So the edge has been planed square and straight; check it with a straight-edge and square. If you are doing a batch of 20, check the first three to get into the swing of it, then check every third edge. Checking means looking for trouble, not hoping for the best. If you don't want to see your poor workmanship, it's easy not to look that hard.

The problem of getting a constant right angle on a jointer with a doubtful fence can be helped by marking the boards as shown in fig. 2. The endgrain mark indicates which side has pressed against the fence, the mark pointing into the junction of fence and jointer table. Keep these marks parallel when assembling, any inaccuracy in the fence should be cancelled out, and the assembled panel will remain flat.

Finer points

On the question of marks, we come to the cabinetmaker's triangle (fig. 3). Used correctly, it can tell you which three pieces out of a pile of 50 go together. It will also tell you which way they fit, what's the inside, the outside, the top, the bottom, the right, the left. By underscoring the base of the triangle in different ways you can identify groups of components. Use white chalk on light boards, red on mahogany or padauk.

If the edges have been passed over the jointer slowly on a fine cut, the edge will butt up to give a good joint straight from the machine. Small components less than 100mm can be left straight, but with longer pieces it might be better to put a slight bow in the edge. The idea is to get the ends to come together first, and then the centre can be cramped. The amount of bow is a debatable point; I have found that one shaving, beginning and ending 100mm from either end, is enough. The plane should be finely set and keen. The iron should be slightly curved, which has two effects; firstly it allows the plane to enter the cut from the side smoothly and delicately, and secondly, the cut is slightly concave across the joint so the points to touch first are the parts you see, the outer edges.

Begin the cut to one side well into the length of the board. As you go forward, move the plane across so the shaving is centred in the throat of the plane. By pressing down it should be possible to take one continuous shaving before easing the plane off the edge. This is a skill worth acquiring, for edge-jointed boards, if they are to split, go at the ends. For this reason, I like to put the ends under a bit of compression. The end grain is absorbing and losing moisture far quicker than the centre of a board, so the ends are working harder than the middle.

Assembly

Edge-gluing a board can be tackled in one of two ways; rub-jointing or cramping. Anyone familiar with this occasional series will know my perverse fondness for animal

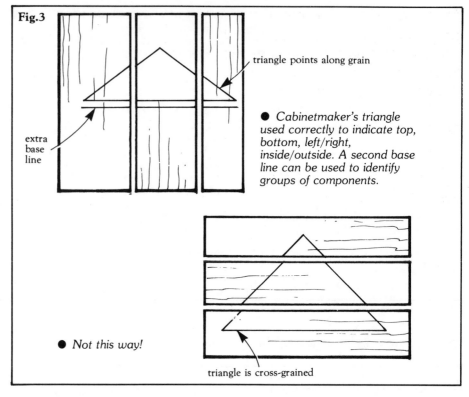

Fig.3

triangle points along grain

● *Cabinetmaker's triangle used correctly to indicate top, bottom, left/right, inside/outside. A second base line can be used to identify groups of components.*

extra base line

● *Not this way!*

triangle is cross-grained

glue; if your job isn't very large and there are a great many edges to glue, animal glue is the stuff of life. The advantage is that a great many edges can be glued very quickly without cramps, but the disadvantage is that it takes a bit of doing if you are unfamiliar with animal glue.

The joint should be dead flat and true. Grip the bottom board upright, either in the vice or in the bench dogs. Make sure the glue is hot and not too thin. The second board can be leant against the first, so both surfaces are there together ready for the glue brush. Brush on a little glue; your first few goes will get glue dribbling everywhere, for you actually need less than you think. Now bring the surfaces together and rub. This is why it's called a rub-joint — the action of pushing to and fro coats both surfaces and expels excess glue. It should only need one or two good rubs before a stiffening is sensed, rather than felt. Now align the boards and let it stand for a moment. The test of a good rubbed joint is simple — can you now open the vice and lift the assembly, holding it by that top board? The action is that fast. Pick up the panel, and gently lay it against two stickers propped against a wall. Other panels can be piled in front, using carefully placed stickers, and then don't disturb the joint for the rest of the day. Although it's possible for very long boards to be rubbed together by two people, I prefer to see large boards put under cramps.

Cramping edge joints together demands a very flat surface on which to stand the cramps — the bench is the obvious place. I made a number of sash-cramps a few years ago when I couldn't afford the proper Record metal T-bar variety; they use much

cheaper cramp-heads and a hardwood bar. These cramps have been a great success and are now used in preference to heavier hardware. The secret, if there is one, is to make the bar from a good tough hardwood; but make it very carefully. If the holes for the locating pins aren't spot on, you will regret your carelessness for many a year.

PVA or white glue is a favourite for a cramped edge joint. There should be plenty of time to apply glue (with a brush not a finger!) to both surfaces. Successful glue-ups are about having everything to hand, a little glue, a little bit of squeeze and no fuss. Most jobs use between five and seven cramps spaced evenly along it. Alternate the position of cramps, so for every two beneath there is one cramp above the job. Then give it a very little squeeze. If the boards don't align properly, either tap them down or pull them together at the ends with a speed cramp. Now a bit more squeeze from the centre and you should be finished.

Resist the temptation to wipe away the globs of glue which shouldn't be there. The assembly can be moved from the bench, but the clamps must remain on the job for at least one hour. The panel can then be removed and stored in the same way as rubbed panels. The globs of glue are best removed when they are rubbery hard, but not yet set, for which a cranked paring chisel is a favourite weapon.

If the job has been done properly, there will be no visible glue line. The joint between the boards will be visible only by the change of figure between one board and the next. If your first attempts are less than perfect, don't despair — when you get it right, the sense of achievement will be all the more enjoyable. ■

Scarfing it

Just a cheap way of making a long bit of wood, you say? Scarfing is a great deal more than that, says Malcolm Wintle — with a host of drawings to back him up

The scarf rarely receives a mention in carpentry manuals, which is a pity because it's a useful joint. With a knowledge of the method and a little care, the average woodworker can make good use of it.

The form shown in fig. 1 is in effect a butt joint with the butt ends cut not at right angles to the grain, but at an acute angle. The faces are glued and the pieces clamped together. It sounds very easy and it is; but there are pitfalls.

Why make such a joint? The scarf has long been common in clinker-built (i.e. planked) boat-building, where longer planks than the ones available may be needed. It's also used when repairing such boats, when a section of planking is scarfed in. If a boat has a plywood skin, scarfing can extend standard sheets, giving a stronger and fairer outer surface than a butt-and-lap joint would. Domestic skirting-boards are usually joined on a long run by a crude scarf joint, generally rough-sawn and not glued. Broken masts, oars, paddles and even broom- and tool-handles can be repaired by scarfing. Bad patches in timber too — knots, shakes, bends, or areas where the grain runs off badly — can all be cut out and the wood re-joined. Then you might come across an unexpected job for which pieces to hand are too short, so you can just join up the available wood rather than make a special journey to a timber yard.

I sometimes need pieces longer than I can easily carry home, so I buy two lengths and scarf them together when I get them on the bench. This actually makes it easier to get the timber straight on a long run. For instance, if a long piece develops a bad bend on the flat, it may be impossible to pull it straight. Planing the edges wastes a lot of wood, as fig. 2a shows (it's exaggerated for clarity). But if you cut the wood in half and scarf together again, the bend can be greatly reduced which in turn increases the useful thickness of wood left after planing (fig. 2b).

The strength of the finished joint is determined by the angle of taper. The finer the taper, the stronger the final result. If the joint is purely decorative, as in a skirting-board or unstressed panelling, then a 1:2 taper may be adequate (fig. 3a), but in a shelf, mast or broom-handle for example, where bending forces have to be withstood, a taper between 1:6 and 1:10 would be more suitable (fig. 3b).

The total length of timber will have to be at least the finished length plus the length of the scarf. To make a strong joint in 25mm timber would require an extra length of wood of 200mm for a 1:8 joint, plus safety margins.

The method

There are two problems in forming the tapers: making the two tapers true and identical, and getting a good feather edge. The stock should be cut slightly wider and thicker than finished to allow it to be trued up square before the joint is started and also for some wood to be left for planing off in final cleaning up. The two ends to be joined are marked with the intended taper (fig. 4a). Save effort by sawing the scrap off on the waste side (fig. 4b). A rigid flat working

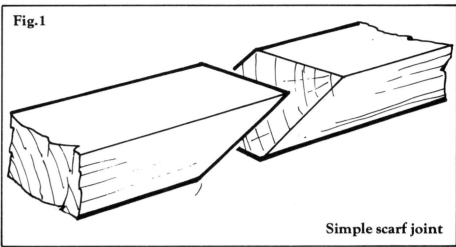

Fig.1

Simple scarf joint

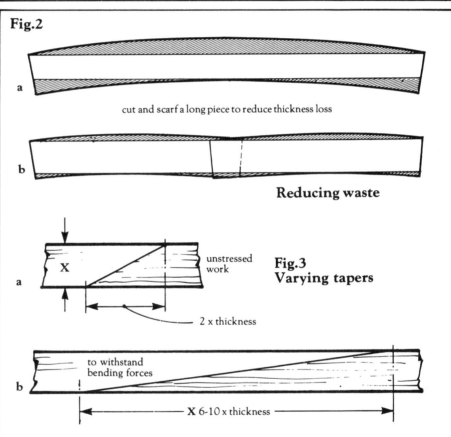

Fig.2

a

cut and scarf a long piece to reduce thickness loss

b

Reducing waste

a

X

unstressed work

2 x thickness

**Fig.3
Varying tapers**

b

to withstand bending forces

X 6-10 x thickness

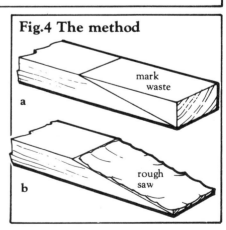

Fig.4 The method

a

mark waste

b

rough saw

surface is essential for planing the tapers; clamp the two parts to be joined one on top of the other as in fig. 5. The bottom, straight flat packing-piece raises the work high enough to be planed over the full length of both tapers, and also supports the delicate feather edge. This piece should be only slightly wider than the work, and its front end should be square to the long sides.

Next, position the two pieces to be joined as shown, one face up, the other face down. The lines of the two tapers are lined up with one another and with the corner (**C**) of the packing-piece. Align the long edges of the two workpieces with one another, parallel with the long edge of the packing-piece.

Then clamp a flat pad to spread clamp-action in two places, to bring the work-pieces together right up to the tip of the upper one, and the lower one in contact with the packing-piece right up to the corner (fig. 5). This is essential to get good feather edges. The final planing line must be clear of the upper pad and of the top of the nearer clamp, and the lower pad must be thick enough to stop the plane hitting the bench before you reach the end of the taper.

Using a sharp plane, cut the tapers back to the mark. It doesn't matter if the final taper isn't exactly what you intended, pro-viding the rough sawcuts are completely planed away. Nor, if a small margin has been left on the overall length of the work-pieces, does it matter if the planing is taken a little too far; apart from shortening the work slightly, the only other result is a slight nick off the corner of the packing-piece.

There are two important points to watch during planing. Firstly, the planed face of each taper must be *quite flat* so they will eventually lie in good contact over the whole area. Second, both ends of each taper must finish at right angles to the long sides of the work. An angled cut (seen from above in fig. 6) results in an error of double the angle when the two pieces are glued together, so you need more planing on the right side **R** to bring the ends of the tapers perpendicular to the long edges of the work. The feather edges are sharp and delicate when you unclamp them, and must be handled carefully.

Gluing

Lay the two pieces flat and offer them up for a trial fitting in the final position. When the pieces are slid together and aligned, the two bevels should come together over the whole area. If they don't, then the planing was out of true, the work wasn't initially planed square, or the pieces weren't clamped up accurately for planing the tapers — or any combination of these. So clamp up again and repeat the planing. You can make slight corrections by planing one of the tapers only, the feather edge supported this time with a single workpiece.

When the pieces meet accurately, mark them across the join (fig. 7b) to aid length-wise positioning when gluing. It can be dif-

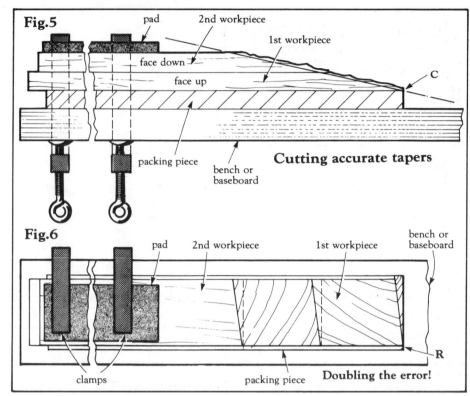

Fig.5 pad   2nd workpiece   1st workpiece   face down   face up   C   packing piece   bench or baseboard   **Cutting accurate tapers**

Fig.6 pad   2nd workpiece   1st workpiece   bench or baseboard   R   clamps   packing piece   **Doubling the error!**

ficult to see when the tapers are mated correctly with a generous layer of glue. Then score thoroughly across the whole of each surface to be glued with a saw or sandpaper to provide a key.

Cascamite is suitable for 'undercover' outdoor work, but if the joint will get wet, a fully waterproof glue such as Aerolite 300 or a resorcinol is best. The clamping secret is that each piece is clamped individually to a common base before being clamped to the other — it's important to get the sequence right or the joint is just squeezed apart. Clamp one piece to the bench (or other flat surface with a good straight edge) so the edges of work and surface coincide and the glued face of the work is uppermost (fig. 7a). Slide a piece of plastic film under the feather edge before tightening the clamp so the glue squeezed out later doesn't stick the work to the bench. Offer the second work-piece up to the first, in a line guided by the edge of the bench, the two previously made

marks coinciding (fig. 7b); then clamp this piece to the bench as well. Put a second piece of plastic film over the upper feather edge, and clamp the joint together with one or two clamps on a flat pad (fig. 7c).

If the joint has been well prepared and comes together correctly, glue will squeeze out all along both sides, but don't clamp too tightly or you'll starve the job of glue and weaken it. Don't clean the excess glue off until it's rubbery, which shows curing is well advanced. With a glue like Cascamite which sets finally like glass, it's easier on the plane to do most of the cleaning-off before the glue is fully hard.

The alternative way to prevent the parts slipping under clamps — temporarily pin-ning them together — apart from leaving holes, puts pins in the way and is best avoided by the fig. 7 method. But it's some-times useful; two well-spaced pins are driven through the upper piece when both are dry and clamped in position (fig. 8). The

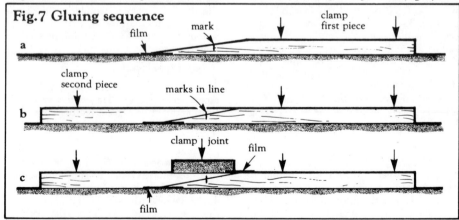

Fig.7 Gluing sequence   clamp first piece   mark   film   a   clamp second piece   marks in line   b   clamp joint   film   c   film

pins should just enter the lower half; mark the joint across as before. Then separate the parts and glue them, and relocate the points of the pins in the holes in the lower workpiece, using the pencil marks as a guide. The pins can be driven in further if necessary and the joint clamped. Remove the pins when the glue has set.

With a good taper (1:8 at least) and careful gluing with good glue, the joint should be as strong as the original wood. It's always worth making one or two practice joints and testing them to destruction, in which you'll see that with a fine taper, it should be the wood and not the joint that fails. If the scarf is so you can remove a bad section at a knot or where the grain runs off, the finished job will certainly be stronger than the original.

If the stock is round (a mast for example), it's difficult to plane the two parts together as in fig. 5, so they must be planed separately after roughing out the joint. It's essential to support each feather edge on a packing-piece as it is planed, and the two parts have to be fitted together by trial and error until each is planed to the same angle and you get an accurate fit all over the faces.

The sequence of clamping is as before, but it is necessary to make shaped packing-pieces like those in fig. 9 to provide a firm bearing surface for the clamps.

Double scarf joint

Sometimes, it's worth considering a double scarf as shown in fig. 10. It uses a smaller additional length of material, and for a given length of joint is likely to be stronger than a single scarf because of the second pair of mating surfaces. A disadvantage is that the faces of the slot have to be finished by hand after roughing out, but this isn't too difficult. I've used this joint successfully to extend a wooden mast.

The slotted part is marked out as in fig. 11. There's a flat at the bottom of the slot, easier than working an acute-angled recess right down to a sharp point. Make the width of the flat equal to the diameter of whatever drill you have around 5-6mm. Drill through the work halfway from each side at **X**, then rough out the tapers by making two saw-cuts to end at the hole. Finish the slot off to the line with hand chisels. The other part is marked out as in fig. 12 with the same width of flat and angle of taper, roughed out by sawing, and finished to the line. This part is comparatively easy as the tip can be left rough-sawn, the tapers can be planed till you get a good fit with the slot, and there's no feather edge to protect. If the faces are planed too far, you'll have to plane a little off the tip. Score and join as before.

Some cosmetic uses

An easier job is the repair of a damaged corner, of a door or door-lining for example. If the damage is more than filler can cope with, you can scarf a new piece in.

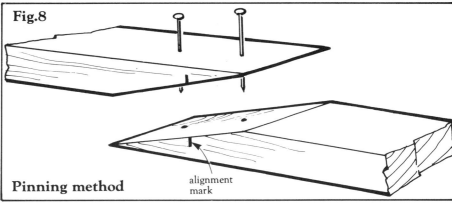

Fig.8

Pinning method

alignment mark

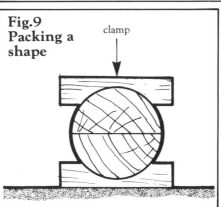

Fig.9 Packing a shape

clamp

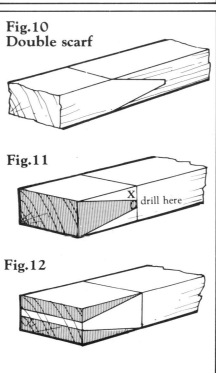

Fig.10 Double scarf

Fig.11

X

drill here

Fig.12

Cut a gash (fig. 13a) out along the dotted lines. Depending on its position, the enlarged hole can sometimes be roughed out with a saw and cleaned up with a chisel, but it's just as easy to do the whole thing by chiselling from each end alternately, enlarging the hole from the centre outwards till the damage is cut out or at least surrounded by good wood. It helps if the

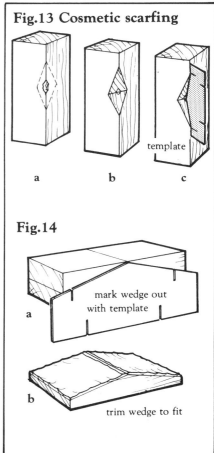

Fig.13 Cosmetic scarfing

template

a   b   c

Fig.14

mark wedge out with template

a

b

trim wedge to fit

angles of the two tapers are about equal, and the line where the tapers meet is at right angles to the edges of the frame or door (fig. 13b). As this is a cosmetic job, a taper of 1:2 or 3 is adequate. It's easy to check each taper is flat by laying the back of the chisel on it, which immediately shows up any bumps or hollows for further paring.

Next make a template of the angle by cutting a piece of cardboard and adjusting it until it's a good snug fit in the angle. Mark the extent of the hole on it (fig. 13c), and mark the width of the hole on the opposite edge of the card.

Mark out a broad wedge with the template (fig. 14a) on a well-seasoned oddment of wood with lengthwise grain, slightly wider than the base of the hole. Cut off the waste on the tapers (fig. 14b) and either plane or chisel the sloping faces until you get a good fit with the hollow. After getting a good fit, don't forget to mark which way round the wedge goes, and also mark across the join as before to help positioning when glued. There's no need to shape the wedge any more on the other faces yet — this is more easily done when it's glued in place. Score across all inclined faces and glue as before. When the wedge is mated with the work and lightly pressed home, check that glue squeezes out all round. Very little force is needed to keep the wedge in place while the glue cures, after which you can plane the excess wood and glue off. If the repair and surrounding area are well rubbed down and painted, the new wood is undetectable.

My most frequent use of the scarf is to repair a piece of wood on the flat. Examples are: cutting out knots in work I'm preparing, cutting out unsightly or resinous knots in existing fixtures, and filling holes in floors under carpets where knots have shrunk and fallen through.

Mark two lines on the work along the grain on each side, clear of the defect (fig. 15a). Starting from the centre, chisel out a shallow vee progressively until there is sufficient depth all over the fault to make a good repair (fig. 15b).

As before, cut a piece of card to make a template for the angle of the base of the hole, and mark the width of the hole on it as in fig. 13c. Mark out the replacement wood as in fig. 14a, but this time the width (fig. 14b) is the same as the hole. After you've cut the tapers, adjust the plug by trial-and-trim to fit the hole easily but snugly; make a locating mark across the join as before. Score across all sloping faces, glue all mating faces and press the plug lightly home until glue comes out all round, especially under the overhang at each end.

Larger repairs

Rotted areas of window and door linings or frames, usually at the bottom, require replacement of rather larger volumes of wood. Awaiting my attention now is a bad patch in an oak porch (fig.16) where the rain has got up into the endgrain and caused shakes if not actual rot. I shall cut out a vee as indicated and scarf in a new piece of oak, using Aerolite. If the part to be mended includes a rebate, the scarfed insert can be shaped before gluing in place, but it may be easier to leave the section slightly oversize and finish it to match after fixing.

I recently repaired a window lining, rotten round a bottom corner, by cutting out the whole corner with about 1:4 tapers, then jointing up a complete new corner on the bench with the rebate roughed out to size and the two scarfs accurately fitting the fixed tapers. It was glued and clamped in place, and finished *in situ* flush with the old wood. It was undetectable when completed and painted. It was much cheaper than replacing the whole frame; and although it took a long time, it was still quicker than waiting for the builders!

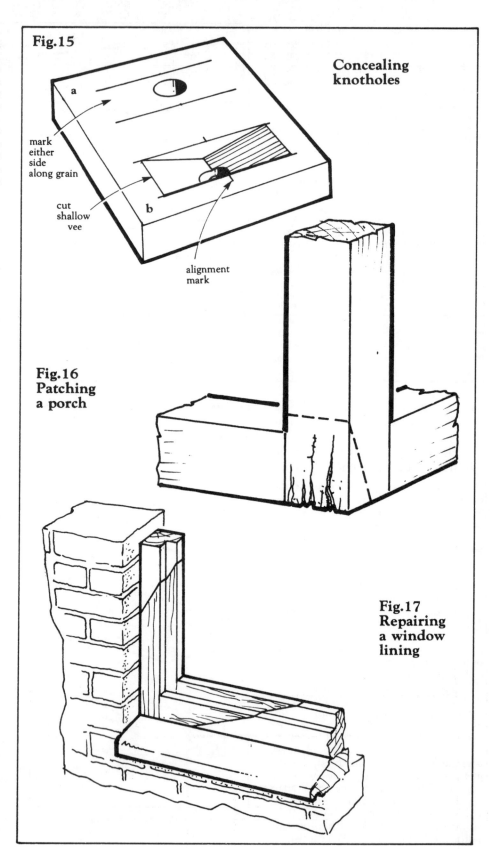

Fig.15

mark either side along grain

cut shallow vee

alignment mark

Concealing knotholes

Fig.16 Patching a porch

Fig.17 Repairing a window lining

Motivation!

I've tried to give an idea of the range of uses of this versatile joint — please don't be put off because it sounds just too much trouble. It really is a case of easier done than said, and once you've tried it, you'll find you can knock off a good joint remarkably quickly. I find it very satisfying, when stripping a job for repainting, to find a scarf joint or repair I've made many years before, forgotten and hidden under the old paint. ∎

WHERE SCRIBE AND MITRE MEET

Stan Thomas offers solutions to the eternal chestnut of joining mouldings

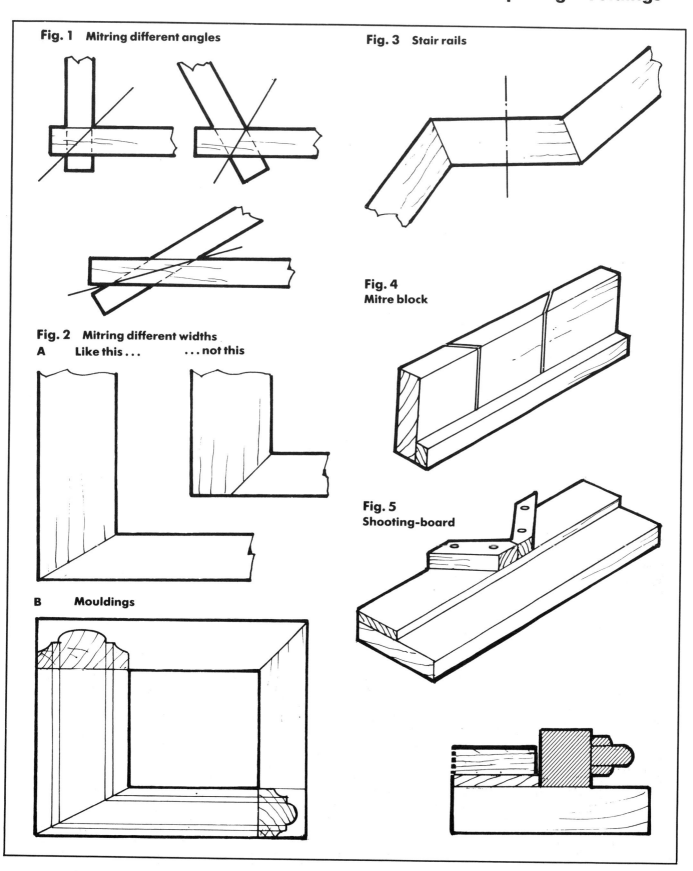

Fig. 1 Mitring different angles

Fig. 3 Stair rails

**Fig. 4
Mitre block**

Fig. 2 Mitring different widths

A   Like this . . .   . . . not this

B   Mouldings

**Fig. 5
Shooting-board**

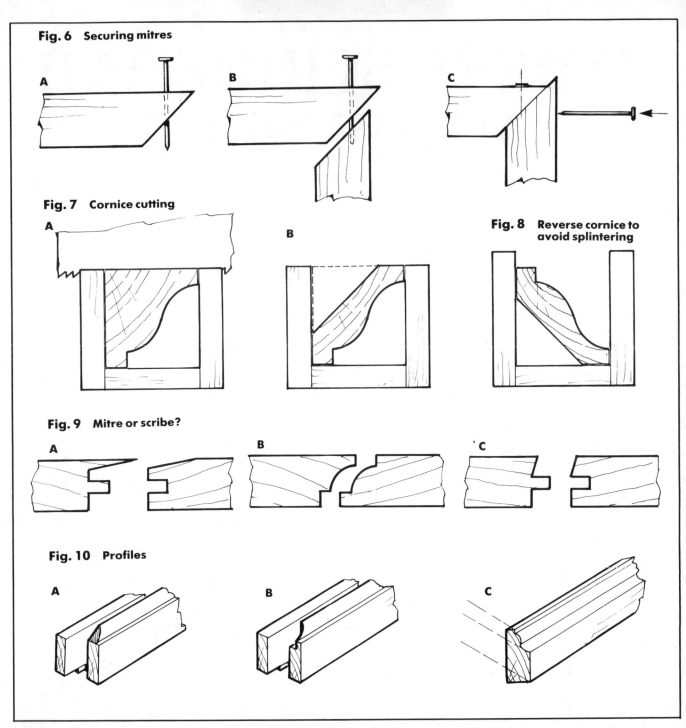

Fig. 6 Securing mitres

A   B   C

Fig. 7 Cornice cutting

A   B

Fig. 8 Reverse cornice to avoid splintering

Fig. 9 Mitre or scribe?

A   B   C

Fig. 10 Profiles

A   B   C

ny luck with your mitres? is a constant jibe in the workshop, in fun of course. I was once told of a picture framer who used tram tickets in his mitres – presumably to pad them out. Apparently his son spent most of his time roaming the streets for such discarded tickets. With or without tram tickets, mitred and scribed joints can pose problems, and a 'bit of luck' is sometimes very gratifying.

I distinctly remember being taught the theories of mitring: using protractors to measure 45° mitres for standard 90° corners and compasses to 'bisect the angle' from a level dado rail to an inclined one. In practice, I learned the easiest way to find a mitre is to overlap and draw a line through the intersection. The principle applies to mitres of differing angles (fig. 1), and situations when the pieces to be mitred are not the same width (fig. 2a). However when joining mouldings of unequal width or section (fig. 2b) mitring will not necessarily work.

The overlapping method works well f the junction of inclined and level dado rails, but for stairs with a turn do not attempt to mitre at an angle on the corner. I find the result is usually an untidy distorted mitre. Instead, level off before the turn (fig. 3) so that the job becomes a simple mitre.

For mass-mitring, a mitre box will of course save time. Remember, though, to mark special purpose-made boxes that are not 45° as such to avoid errors. Skirting mitres are cut using a mitre-cut (fig. 4) and for cleaning-up mitres a shooting-board is very useful (fig. 5). For a shooting-board to work accurately ensure that the guide does not rise above the blade by more than ¹⁄₁₆in and that the blade is straight and square.

Securing mitres can be a headache, and we have all at some time or other got into the most frightful situations. The most common fault is to nail at right angles to the mitre, and not the correct way (fig. 6). Tap the nail or pin perpendicular to the piece (fig. 6a), put the other piece in a vice and 'bite' the nail in off-centre (fig. 6b). Con-

tinue to tap in the nail until flush and if the mitre still overhangs, nail from the opposite direction to compensate (fig. 6c).

Cornices cause terrible trouble, mainly when you attempt to cut mitres flat, as you would for architraves or border strips. Have you ever noticed that though the mitre is a true 45°, the joint has a prodigious gap? If the cornice has a right-angled section (fig. 7a) cut the mitre in a purpose-made box, using the same method for cornices without cornered sections (fig. 7b). To find the length of cornice required mark on the ceiling with a short piece of cornice where the mitres meet. Measure from the point where the cornices meet on the ceiling rather than the wall, and cut in a mitre-box.

Sawing through cornices in this way can cause splintering so reverse the cornice (fig. 8) as though the cornice is being put around the floor. As you will soon discover, all the angles must also be reversed. Be prepared to make mistakes by having plenty of spare cornice.

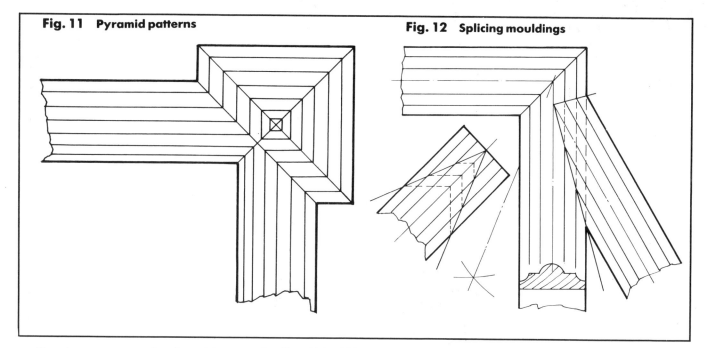

Fig. 11   Pyramid patterns

Fig. 12   Splicing mouldings

To mitre or not to mitre is a debate reserved for internal angles. The alternative is to butt the joint, scribing one piece to fit the profile of the other. As a rule a joint that creates a 'feather-edge' is mitred (fig. 9a) and the rest scribed (figs 9b,c).

Many carpenters use template gauges to scribe profiles, but when the pieces to be joined are identical in size and section there is a simple method. Cut the piece to be scribed with a 45° mitre, as for an internal angle (fig. 10a). Chisel or cut out the bevelled area (shaded in fig. 10a) to produce the desired profile (fig. 10b). This method can be used for skirtings, sawing out the profile with a copying saw or bandsaw once the scribing line has been found with an internal mitre.

Multiple mitres can create decorative features if cut accurately, in picture-framing, cabinet making and carpentry work. Four pieces, mitred like arrowheads (fig. 11) form inverted or normal pyramids. On ceilings, patterns can be created by splicing large astragal mouldings (fig. 12). The principle is identical to standard 45° mitres, ensuring that the angles on corresponding mitres match. Joinery novices learn the mitre joint early, but its usefulness broadens in tandem with skill and imagination. ∎

A cottage door

Bob Grant, who is a sizeable Saxon, explains how he set about making a door for a Welsh cottage with doorways evidently designed for a compact Celt

Pictures by John Peacock

It is one of my fanciful and completely unsubstantiated theories that the further west one goes in these islands then the smaller in stature its native folk become. From the stolid Saxon stock of the eastern and southern shires, smaller people, possibly of the older British race are to be found in Wales, and of course there are some rumours of wonderful little folk across St George's channel! Be that as it may, it was no real surprise to me when a good friend asked me to make a replacement door for his cottage in Wales to fit a frame 5ft 9in by 2ft. The building had once belonged to a miner and if not from his occupation he must have acquired a permanent stoop getting through his door, unless of course my theory has some basis in fact. I made the door shown in the accompanying photos as a forthright piece of joinery in the country tradition, though with some modern modification. My scale drawing shows the construction used; an 1⅛in thick mortise and tenon framework was faced with ½in thick boards of alternating 4in and 6in widths. These were grooved on their edges to take a hardboard tongue making the door chink proof. The boards were fixed to the frame by screws arranged in a staggered fashion, counterbored and covered with a raised pellet in simulation of the old fashioned rose-headed clout nails once used for the purpose.

All board edges and frame members were well chamfered off and as the door was to be left clear finished I went to some pains to select the tonal value of the boards with some reddish coloured pieces placed in the middle. The finish was three coats of W. S. Jenkins' 0.004 pale outside polish ('Jeco' Works, Tariff Road, Tottenham, London N17 0EN) an excellent clear finish. The door furniture is to be added in situ and I sawed off the horns before the door left my workshop. I would say that the construction employed for this small non-standard door would not suit a standard 6ft 6in × 2ft 6in door which would probably require wedging and bracing. ∎

Cutting list. Nett sizes

No	Description	Material	L	W	T
2	stiles	Joinery	5ft 9in	3¼in	1⅛in
1	top rail	quality	2ft	3¼in	1⅛in
1	middle rail	Russian	2ft	4¼in	1⅛in
1	bottom rail	red deal	2ft	6½in	1⅛in
3	boards	" "	5ft 9in	4in	½in
2	boards	" "	5ft 9in	6in	½in
4	tongues	hardboard	5ft 9in	½in	⅛in

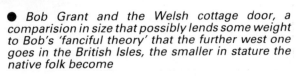

● Bob Grant and the Welsh cottage door, a comparision in size that possibly lends some weight to Bob's 'fanciful theory' that the further west one goes in the British Isles, the smaller in stature the native folk become

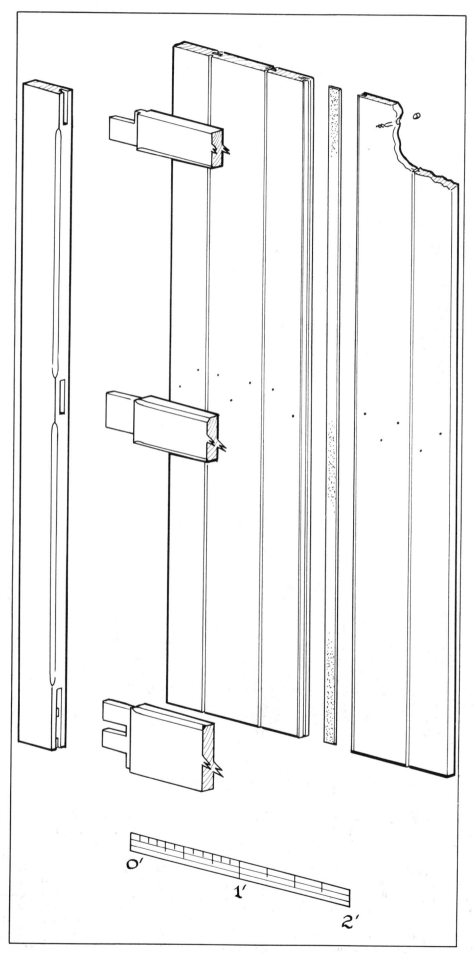

● *Above: the finished door. Below: a detail showing raised pellet screw plugs and hardboard tongue linking the boards*

MINIATURE MARVELS

Doll's houses and scaled-down replica furniture are fast becoming collectors' favourites and Den Young is famed for his Lilliputian manors and mansions. Michael Terry went to meet him

▲ Den Young's stock model: an Elizabethan manor house

► Magnificent William and Mary mansion, recently completed for a collector at almost £1000 per room

en Young is living proof that you don't have to have certificates to become a master of your craft. Over the past 20 years he's made a good living and won international acclaim designing and building replica doll's houses and furniture exact in every particular — and without the benefit of any formal training.

He lives in Willingham, near Cambridge, and recently completed a scale model of a 23-roomed William and Mary mansion, commissioned by a woman in Miami for £20,000. Not only does Den look the part of the classic fairy-tale toymaker with pipe, and bushy grey sideburns, but he's also blessed with an infectious laugh and an engaging manner. Sadly, he's not had any daughters or grand-daughters for the benefit of whom he could indulge his remarkable woodworking talents.

Den's attention to detail is obvious from the William and Mary mansion. The dome on its roof-lantern uses tiny, individual tiles made of real copper, the patterned parquet floor in the ballroom is made up of 1549 pieces of perfectly fitting wood and the symmetrical rows of miniature sash windows actually pull up and down.

It's a creation of epic proportions. Standing 69in tall, 66in wide and 34in deep, the model mansion was too large to fit inside Den's workshop, so it had to take pride of place in the family garage.

The outside walls of the model convincingly simulate ochre blocks of Bath sandstone and the front and back facades both open to reveal the imposing interior. The front door leads into a spacious hall; the impressive stair-case, with wrought-iron lamps on newel posts, took 200 hours to make. There's a delightful cast-iron kitchen range, toilets with cisterns and wooden seats — Den's vision is of a home lived in by the same family over two centuries — marble busts, fires that flicker and 42 lamps that light up. The wiring is skilfully concealed.

Den reckons that the complete project will have taken 4000 painstaking hours. At a price which includes materials and therefore represents less than £5 per hour, the lady in Miami is not getting too bad a deal!

DEN, NOW IN his 60s, took up dolls'-house making 20 years ago by sheer chance. After service in the Second World War as an RAF sergeant flying Spitfires and Hurricanes on reconnaissance over North Africa, he became a GPO engineer in peace time. Then, tiring

◀

of Civil Service routine, he decided to take up full-time the spare-time hobby which had come naturally to him since he was given a tool set at the age of four — woodworking.

He then made a good living selling inlaid coffee tables, lamp standards and wooden bowls. Listening in his workshop one afternoon to BBC Radio's Woman's Hour, he heard an American woman's impassioned plea for someone to make decent miniature antique furniture for her doll's house. Den immediately wrote asking her to provide a list of her requirements. He's never looked back since.

His first doll's house was the prototype of what was to become his stock model: an Elizabethan manor house which now sells at around £2000. Den showed it at the ancient Cheese Show at Frome, Somerset, in 1964 and won first prize. He received plenty of local media publicity, including TV, and the enquiries started to flow in. The timing was impeccable. Den's discovery of his new craft coincided with a revival of interest in the serious collecting of replica doll's houses and miniature antique furniture.

Today it is a thriving world-wide market. In America it rates as the second most popular hobby for women. The model items, however, are never destined for nursery playrooms. They are collectors' pieces; heirlooms, skilfully fashioned works of art admired for their magical, microcosmic qualities. The collectors demand the very best in accuracy, quality of finish and durability and are prepared to pay top prices.

Den's workmanship is a case in point. Roofs on his model houses have lofts with authentic trusses, king posts, queen posts, rafters and joists. The thatch on one of his replica cottages has separate trusses of real straw all made to scale; and a 16th-century inn he made for a building contractor's wife who is assembling a model-village High Street has a miniature beer engine that actually works!

Even the joints on the model pieces of replica furniture Den builds are real mortise-and-tenons in miniature. Fragile though they may seem, Den gives his assurance that if four of his exquisite Windsor chairs were strategically placed, they would be strong enough to bear the weight of a man. To achieve such high standards requires hours of dedicated research and skilled craftsmanship, and it's the reason why commissions have poured in from as far afield as America, Canada and Australia. He's even doing his bit for British trade overseas with appearances at 'British Week' exhibitions at leading department stores in America and Japan.

But Den is very modest, some would say nonchalant, about his rare talent. 'Miniature work is merely about cutting, sticking and possessing a steady hand and good eyesight. All you need is an eye for scale and the ability to use simple carpentry tools.' Those in the know judge Den more seriously. Michal Prouse, owner of the specialist Covent Garden shop 'The Dolls' House' (and arguably the woman who set in motion Britain's post-war revival of interest in doll's houses) rates Den among the masters of his craft. Vivien Greene, wife of novelist and playwright Graham Greene, has congratulated him on his work. And given that Mrs Greene is President of the Doll Club of Great Britain, has two definitive histories of doll's houses

under her belt, and owns a priceless collection of doll's houses and contents, it is an accolade indeed.

Den operates out of a workshop at the back of his Willingham house and, as he says, basic carpentry tools are the order of the day. He uses a bandsaw, a Black-and-Decker electric hand-drill and a range of modelling knives. But his most important tool is his Myford ML8 lathe which he's had for 35 years and which he uses for turning pieces such as balusters and legs for furniture. The lathe has an adjustable saw-bench. He also has an array of specialist tools custom-made by him to meet specific tasks which relate to small-scale work, such as miniature beading on miniature chair legs.

The woods which he uses on his models are, where possible, those used in the period houses of the time — mahogany, oak, sycamore and teak are incorporated in the William and Mary mansion. But he's found that the ideal woods for small-scale work are those which are dense, strong, with very little grain visible and have an ability to absorb stain evenly.

Whereas Den meticulously researches the historical and technical details of the houses and furniture he builds, he uses no detailed drawings or set plans — not unless you include the occasional rough scribbles found on the back of old envelopes lying in his workshop. 'I've been blessed with an in-built sense of scale,' he claims. 'I just build as I go along.' His basic technique is to first cut and build the base, side walls and room divisions so that he has a hollow box with a grid in which to fit the pre-made floors, fittings and furniture.

And how does Den market his wares? He puts it down to word of mouth. But close questioning reveals that he also advertises in specialist-hobby magazines at home and abroad, attends crafts exhibitions and keeps the British Overseas Trade Board and his local tourist board fully informed. He also distributes through specialist shops in London and the regious.

But he makes the point that the essential characteristic of the market is that it is demand-led. It is the collectors who set the fashions and seek out craftsmen to build their orders. The doll's-house tradition in this country goes back 300 years when Anne Sharp, daughter of the then Archbishop of Canterbury, was given a doll's house by her godmother, the future Queen Anne. The house can still be seen in the Strangers' Hall Museum, Norwich.

Den Young joins a long line of practitioners which includes such eminent names as Sir John Vanburgh, the 18th century architect who built a magnificent example for the Yarburgh family of Yorkshire, and Sir Edward Lutyens who during the 1920s masterminded the world famous Queen Mary's doll's house. The present-day revival has also given rise to a fast-growing number of amateur builders who are gaining a reputation, even among experts such as Den, for the high standards of their skills and creativity.

In his time Den Young has made more than 40 doll's houses and thousands of individual pieces of miniature furniture. For him it's been 'fun, exasperation and being my own boss.' And his only regrets? 'That I didn't start 20 years earlier.' ∎

The building contractor

Tony Sattin went to see a man who shrinks the best of British architecture to tabletop size

● *Bruce Coombes has a particular passion for miniature inns because of the social history which fills every corner.* **Below** *is the Spaniards, a well-known north-London landmark*

The first and most striking thing about Bruce Coombes is his passion for his work. Whether pointing out the model buildings ranged around his showroom-workshop in Frome, Somerset, or flicking through his albums of past commissions, he is animated. He loves talking about his models and the history that surrounds them.

This is not an idle observation, because one of the essential qualities for a modelmaker — Bruce Coombes specialises in building model period houses and architectural structures to scale — is enthusiasm: enough enthusiasm to survive the hours of painstaking research and weeks of delicate construction. Most of his stock models have taken between six and eight weeks to complete.

Born in London in 1917, he completed a tool-and-die apprenticeship and gained experience in several different fields before he started teaching technical studies and crafts at Bloomfield School, Woolwich, in the late sixties. It was there that he began making models — as teaching aids, to help bring history alive and to demonstrate construction techniques through the centuries. He has now made a series of models of Tudor, Georgian and Victorian houses, which have been bought by the Schools Loan Service. They are made from a variety of woods, including oak and mahogany; the windows are glazed either with glass or, if the models are to be used by children, with Perspex. His unusual scale is $5/16$ or $3/8$ in to the foot.

Another educational series he has developed demonstrates road communications with fine scale models of a coaching inn, toll-house, blacksmith's forge, wheelwright's shop and village store. And, to give movement to the series, there's a working $1/12$-scale model of a Royal Mail coach, its wooden structure mounted with iron shackles on to timber axle-cases. The wheelwright's shop is an excellent example of the lengths to which Bruce Coombes will go to recreate a building and its contents. Open the doors to the workshop, and inside are the workbenches and tools of the trade — all fixed to the surfaces and racks in case they get lost or broken.

By the early 1970s Bruce had moved to a school in Bath, and it was then that the *Sunday Times* carried a feature on his models. The subsequent attention and flood of commissions allowed him to retire from teaching and devote all his time to developing his talent for modelmaking. But the commercial demand for his work didn't make him change his techniques. Although his workshop now houses an engineer's lathe, a woodworker's lathe, a bandsaw and a small drilling machine, he doesn't do anything with them that he wasn't already doing with hand tools. 'All the machines do', he points out, 'is make things quicker.' Unlike many other areas of woodworking, modelmaking doesn't have to involve any great expense, and it can be done on the smallest of worktops.

His new market allowed him to expand his range, and he was commissioned to produce scale models of a number of private houses for their owners. Of one of them — Duart Castle, in Mull, Scotland, made on a scale of $3/16$ in for its owner Lord Charles Maclean — he is especially proud. For such a commission Bruce, usually assisted by his wife, likes to spend some time at the house, not only to measure (they take the dimensions and descriptions of every room and passage) but also to get a feel for the place. 'You have to use a certain amount of discretion when reconstructing,' he insists; but you also have to know the building you are intending to model.

Models of houses and public buildings are usually intended as presents. One proud father commissioned a model of Burbage's Globe theatre (1599) to commemorate his son's appearance in one of Shakespeare's plays.

Commercial organisations also showed an interest, and a number of companies (both in England and abroad) have commissioned models. Some form part of a promotion — the Japanese purchased models of a Cotswold stone house, a Tudor half-timbered house, a Victorian artisan's house and a Georgian shop, to display at British Week in Tokyo in 1975, and a department store in New York commissioned a stunning Tudor house as a central display piece. Some are emblems for products — the Black & White whisky company ordered a working model of a horse-drawn whisky dray.

Bruce Coombes has also executed a number of models of inns and taverns, usually for the licensee or landlord. This area of his work obviously excites him, and he does a great deal of research for it. 'I like to know the stories that come with the inns.' His models are exact and carry some of the history of the real buildings with them. His enthusiasm for the inns reflects his deep interest in social history; and, as he says, 'Every inn has got some history attached to it.' Along the shelves of his showroom are models of the Spaniards Inn, the much sung-about Bull and Bush in north London, and the King's Head in Aylesbury. Some are intended as educational pieces, and so a section of the roofing can be detached to reveal the structure — built, as in the original, of oak (although he uses pine if it's not going to be seen).

● A Coombes interior is carefully detailed down to counters, labels, pots and pans

His sense of history pervades his work altogether. Both his Nuremberg kitchen and his grocery shop are meticulously accurate in their furnishings and details; pans and kettles are made from copper or brass, and each packet is properly labelled. It is through these pieces that the modelling tradition can be traced: like the other models in the range — an English butcher's shop, a Victorian bathroom, a milliner's shop and a pleasure-garden kiosk — the grocer's shop was first made as a training aid for young ladies before marriage; it was to give them an idea of how a household was run and provided for, and to show them things they might never have seen otherwise.

By the end of the 19th century, toymakers in Nuremberg were reproducing the buildings as toys for children. The doll's- or baby-houses, as they were called, were originally designed for boys to play with, although they have a more general appeal now. The people who commission the models in this range do so for their value and appeal as collectors' items, and only occasionally for use as toys. (Bruce also provides miniatures, mostly furniture and brass- and copper-ware, for members of the International Doll's-House Club.)

The ability of Bruce Coombes' models to record social and industrial history is clearly shown in his scale reconstruction of Bridgewater Docks as they were in 1900, showing the warehouses, railway lines and roads, which is now exhibited at Bridgewater's Admiral Blake Museum. The list of his other commissions includes models of Newcomen's steam-engine, canal scenes (complete with lock-keeper's house, lock gates and barge or narrowboat), a complete medieval village for the Loch Lomond Bear Park, and a number of buildings for the army's officer training colleges. There seems no end to the different ways his models are used. This was obviously one of the things that first attracted Bruce Coombes to modelmaking, and it has continued to fascinate him.

At one time he called himself an artist-craftsman because, he argued, he was a craftsman in skill and an artist by inheritance (from his father and grandfather) and by training (at the Harrow and Lime Grove schools of art). But he seems to have little time for or interest in that kind of debate now.

He calls himself a historical modelmaker and a specialist — less provocative, perhaps, but just as apt.

In keeping with a noticeable trend among independent specialists in a whole variety of occupations, Bruce has recently opened a shop (he works behind it) at 17 Paul Street, Frome, Somerset. It is strange but pleasing to see a window filled with models in a row of shops selling more mundane products such as clothes and food. Inside he is busy at work on his latest commission, for the Castle Cary Museum: a Roman temple, based on the one uncovered at the Creech Hill site, which is typical of rural Roman temples found all over the country. Piled on his worktop are books on Roman architecture and guides to Roman sites and archeological digs. If you go in you might find him researching a design for the mosaic on the floor, or wondering whether there should be a frieze beside the architrave, or just gazing at his already completed models — reminders not only of ages gone by, but of life-styles that went with them. ■

Clever cleaner

● *Mark 1 hood with additions; mark 2 with its offset design is 90% efficient in crosscut mode*

● *For ripping, Don connects a vacuum hose to the dust spout. It's 95% efficient; detail shown opposite page, bottom right*

Extracting dust from radial-arm saws is notoriously difficult and rarely efficient. Don Solman's home-made solution is based on a classic amongst vacuum cleaners

I built my workshop to combine both woodwork and silversmithing, but they are not really compatible because of the dust. If I want to do some silversmithing it's a 45-minute task to clean away 3-4mm of dust from the silversmithing bench and tools.

Most of this dust (sawdust and fine dust) is created by the radial-arm saw, which backs up to the wall. The sawdust hits the wall and spreads everywhere. I have tried hoods with chutes to direct it into a container, but without much success.

I decided I had to get an extractor, but there were two constraints; cost (I am always reluctant to spend large sums of money on my hobbies) and — the real deciding factor — available space. There's just no room for a large but efficient free-standing extractor. The cost, depending on size, ranged from about £80 up to £450. The next stage was inevitable. The thought was already running through my mind: 'I'm sure I can make a reasonably efficient extractor for a fraction of the cost'.

Raw materials

The heart of an extractor is a good motor and fan blade, so I started looking at vacuum cleaners for an efficient motor that could also be easily adapted. I reckoned the most suitable was a Hoover 'Constellation' (I believe they're no longer made), the spherical type that glides along on a cushion of air. This particular model has excellent suction, and it could be easily modified

because it's made in two halves hinged together. The bottom half houses the motor, switch and two filters. It didn't take long to pick up a secondhand Constellation cleaner for £8.

The conversion

The basic idea is to junk the top half of the cleaner and fit the motor unit upside down on a new bin. The more I studied the cleaner the more I saw it was going to be easier than I thought. The hinge, toggle clamp and dust bag bracket had to be removed from the bottom half; they were riveted on with hollow rivets, which made it easy to drill the heads off. To do this I removed the three self-tapping screws that hold the filter plate to the bottom half, then lifted the motor about 20mm and pushed it to one side so the rivets could be drilled out. I plugged up the holes left by removing the rivets, using pop rivets — quick and simple. I removed the two small locating lugs that are spot-welded to the filter plate by centre-punching the spot welds and drilling out. An ⅛in drill was large enough.

Before re-assembling, the three round-head self-tapping screws had to be replaced with countersunk screws, as this is where the unit sits on the bin and you need a flat surface. The plate isn't thick enough to countersink normally, so it had to be press-countersunk. Get a large centre punch or something similar, hold the plate on a piece of wood (endgrain) and punch it deep enough to accept the countersunk head.

A seal was necessary between the motor housing and bin to keep up full suction. I made it by removing the rubber seal from the top half of the vacuum cleaner and cutting round the outer edge with a sharp knife to produce a flat rubber seal, which I fitted and stuck into place with contact glue. The motor housing was then complete and ready to be fitted to the bin. I did intend to remove the base ring but realised it made a perfect carrying handle, so I left it on.

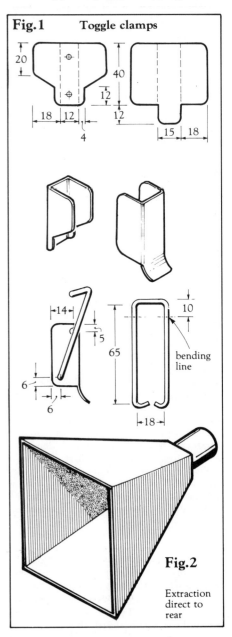

Fig.1   Toggle clamps

20

40

12

18   12

4

12

15   18

14

5

65

bending line

6

6

18

10

Fig.2

Extraction direct to rear

The bin

The bin needed to be 12in diameter, which I thought would be difficult to get — but I asked some friends who might have access to throwaway bins at work, and five were produced, all 12in diameter! I chose a tinplate one because it was the ideal height (14in); it would sit under the saw, and it has a reasonable volume.

I put the motor housing on the bin and took measurements for the toggle clamps, which I had also decided to make. Some 20swg mild steel sheet I had knocking about was suitable for all three clamps.

Fig. 1 shows the dimensions. Once I cut the metal (easily done with tinman's snips), I clamped the inside piece in the vice and bent it over a 12mm square bar (a piece of hardwood would do), and bent the outer piece over a 15mm square bar. The two pieces were then put together and drilled as a pair. The position of the holes is important, to ensure the toggle snaps over and clamps down. The size of the holes should suit the available rivet, bolt or wire. The clips were made from a 10swg (⅛in diameter) wire coat-hanger. The three toggle clamps were spaced out round the bin and pop-riveted into place.

I removed the hose connector from the top half of the cleaner by drilling out the two hollow rivets and spot welds. I used the holes created in the flange when I drilled out the spot welds for pop-riveting it on to the bin. Using the outer plate to mark the shape and position of the hole, I cut it out with tinsnips, and as the flange is flat I cut a piece of plywood the required diameter and G-clamped it on the inside, with another piece of wood on the outside. This created a flat surface so the hose connector could be pop-riveted in place.

Hoods and fitting

The dust extractor was now complete. It didn't take too long, but I did spend a great deal of time experimenting with the extractor hood for the crosscut mode of the saw. There's no doubt the most efficient is a hood that directs the sawdust to a point of extraction at the rear (fig. 2). My saw backs up to the workshop wall, so the point of extraction is at the bottom of the hood. This is where the problem was created. The first hood I made had a flat back and I thought the dust would drop down and be sucked away, but the sawdust hit the back of the hood with so much force that about 70% rebounded out.

I tried again, and made mark 2 (fig. 3) with acutely sloping top and sides to direct the sawdust to the point of extraction. This was about 70% efficient, the rest of the waste rebounding out. To overcome the bounceback I added inwardly sloping baffles (fig. 3) at the front. This has improved the unit to about 90% efficient, and unless I spend a lot more time I feel it's as good as can be expected. The photos show

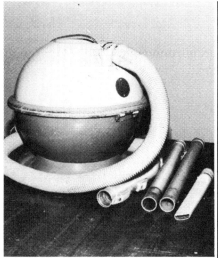

● *The Hoover Constellation – what price extraction for £8?*

● *Above, how it looks when it's ready to go. The fan and motor unit is inverted. Below, cam clamps hold the hose for in- or out-rip positions*

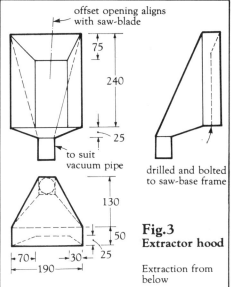

**Fig.3
Extractor hood**

Extraction from below

hood mark 1 with experimental additions, but mark 2 has now been installed. I have the facilities to gas weld, so I made the hood from 20swg. mild steel sheet, but with a little ingenuity it could be made from plywood, hardboard or any suitable sheet material.

For ripping, I put a piece of tube in the rubber dust spout on the blade guard, held with jubilee clips, and with the extractor connected at least 95% is extracted. The changeover from crosscutting to ripping only takes seconds, and to support the hose I made two simple cam clips, one for in-rip and the other for out-rip positions. It also attaches to my belt sander and power planer, a bit cumbersome but nevertheless efficient.

This was definitely a worthwhile project, and the total cost to me was £8, plus a couple of pints for the bins. It has made my workshop environment healthier, and now there is no great build-up of dust. It's efficient and portable so a general clean-up can take place more frequently; even the car gets vacuumed now! ∎

Smoke your own

An interesting special for the Christmas cuisine — benefit from guest cookery editor John Turner's sagacity and add an individual shavings flavour to your cheese

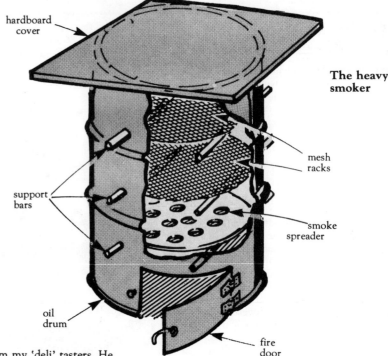

hardboard cover

The heavy smoker

mesh racks

support bars

smoke spreader

oil drum

fire door

I'd long thought about having a go at smoking my own food, cheese in particular, but it was having a floor full of apple shavings that launched me into action. I filled an 8in-high flowerpot with them, set them alight, and put the pot in a clean oil drum. I had cut some ash laths ½in longer than the drum diameter, and I braced these into the ridges, and balanced some more small-section pieces across these as a makeshift grid.

This is when I learnt lesson one. Do all the leaning into the barrel and fiddling about that you have to do *before* you light the shavings.

Eyes smarting, I ran to fetch the pound of tasty cheese we had in the fridge, and balanced it on the sticks. The wind blew the smoke out as fast as it was generated so I shook out an old sack and covered the drum with it; 10 minutes later the shavings went out.

Lesson two: carbon dioxide is heavy and extinguishes fires. Solution — drill some holes round the bottom of the barrel.

Two hours later I tasted the cheese, refilled the flowerpot and put it back to get a bit more flavour. Three hours after that I was jubilant. The cheese was delicious — if a little strong.

Next day I bought 3lb of mild and tried again. I also put two bacon rashers in to try that. Smokey those rashers certainly became, nice when chopped into a sauce — cauliflower with smoked cheese and smoked bacon sauce, delicious — but bacon really needs smoking as a joint before slicing. The cheese was such a success with friends and it seemed so easy I immediately did another 3lb.

This time I took slices of it to a couple of local delicatessens, to get an opinion and investigate the idea of supplying them. I carefully memorised the wholesaler's phone number on the cheese block in one shop, and wrote it down once I got out of the shop. When I rang him to ask if he could supply cheese for my new smoking business, he suggested he might buy it back once it was smoked. This seemed a brilliant idea, since distribution costs were already threatening to destroy my potential profits.

The wholesaler came to see me, liked the cheese and heard the reports I had received from my 'deli' tasters. He suggested it would be easier to pay me to smoke it, rather than selling it and buying it back; so I found myself holding 40lb of cheese, waving good-bye to trusting salesman.

It was raining, so I moved my smoker indoors. It was also obvious that 40lb of cheese was going to take up more space than 3lb, so I wedged in another rack, only to discover that the cheese took up so much space I couldn't get the flowerpot in. So out it all had to come; the dog knocked the flowerpot over and broke it.

I had a failed applewood bowl lying round, so I drilled some holes in that, filled it with shavings and lit it; bending into the smoke, I braced in the racks, put the cheese in and covered it over. The shavings in the bowl burnt a bit fast, and though the cheese didn't actually melt, it did take on some of the shape of the sticks and coloured somewhat patchily. Visions of paying out fat cheques and finding myself with six months' supply of cheese began to flash uncomfortably in my mind.

A remedy was needed — and quick. A smoke spreader? Cutting a circle from an old roofing sheet with scissors (hard work but needs must), I punched it full of holes and put that in the barrel.

Now what to put the shavings in? Metal causes condensation and extinguishes the smoulder, no more flower pots . . . what? Ring round the libraries: a book on smoking? No, not giving it up; *food* smoking. Yes? I'll be right over.

I set to and re-equipped myself, going by the book.

Proper 1in welded mesh racks, iron bars, more holes in the barrel, a door cut in the bottom, self-tapping screws, a hinge, a heavier lid to cover — but for the shavings container, no easy answer.

Try the wooden bowl again, this time controlling airflow into the barrel; I also put a yoghurt-making thermometer in the top. Chuck that sack, dust on the cheese doesn't look good.

This time it burnt too cool, and the cheese smelled a bit sharp as a result, so I discarded the lid and decided on a clean candlewick cloth to cover.

Still doesn't look right, 40 quid's worth of cheese . . . what to do?

Ring round the market traders: Look, I may have some good smoked cheese coming up, a pound a pound, doesn't look perfect that's why it's not going out the usual way, but it tastes good, the price is right, you interested? Good. Yes, I'll let you know.

Smoked cheese seems best about four days after it comes out, so I bagged up the results to season. On Wednesday I'll open the bags, cut one block in half and taste it. I'll look the other blocks over, and any that meet a high standard will go to the wholesaler. Some I shall swop with a friend for an old fridge — the wholesaler only comes past once a week — some will go to the market unless there's been a flavour disaster, then . . . well, suck it and see, as they say. ∎

● Cheese is less complicated to smoke than meat. The book from the library is called *Home Smoking and Curing* by Keith Erlandson, Barrie & Jenkins 1977.
● Don't put the smoker in your workshop unless you want a sore throat!

Not so dusty?

The Health and Safety Executive Report *Manufacturing and Service Industries 1984*, makes disturbing reading for woodworkers

'Two young people were working for a self-employed furniture restorer. He had a wide range of woodworking machines, some of which were rarely used, with many unguarded danger points. The major concern was the use of a home-made radiant heater for flashing off solvents from french-polished furniture. The element of an electric fire was screwed to a piece of timber approximately the size and shape of a cricket bat. The element was completely unguarded and was held near to the polished furniture. An immediate prohibition notice was served and the drying of french polish is now carried out more safely.'

13 people died in the timber and timber-related manufacturing industries in 1984, and six in 1983. The statistics break down in more detail, of course; 40% of woodworking machinery accidents in an H&SE study occurred on circular sawing machines; in 57% of the cases, the inspector considered the accident was because guards had been removed or were defective. There was a disproportionately high percentage of accidents in small firms employing up to 25 people.

What about dust?

'Exposure to wood dust has received particular attention during the year because of concern about potential long-term effects on health,' says the Report. *'The problem . . . was most acute in factories manufacturing reproduction furniture and generally employing fewer than 30 people. Inspectors found dust accumulations on floors three and four inches deep, piles of shavings several feet in depth and ledges and fittings covered with up to seven inches of dust.'* Credit where it's due — six High Wycombe factories, inspected in 1977 and 1983, showed a 'statistically significant decline in exposure to wood dust'.

The H&SE Woodworking National Industry Group has produced a leaflet on the subject — a Guide for Employers. The whole theme of the H&SE's work is that it's up to the employer to provide safe working conditions. **But:** real detail on the actual hazards that face the woodworker — self-employed, small professional, semi-professional and indeed the enthusiastic amateur — is lacking. *'Exposure has been associated with the following health hazards,'* the leaflet warns; *'● skin problems ● obstruction of the nose ● asthma ● a rare type of cancer of the nose.'* And, of course, fire and explosion.

In November's *Woodworker*, we appealed for a medical angle. Someone out there, we reasoned, must be a doctor and a reader who loves wood and woodwork; and **Dr Bob Clewlow** has replied.

I HAVE BEEN much interested in recent articles and comments about dust hazards.

I've had to stop working with yew because the dust always causes me severe headaches, nausea and chest pains, which can persist for several weeks. I began to notice that with each successive exposure the symptoms became worse, and could only assume the effect was cumulative. I concluded that it would be wise to think of the problem not as an allergy but as permanent damage.

Although it's always wise to wear a dust-mask, fine particles remain floating long after the mask is removed. The main effort must be to collect the dust effectively at source. Vacuum-cleaners and dust-extractors with nozzles close to the source will remove most of the fine dust which is the main hazard.

May I recommend some very informative reading on the subject? 'Toxic Woods' by Brian Woods and O. P. Galnan, supplement 13 to the British Journal of Dermatology, vol. 95, 1976, Blackwell.
Ken Keleher, Whitby

● *Yew dust – readers' letters continue*

WORKING WOOD — AND BREATHING IT

Dr Bob Clewlow deals in depth with the hazard to your health

The traditional image of woodworking is not usually associated with industrial disease. The odd gash or bruise is all the traditional joiner working with plane, chisel and mallet expected, but the introduction of lesser-known timbers, manufactured boards, and sophisticated power tools has brought previously

● *The report – does it tell you enough?*

unsuspected dangers to health. Industrial users are strictly governed by safety regulations, but the personal responsibility that these regulations demand is often neglected — or worse, ignored — by small businesses and owners of home workshops.

Any cutting of timber inevitably produces particles of waste wood. Their size depends on the nature of the wood and the operation. In general, the harder the wood, the finer the dust; routing, bandsawing, and, obviously, sanding all produce a very fine waste, which in the case of sanding is probably mixed with abrasive powder too. Many power tools and woodworking machinery generate a draught which causes the fine dust to be whipped up into a highly penetrating aerosol suspension, and it's in this state that the dust can be damaging. There's no reason to believe that poisonous fruit in a timber species leads to a more toxic dust. Yew and laburnum both produce toxic berries, but there is no evidence that their dust is any more toxic than other timbers. Certain species produce toxic vapours while they're being worked; teak can give off an irritating vapour when friction-heated during turning, and cocus wood (once used extensively to make spinning shuttles in the cotton trade) gives off a volatile alkaloid when worked, which has an excessive slowing effect on the heart-rate.

In the early days of mechanisation and automation in the furniture industry, workers displayed a very much higher incidence of nasal cancer, especially around High Wycombe. The now-widespread use of efficient dust extraction plant has minimised this problem, and I don't think there is a significant risk to the small workshop user.

The major problems that result from wood dust come generally under two headings: the direct irritating effect, and the effects produced in sensitive subjects. The direct effects are likely to affect anyone coming into contact with dust; the particles enter the nose and pharynx through inhalation, and get in the eyes, when they can cause severe irritation and conjunctival reactions. This can be counteracted by using close-fitting goggles, and a Martindales face mask for particularly dusty operations. Sensitivity to wood dust can produce a severe swelling of the eyelids which may persist for some days and is likely to recur on subsequent exposure.

Skin contact can cause sensitivity problems, and avoidance is difficult. It's hardly practical to carry out the majority of woodworking operations in protective gloves. There are two main types of skin problem associated with handling sensitising substances. The first is an acute sensitivity reaction, when the skin develops a red, raised, itchy blistering rash similar to nettle rash, and is more likely to be due to a direct reaction to oils or resins in the wood than to an allergy. This sort of reaction settles fairly easily with homely remedies. The second type of reaction is more long-standing, and is due to prolonged exposure to one type of dust, to which the worker

becomes sensitised. A chronic dry dermatitis then develops, often with cracking and fissures in the skin. This is much more difficult to treat, and requires the attention of a doctor. If it occurs at work, it could be recognised as an industrial dermatitis and thus qualify for industrial compensation. Skin sensitivity problems are not common in wood-handlers, and species likely to cause problems are those producing a very fine dust, for example ebony and rosewood. Interestingly, clarinet players may get reactions in their lips from sensitivity to the grenadilla wood used for reeds. Wood dust and shavings that have been standing for a long period can become damp and form an ideal home for mites. These tiny creatures cause rashes by biting those handling infested material, so this too presents a minor irritation.

Sensitivity to wood dust causes the most serious problems in the respiratory tract, where the damage caused by inhalation of the aerosol-fine dust is worst. The different sections of the lining of the respiratory system, which runs from the nose to the final honeycomb tissues of the lungs themselves, respond differently to toxic substances.

The upper levels are lined with mucous and hair-cells which trap and eliminate foreign particles. The acute feeling

of congestion in the head, sneezing and running catarrh that you get when dust enters the nose and throat is because these cells have been temporarily immobilised.

Further down the respiratory tree, in the small air passages, the response is a different one. Here the walls of the small air-tubes are lined with a muscle coat, and the presence of foreign matter, especially organic, causes an allergic constriction of the muscle tubes and a possible attack of bronchial asthma. The sufferer need not necessarily be allergic, though he or she usually would be, and would also need to have been exposed to similar sensitising material in the past. Long-continued exposure to small amounts of organic dust can produce a chronic 'late onset' asthma, which causes persistent shortage of breath, and occurs especially on working days. Asthma due to inhalation of organic dust at work is also now recognised in certain groups of workers as a notifiable industrial disease.

There is a whole group of diseases, known as the **pneumoconioses**, which are a result of dust in the final saccular portions of the lung tissue. Here the response to foreign substances is different again. Cells known as **macrophages** in the tissues absorb the foreign particles, and in doing so generate inflammation, the nature of which depends on the

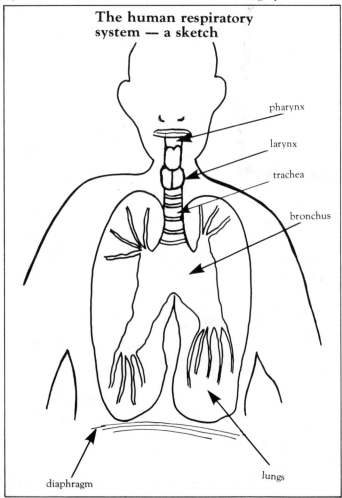

The human respiratory system — a sketch

pharynx

larynx

trachea

bronchus

diaphragm

lungs

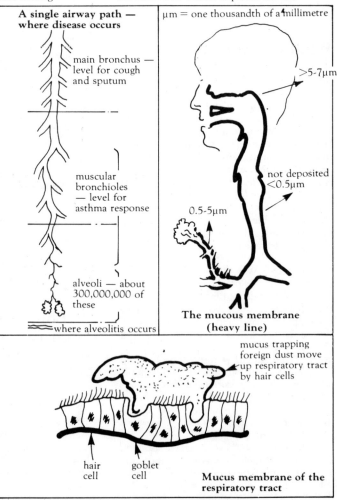

A single airway path — where disease occurs

main bronchus — level for cough and sputum

muscular bronchioles — level for asthma response

alveoli — about 300,000,000 of these

where alveolitis occurs

µm = one thousandth of a millimetre

>5-7µm

not deposited <0.5µm

0.5-5µm

The mucous membrane (heavy line)

mucus trapping foreign dust move up respiratory tract by hair cells

hair cell

goblet cell

Mucus membrane of the respiratory tract

Not so dusty?

inhaled matter. The damage caused by the inhalation of foreign matter depends upon various factors:
● The size of the particle (0.5-5μm)
● The density of the particle in the inhaled air
● The chemical nature of the particle
● Individual tolerance
● Allergic tendency in the person exposed
● Previous exposure to the substance.

Because of the varied chemical structure of wood dusts, there is no constant clinical picture for wood dust pneumoconiosis. There have been reports of dust diseases arising from the inhalation of the dust of mahogany, oak and iroko, but blood tests on the sufferers failed to reveal any allergy to the timber itself. Most allergies to timber or its products are in the group known as **extrinsic allergic alveolitis.** This is a massive inflammatory response in the lung tissues, occurring about eight hours after exposure, and appearing as an acute respiratory difficulty with chest-pains and aching limbs. Although the acute stage may settle quite rapidly, breathlessness and cough may persist for weeks or months, and may progress to permanent lung damage. It's a similar condition to that which occurs in farmer's lung, and results from inhalation of fungus spores in timber. Investigation of the victims very often shows their blood to have antibodies to microscopic fungi in the material they handle. The description given by the correspondent mentioned in 'This Month', *Woodworker* Nov. 85, of his troubles turning an old piece of yew sounds very much like this condition, and could well be explained by his old and dusty timber. Because of the potential in these sorts of disorders for permanent and serious chest disease, it's

important for anyone with respiratory problems who is exposed to wood dust to seek medical advice quickly and to tell the doctor that dust inhalation might be a cause of the symptoms.

Many workshop hazards are self-evident, and with reasonable methods can be avoided or eliminated. It seems that medical authorities in the past have failed to recognise the possible hazards of wood dust, or they have been overlooked on the shop floor (except by industrial timber users). It's more than possible that wood dust can prove a health risk not only for those with allergic tendencies or chest disease, but for healthy people too.

Some protection can be given by commercial face-masks, but many of the smaller particles can pass through their pores. Dust extraction machinery is hardly practicable for the home user, though it may suit the small commercial workshop. If you experience serious chest problems on exposure to wood dust, you should seek medical advice and be sure to point out the nature of the exposure. If you do have serious chest disease, you'll have to avoid that particular timber; you might even have to avoid wood dust altogether, which means — god forbid — you might have to give up woodwork; unless, of course, you can come up with strictly dust-free techniques! ■

References
Franklin, *Medicine* Oct 82
Hutchinson, *Health in Industry* (Penguin)
Oxford Textbook of Medicine
Schleuter, Fink et al, *Annals Int. Medicine*, 77, p.907
J. Slavin, *Allergy & Clinical Immunology*, 1978
Turner Warwick, *Thoracic Medicine*.

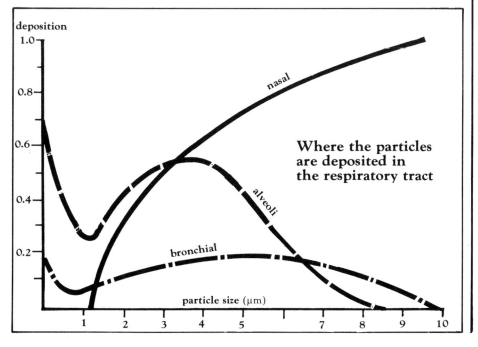

Where the particles are deposited in the respiratory tract

deposition / particle size (μm) / nasal / alveoli / bronchial

A coffee table

Gift for a god-daughter

Bob Grant presents a stylish coffee table which he designed and made in Columbian pine as a wedding present for his god-daughter

Picture by John Peacock

Godchildren are a spiritual charge but when one of mine married recently and settled down in a neat little house in the West Country I offered a more tangible service and said that I would like to contribute to the new home.

A pine table of the refectory type was wanted the size to be no more than 3ft × 2ft × 18in and the rest was up to me. The photograph shows my response and the accompanying scale drawings and cutting list should assist readers who may want to make a similar piece. It is some years since I have worked in good, clean British Columbian pine (though it has its moments of devilment and can split at the most awkward times and places) and I had quite a job finding a supply suitable to my wants. The design would look well in any wood.

Shouldered mortise and tenon joints are used in the construction of the pedestal ends whilst the top spreader bars are lap dovetailed on as shown in the plan view drawing (top half removed). The curved underframe stretcher rail may be set out by springing a lath some 1in up in the centre and the fancy wedged mortise and tenon joint which protrudes through the pedestals is shown in detail in sketch and photo.

The arriss on the pedestal units is worked into a moulding using a portable router fitted with a ¼in rounding over bit with

guide pin and set down to form a step.

The edges of the top and underframe rail are similarly worked with a cove moulding. The top is butt jointed up from a number of narrow boards (I carefully selected these for their even grain) and this is held down to the substructure by metal fixing plates suitably slotted to the whole and it would be advisable to coat the top with a heat resisting variety. I did this on the original and then cut the shine off with 0000 steel wool, buffing the top to a pleasing matt finish. ■

CUTTING LIST (SIZES NETT)

No	Description	L	W	T
2	standards	16in	3in	1⅛in
2	cross bars	20in	2½in	1⅛in
2	feet	20in	3½in	1⅛in
2	spreader rails	26in	1½in	1in
1	underframe rail	28in	ex3in	1⅛in
1	top	3ft	2ft	¾in

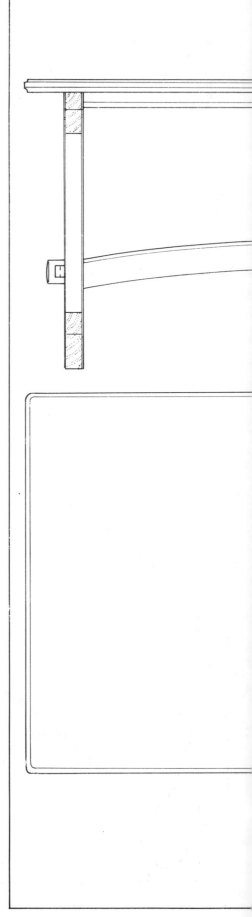

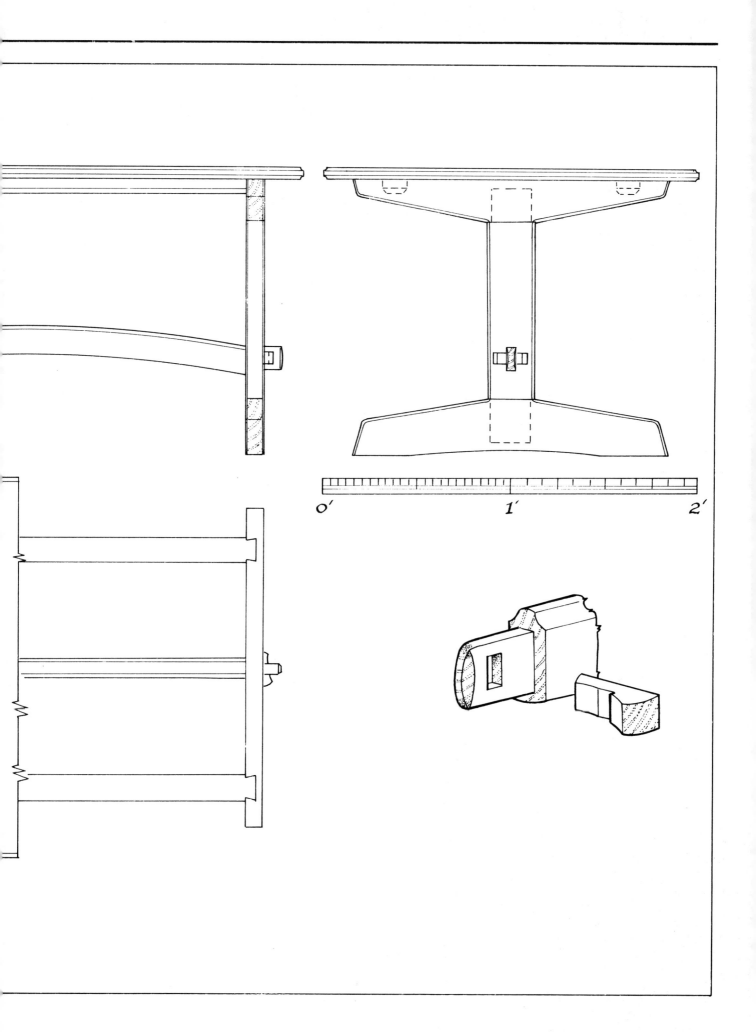

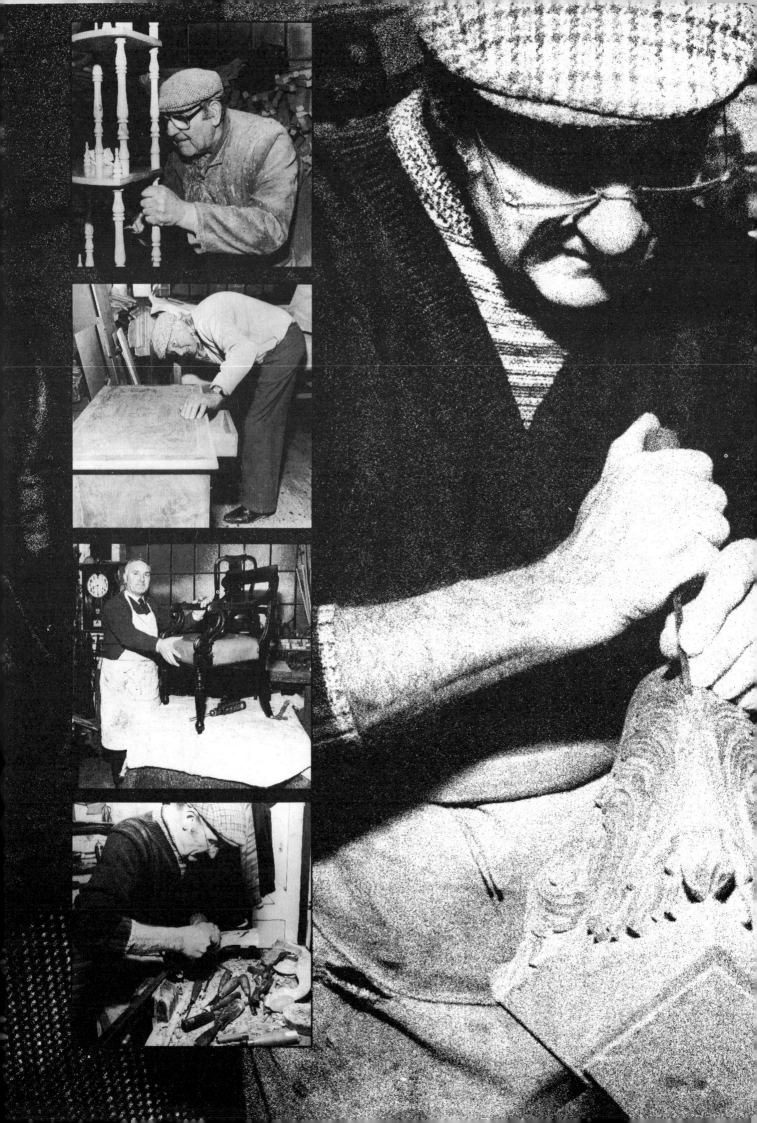

TIMES PAST, TIMES PRESENT, TIMES FUTURE?

John Hemsley visits a cluster of traditional wood trade workshops in London's East End and discovers a modern maker in their midst

For 150 years the East End of London has had a thriving furniture-making tradition. The trade was characterised by small workshops and intense specialisation – carvers, turners, polishers, concentrating on what they did best and fastest – with middlemen coordinating, assembling and selling on the final products. Though the trade has diminished sharply in the past 25 years, with rent increases forcing the craftsmen to look outside the metropolis for cheaper premises, some of the old-style workshops still exist.

One of these is Sunbury Workshops, a delightful mews of 30 tiny workshops purpose-built for the furniture trade more than half a century ago. The workshop block is crammed with craftsmen in wood and allied trades – trade turners and carvers, fret cutters, upholsterers. Most work in traditional East End fashion, spending long hours using a single skill – like Vic the carver, who produces a highly decorated claw and ball cabriole leg in four hours

Carver Vic Deeks (left and bottom far left) started carving at 14 and says he'll never retire: 'I'll die on the bench.' Far left, from top: Harry Crook, the turner of whatnots; Lou Feldman, erstwhile maker of aircraft, now cabinets; Bill Spiller, restorer. Below, Matthew Collins attends to a cabinet base

flat, and then starts on the next... He has earned his living with a limited range of carvings for 46 years.

Matthew Collins is a modern anachronism in this setting, a cabinetmaker who designs and makes, seeing projects through from beginning to end. He's 24 years old and has been a self-employed professional for only 12 months.

He used to work in a bank, but struggled to make furniture on a B&D Workmate in his spare time. Then he discovered WOODWORKER, got hooked on wood and launched himself on a journey of self-realisation that has taken him to furniture college, working for a Gimson/Barnsley tradition designer/maker and now esconced him in his own tiny workshop.

Tiny it is, like the rest of them in the Sunbury block. In the 255 sq ft is a 10in Wadkin sawbench, a Sedgwick 12in planer/thicknesser, a Whitehead Linisher belt & disc sander, a Sedgwick mortiser and a small Wadkin Tradesman bandsaw – Matthew likes his machinery to be British, cast iron and solid! Racks on one wall are laden with English hardwoods, particularly chestnut which is his current favourite. In a corner is a miniscule open fire on which he throws offcuts to keep the frost away.

He likes being in the East End. He has lived in the area since he was 16, and the

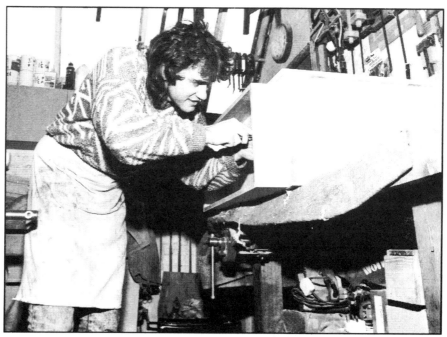

Tower Hamlets location mean that renowned tool shops like Tyzacks and Parry's are just a stroll away. He is keenly aware of the heritage of the Sunbury Workshops: some of the trade craftsmen have been there more than 30 years, others have taken up a workshop which their father or uncle had.

Matthew did not immediately feel accepted in this traditional setting. 'It took a while before anyone here trusted me,' he concedes. 'Then one upholsterer gave me a job, I did it well and I was soon inundated with work.' Now the other craftsmen realise that Matthew can, and will, turn his hand to any work in wood – general joinery, restoration, making for other furniture designers, some trade reproduction work (bread and butter for East End furniture making today) – when he's not working on his one-offs and small batch runs.

Matthew's beginnings were certainly different to most of the people in Sunbury Workshops. 'Working in a bank when I left school was an easy option. But I detested it.'

Living in a council flat on the Isle of Dogs, he started buying hardwood and making furniture for his home. This practical handiwork, combined with the lure of what he found in the magazine, caught him up in the enthusiasm of a lifetime. He thought about college, and his work was good enough for him to be offered a place at Rycotewood as well as his choice, High Wycombe, for the Fine Craft Diploma course. It was a three year course, but

family responsibilities forced him to leave after two; he did complete City and Guilds in chairmaking (Advanced Craft Part III) and cabinetmaking, in both of which he gained distinctions.

On leaving college he got a job with an east London company, Giles Thomas Furniture, which concentrated on contract furniture and one-off items designed in the Gimson/Barnsley tradition by Giles Thomas, whom Matthew regards as one of the finest current British furniture makers.

After working at his own speed at college, Matthew found furniture making outside made far more demands on him. 'My first job was a tea trolley that had 140 handcut dovetails, and Giles set me a tight time limit,' he recalls. The firm did a fair amount of joinery as well, reinforcing Matthew's own opinion that the common elitism of cabinetmakers is quite unjustified. 'There's a lot of people doing quality work in the wood trade, from carpenters to carvers,' he points out. 'The Barnsleys were involved in building work as well as furniture. Personally I can get just as much satisfaction from a really nice staircase as a chest of drawers with handcut dovetails.'

That satisfying period came to an end for Matthew after 18 months. The Giles Thomas workshop, on the Isle of Dogs, became worth more as residential property as yuppies discovered east London. Giles turned down many offers but finally sold up.

Flexible as ever, Matthew turned to building site work (second fitting) to earn

enough cash to set up his own workshop. 'I enjoyed working for Giles, and I decided the only way I could be as happy again was working for myself.' When he finally took the big step, he got a £1000 grant from the Prince Charles Trust to help him start up.

Now he does one-offs and small batches. One of his latest commissions was eight Arts-and-Crafts Movement style chairs for a customer in Boston, Massachusetts, involving considerable handwork; he reckons they've taken him about a week apiece. He fits in other jobs around them as well. 'I regard myself as a maker and not a designer,' he says, 'though I make mainly to my own designs.'

Matthew likes his workshop and the friendly atmosphere of working alongside other craftspeople in allied trades. His rent, at £25 a week plus £10 rates at the moment, is cheap by London standards. But it may soon change. The Sunbury Workshops used to belong to the GLC, and were transferred to the London Residuary Body (after the GLC abolition), which sold them off. In the last six months the block has changed hands twice. Conversion or redevelopment would almost certainly bring in more revenue to the owners. The tenants are combining to fight any such moves: they recognise that not just their livelihoods are at stake, but a living craft tradition. ∎

Reflections on a bench

Alan Peters, held by
many to be this
country's finest
designer and maker
of good furniture, has
designed a simple
garden bench,
exclusively for
Woodworker

Gardening

The garden bench is a humble enough piece of furniture, found usually in a ruinous and rotted condition and invariably uncomfortable to sit upon. The purpose of commissioning a craftsman and designer of Alan Peters' standing to design, specially for *Woodworker,* something as prosaic as a garden bench was twofold.

Firstly we asked him to rethink the shape and construction of the traditional garden seat, and secondly to produce a design of his own which readers could make up for themselves.

The immediately significant impression of Alan's resulting bench is that it appears little different from that time-honoured construction of a garden bench that has been arrived at empirically over a great many summers of idle contemplation in the world's gardens, great and small. However, closer inspection shows that, while its slatted surfaces create a traditional impression, much thought has been given to the actual shapes and profiles that the slats present to the seated human figure.

Alan Peters' design illustrates well his profound respect for the traditions of the past. He is not a man to throw out all preconceptions and he doesn't seek to be controversial or *avant garde.* Rather he chooses to review preconceptions in design within the context of his own original ideas, and makes his changes delicately, thoughtfully. It is apt here to repeat what he has said about his work in general:

'While my furniture is unashamedly of the late-20th century, it does not ignore the best traditions of the past. The care and attention given to my work can never make it cheap, but the challenge of designing within a modest budget has often produced for me the most satisfying work, for I enjoy making simple things well.

'Of course a craftsman's work should be distinctive, and excellence should be his goal, but at the same time I do not believe it is the natural role of the craftsman to find the most expensive and time-consuming solution to the simplest design problem.'

The garden bench project has proved to be a most rewarding and revealing exercise for *Woodworker,* and Alan Peters tells us that he is well pleased with the results too. So now we invite you to make your own garden bench from which to survey the pleasant hum of a summer's afternoon.

Here, in Alan Peters' own words, is his rationale in designing the garden bench, along with details of construction

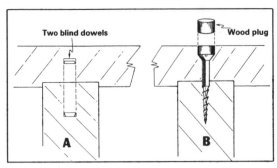

● *Notch seat and back slats in by ⅛in. This gives accurate location for assembly and added strength. Fix slats either with blind dowels (A) or screw and plug (B). If you use blind dowels, each slat must be glued and cramped in turn*

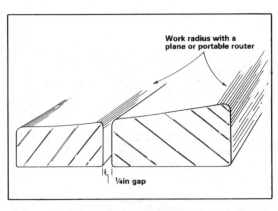

● *A quarter view shows how the back slats are notched into the back supports*

● *Keep seat slats close together with gaps of only ¼in. This will avoid an uncomfortable seat. Cut the angle on a tilting arbor circular saw or whittle away with a jack plane and finish from a sharp plane*

Design aims

An attempt to achieve:
1. A high degree of comfort in a rigid structure
2. A piece of furniture which looks and feels good
3. A seat which can withstand extremes of weather and a degree of human abuse
4. A design within the ability of the committed amateur to achieve, but at the same time possessing those qualities that distinguish the work of a craftsman.

Approach

I began by examining what is wrong with much outside timber seating, which falls basically into two categories:
1. The traditional garden or memorial seat, with arms and upright slatted back which has remained largely unchanged over many, many years. It serves its purpose reasonably well, but is invariably uncomfortable because its ribbed seat and back do not follow the contours of the body and give support where needed.
2. The modern bench, designed on drawing boards for local authorities and institutions. Its aggressive sharp edges and flat planes invite equally aggressive youngsters to soften and humanise its lines with the aid of knives.

I hope that the bench I have designed will invite the human hand to caress rather than deface, and provide comfort rather than torture.

Timber

Choice of timber is vital for the success and maintenance-free future of this project. Any one of the following timbers is ideal, being largely rot and weather resistant:

Hardwoods
Teak
English oak
Sweet chestnut

Softwoods
Western red cedar
Cedar of Lebanon
Larch
Macrocarpa

Failing one of the above, tanalised top quality softwood building timber could be used.

Construction

It is quite feasible to make this piece without the use of machinery if the timber is purchased pre-cut to size. In making the prototype I made full use of a tilting arbor circular saw, hollow chisel mortiser and portable router, with the main purpose of saving time. What is important is the quality of the joints, and the attributes of comfort, appearance and durability of the finished piece. The methods used to achieve these are of no great significance provided they give the maker satisfaction and pleasure.

One note here: before finally fitting down the seat and back slats, sit on it, and correct any uncomfortable projections, before finally glueing. I adjusted mine to suit me at 5ft 9in – yours too might benefit from a personalised 'tuning' into final shape. Simply take off the offending slat, plane off the amount required, refit and try again. It's your bench, and your comfort.

Finish

Resist the temptation to use glasspaper. It is far better to aim for a razor sharp edge to the plane and chisel. Good craftsmanship is what is appropriate to the job in hand, and therefore a boardroom table finish for timber exposed to the elements is no proof of craftsmanship.

All the timbers mentioned need no finish or treatment; if left alone they will mature to a lovely silver grey, and the wind and rain will do it for nothing. If you feel you just *must* apply something, then use an oil or preservative which allows the timber surface to breathe. Avoid at all costs polyurethanes and varnishes unless you want a maintenance job for life.

Adhesives

Use waterproof resin glues, not PVA based nor traditional animal glues.

Maintenance

Provided the right timbers are chosen, there need be no maintenance beyond brushing off any moss that might appear after a particularly wet period. However, if it is possible, it is preferable to move garden furniture under cover during the worst winter months. ∎

Alan Peters was born in Petersfield, Hants, 50 years ago. His home was close to the Froxfield workshops of Edward Barnsley, to whom he was apprenticed from 1949 to 1956. Thereafter he studied for two years at Shoreditch College, collecting a distinction at the end of his craft teacher's training course, followed by a year at the Central School of Arts and Crafts in London with a scholarship to study interior design.

In 1962 Alan Peters set up his first workshop as a furniture maker near Hindhead in Surrey, and 11 years later moved to his present workshop just outside Cullompton in Devon, overlooking Dartmoor.

In recent years he has visited Japan, South Korea and Taiwan, experiences that have stimulated a marked effect on his design work. Of his travels in the Far East he says: 'The simplicity and beauty of much that I saw has had a profound effect on me and the results, for better or for worse, are percolating through.'

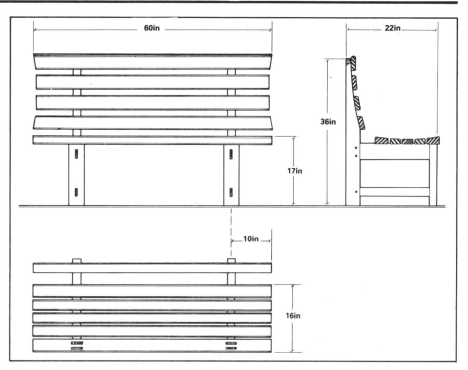

Cutting list (finished sizes)

No	Description	L	W	T	Notes
2	Back legs	36in	3½in	1⅞in	All out of 2in
2	Front legs	17	3½	1⅞	stuff as thick
2	Rails	21	3½	1⅞	as possible.
2	Stretchers	21	1⅞	1¼	1⅞-1¾
	Seat				
2	Outer slats	60	3½	1⅞	As thick as possible
2	Inner slats	60	2¾	1½	
1	Centre slat	60	2¾	1¼	
1	Centre tie	14	1¾	⅜	Hardwood
	Back				
2	Outer slats	60	3½	1¼	
2	Centre slats	58¾	3½	1¼	

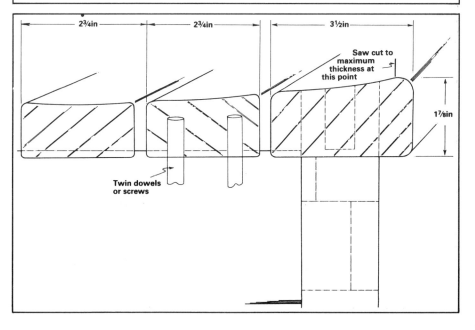

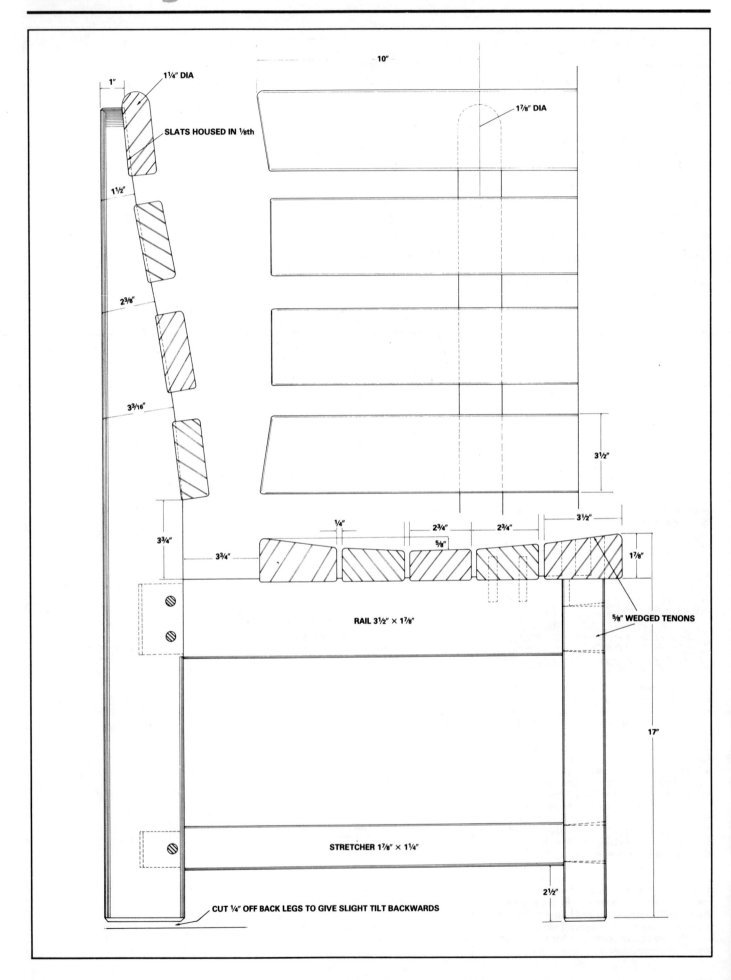

1"
1¼" DIA
10"
1⅞" DIA
SLATS HOUSED IN ⅛th
1½"
2⅜"
3³⁄₁₆"
3½"
¼"
2¾"
2¾"
3½"
⅝"
3¾"
3¾"
1⅞"
RAIL 3½" × 1⅞"
⅝" WEDGED TENONS
17"
STRETCHER 1⅞" × 1¼"
2½"
CUT ¼" OFF BACK LEGS TO GIVE SLIGHT TILT BACKWARDS

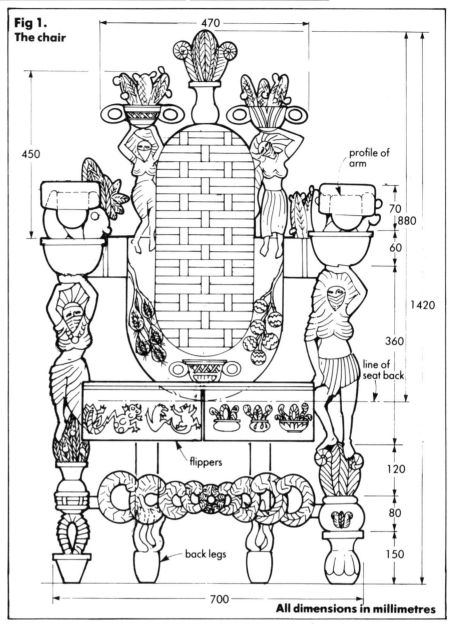

**Fig 1.
The chair**

All dimensions in millimetres

I have been interested in carving from the Indian sub-continent, Oceania and Africa since I was introduced to it at art school. I have since spent time travelling to see the carvings in their original settings and have been able to experience work from these countries in London's museums. I still find now that when I see works that really excite, I want to rush home and start carving. I'm constantly amazed by their complexity and strong imaginative forms. It is certainly important to study and observe great works of art, but one must not become too heavily influenced by them, rather than devoting time to creating and developing one's own ideas.

The subject matter for my pieces has grown out of the fusion of images of everyday objects and sculptural forms, which I may carry around in my mind until the time is right for them to come out and be created. My interest in gardening, I'm sure, influences my carving, and includes so many sculpturally organic shapes, which I use and carry through into my work.

Obviously not all ideas can be expressed three-dimensionally and carving does have its limitations. Some images are stronger three-dimensionally than others. In my work I do try and combine a cluster of images, not always related, to help give an almost overwhelming intensity of contours, rhythms and images. This is an advantage with making furniture. The viewers can now involve themselves physically in the piece: sitting in it, eating from it, whatever. This physical activity breaks down the initial problem so many people have with sculpture – an object you can relate to as opposed to an intimidating object with no practical use.

Chair

The chair is made from 11 pieces of oak, excluding the adjustable construction under the chair seat. With the front two legs I wanted to portray a sense of strength, almost like pillars holding up the arms of the chair; but using images one would not initially associate with strength but an image of suppressed strength – strong matriachal women. The backrest of the chair has similar imagery to the front legs. The chair also has carved cacti growing in difficult conditions, but developing further into strong, voluptuous, healthy plants.

The back legs are in the shape of occupuses climbing up the leg of the chair to give a sense of movement but keeping the

image solid and chunky, as the chair's weight leans back on them. The back of the arms are bowl-shaped with cacti and plants growing in them, curving out from behind the chair. The arm lengths also have bowls carved along them. The pillar-like legs are holding up empty bowls which the sitter can fill with their hands, cups or glasses. This I hope adds to the feeling when someone is sitting in it, of the weight portrayed in the suppressed figures.

The seat has a slight indent carved for the buttock shape. The front flippers are adjustable for comfort and have shallow-carved images of plants and animals.

I wanted the chair to have a strong narrative image, with the sitter having an active role in the overall effect.

Table

The table begins with four cacti; growing out of a plant pot supporting a large circular bowl. This is decorated with relief carvings of rich healthy plants, fishing hooks, fish, eels, and knives and forks. The bowl has four handles, each one with a different design. Out of the bowl grows another large cactus with four off-shoots.

The top is divided into four separate pieces with a dish carved into each section.

These dishes are surrounded by numerous patterns, smaller containers, spoons, fish, flowers and curving snakes disappearing into the bowls. I wanted the table-top to have an almost lacey feel about it, so you could see through to the construction below. From this the stems grow up through the table top to give a sense of continuous growth through the whole piece.

The top centre piece of the table is again a prickly cactus, creating an abstract form of a man holding a swishing fish which has been plucked up from one of the dishes in the table. The fish is smooth and glossy, with it's mouth open holding a collection of spoons and forks which are to give an impression of water spouting from it's mouth. These spoons and forks can be removed from the fish's mouth and used to eat from the table-top. The table is made up of 23 pieces, of elm, oak and hawthorn.

I hope the table portrays the sense of excitement one experiences when sitting at a table lavishly covered in exotic food, but also conveys a sense of cynicism that our enjoyment is at the expense of other living things.

Tools and materials

The majority of my work is carved with just

Furniture or Fantasy

a mallet and an assortment of gouges and flat woodworking chisels. I use a jigsaw and electric drill but these tools are used at the beginning, removing wood and preparing it for carving. The wood I use is collected from many places: people's garages and sheds, storm damaged timber, and even from skips and dumps, which can work out very cheap. I do not use any tropical timbers. The timbers must be well seasoned as weeks of hard carving can be ruined by large cracks. The main thing you need, carving in my type of style, is patience.

Planning

To begin a large piece, the planning is usually made up in three stages.
● Deciding upon the theme (idea, emotions, forms)
● Experimenting with images (sketches, photographs, models)
● Calculations and practical problems (size, length of time, type of timber to be used)

Construction

I start drawing, very roughly, ideas on to paper of the overall feeling I want to portray. You can be confronted at times with the dilemma of how honest you can, or want to be. At this stage if I'm having problems with developing the idea into the three dimensions I will construct out of paper a maquette, which will help me see the design in the round. Working with paper is useful as it has few of its own characteristics to confuse the idea. This is not the case when using clay because it's own qualities can confuse things.

I will then construct the piece roughly and put it together so that it works as a whole, before any detail is added. All the timbers I use are hardwoods as the grain is tighter, and permits finer detail. When this detail is being developed, keeping your chisels sharp is an absolute must. A blunt chisel will not cut through the timber cleanly and it will make it difficult to carve any pattern. Amongst other things sharp chisels make carving far more enjoyable.

Nothing is glued until the end so that I can keep changing pieces if necessary. However far you may have come with the piece, it is always important to dominate it rather than, as the piece progresses, becoming overpowered. Also try not to worry about the time you have spent on the piece but keep developing and enriching it. It takes courage to remove a section you're not pleased with – containing many weeks work – but this is where one of the skills of the maker lies: in having the capacity to keep improving the piece and not becoming too possessive. Photographs of your work during production are a useful way of seeing this, and remind you when decisions about direction were made.

The finished product

Maybe the tribal sculptors had it easier than us as they made things for reasons, other than Art, making the subject matter clear. That is the importance of having an overall design at the start and not letting the natural beauty of the wood to dominate the design. Beautiful timber is often used to compensate a weak design. Such compromise is clear to the viewer. I try to keep my work rich and active in images, hopefully portraying emotions for others to experience and enjoy. ∎

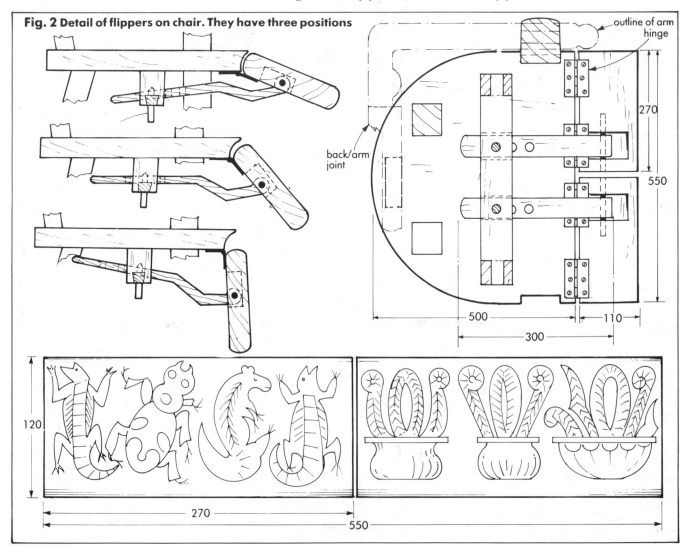

Fig. 2 Detail of flippers on chair. They have three positions

outline of arm hinge

back/arm joint

270

550

500

110

300

120

270

550

This Edwardian mahogany writing-table is an example of a piece incorporating curved drawer-fronts

INTO SHAPE

A cabinetmaker of the old school, Mark Kenning looks at curved drawer-fronts and basic construction methods – including a no-cramp lamination process

T here are several ways of making a shaped drawer-front, depending on whether it is out of solid timber or laminated with thin plywood and/or constructional veneers. The method also depends on the available equipment and whether you are doing one-off or repetition work. For quantity production of solid drawer-fronts, a heavy-duty bandsaw is a must; for volume laminating you would need well-made jigs and heavy-duty hand cramping tools, or better still, a 'daylight' press. Vacuum pressing only requires 'saddles' (generally the bottom halves of jigs). But

here I want to look at some of the ways of making a shaped drawer-front without jigs, heavy-duty bandsaws, presses or even any cramps at all.

The bow or convex shape can also be used as a hollow or concave. It's the easiest to make, and the most common, so I will concentrate on this.

Finding the shape

Whatever method you use, you need to make an accurate full-size template first. I use an unscientific but perfectly satisfactory procedure for this, and have done for many years. First draw the rough shape free-hand

until you're satisfied that it's very near to what you want. Then you can find the final curve by geometry, or as I do, by trial and error. If you can get hold of a large pair of compasses, you can find the centre of the rough arc and mark the true shape, but otherwise you'll have to make a 'radius stick', which is preferable to compasses anyway, in my view.

The radius stick is simply a lath of any waste wood – solid, plywood or hardboard – about 1½in (38mm) wide and several inches longer than the required radius (fig. 1). Cut a flat point at one end, then find the approxi-

mate radius length, again by trial and error, and hammer in a panel pin at that point centrally to the width. Place the point on the centre line of your rough arc and check by swinging the stick to and fro. Now you can find the exact radius, just by moving the pin up or down the stick until it's right.

The template itself is best made from 3 or 4mm plywood or hardboard, at a pinch. It should be at least 2in (50mm) longer than the finished length of the drawer-front, with one long edge planed straight. Square across a centre line from this edge and mark a reference line

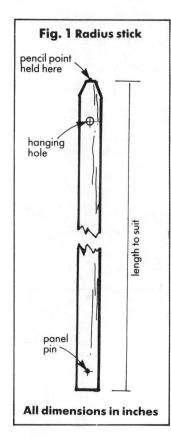

Fig. 1 Radius stick

pencil point
held here

hanging
hole

length to suit

panel
pin

All dimensions in inches

Solid timber construction

Using the template, mark and cut enough pieces off a plank of 1in (25mm) prepared timber. For a 6in wide drawer-front you'll need seven pieces. No need to clean up the saw cuts at this stage. The 'offcut' pieces of the plank can be joined to give extra sections (fig. 3), and of course the boards you start with can be jointed up to get extra width – rub joins only, in both instances.

Do a trial run by placing the pieces one on the other. Choose a piece without joins, if possible, for the top one. You will now be able to see whether any are badly miscut or misaligned, and to replace any which are. For the method that uses cramps, now skew drive a 1½in (38mm) panel pin into the endgrain of each piece (not the bottom one) so the points just project (fig. 4).

Line the bench with plenty of old newspaper to stop it getting fouled up with glue. Lay the first piece on the bench and spread glue on that and on the mating

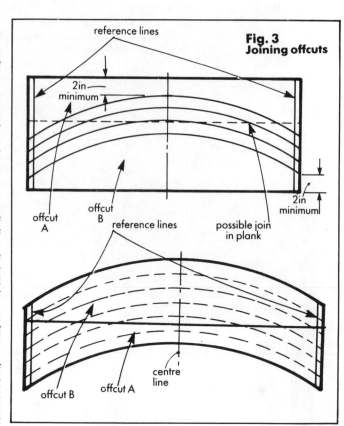

Fig. 3 Joining offcuts

reference lines

2in minimum

offcut A

offcut B

reference lines

possible join in plank

2in minimum

centre line

offcut B

offcut A

each side of it to equal the exact length of the front (fig. 2).

Pin this board under the radius stick in the appropriate position, making sure that the centre lines of template and stick line up. Hold a pencil at the point and trace the curve. Adjust it if you need to, until you're satisfied with the radius. Replace the pencil with a sharp Stanley knife or something similar, and lightly score the ply or hardboard. Return to the starting point, score a little deeper, and continue until the wood is cut. You should now have a perfect curve, needing no more than light sandpapering. Marking out with a pencil and then hand cutting would need a spokeshave at least to trim up, with no guarantee of accuracy.

Do not use the same radius for cutting the outside and inside lines of the thickness of the shape, because the two curves differ slightly. Either shorten the stick or, better still, set a cutting gauge to around 1in (25mm) and run it round the curve from both sides several times. Finish it off with the knife if you need to. When the template is completed, check it by marking the shape on a clean surface then reversing it. It should fit perfectly.

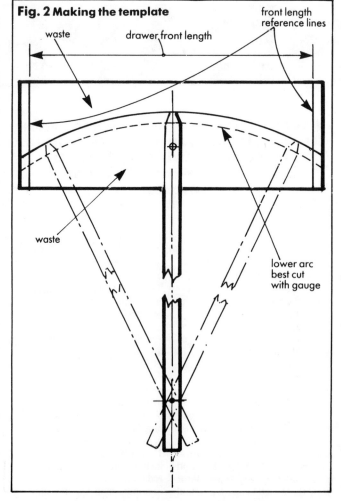

Fig. 2 Making the template

waste

drawer front length

front length reference lines

waste

lower arc best cut with gauge

surface of the next one. Use a PVA like Evostik Resin 'W' or Unibond. Bring the pieces together, and holding them firmly with one hand, tap in the pins. The projecting points will stop them slipping about under pressure. The pins will need to be withdrawn later, so leave enough sticking out for the pincers to get a good grip.

Build up in this way until the top piece has been pinned. Since there are bound to be discrepancies in the cut surfaces, try to line up the concave faces as accurately as possible, since this is the more difficult one to level and clean up later.

Turn the glued assembly over so that it stands like an arch, and apply cramps top to bottom at say, 4in intervals, working from the centre outwards. If the top-to-bottom dimension of the drawer-front doesn't give you tolerance to plane off the indentations made by the G-cramps, use pieces of scrap wood for pads.

Wash off the excess glue (it should run out from the joins quite freely) and check the join lines; they should be hairline. If need be, tighten up the cramps a little more and/or apply more cramps, from the other side this time. If all is well, put the

assembly aside to set.

Solid timber, no cramps

Cabinetmakers do not normally use this method – of building up shapes from solid timber without cramps – but against the disadvantage of slowness it has its advantages. Obviously the number of cramps you have to hand limits the amount and size of drawer-fronts you can do at once, whereas the crampless method leaves you (theoretically) unrestricted. It's very useful for large shaped structures like giant model ships, or other applications where the cramps you would need would be too many and too big.

The shape is built up the same way, in horizontal layers, but instead of using cramps each layer is glued and *screwed* to its neighbour one at a time. When the first layer is set you undo the screws and glue and screw the next layer, until the required height is reached. With the right temperature you could do two gluings a day, one first thing in the morning and another last thing at night, which would halve the time, but this is something you must decide for yourself.

A good rule-of-thumb test to find whether the glue has completely set is to dig a fingernail into it (there is bound to be some on the ends at least), and if you can't make an impression then it's safe to extract the screws. Be sure to remember the first piece becomes the top edge of the drawer-front, as this is the only one that doesn't show screw holes.

With both these methods the faces of the shape will require careful shaping and cleaning up with spokeshave, files and glasspaper, or a compass plane if you have one. Another way to build up shapes from the solid, without using either cramps or screws, is to glue small pieces together bricklaying fashion. It's an entirely different technique, useful in certain specialised work but totally unsuitable for drawer-fronts.

Laminating without cramps

Laminating with plywood and/or constructional veneers is the usual method of making shaped drawer-fronts these days. If it is done correctly, it makes a strong and permanent component which doesn't suffer from atmospheric changes in the same way as the solidly constructed shape will. The faces are perfectly formed and require no further levelling, indeed this would be undesirable. On the other hand, a laminated shape is more difficult to dovetail by hand and the lamination lines, at the ends anyway, can't be satisfactorily hidden, so the method is unsuitable for good quality reproduction work.

The usual method entails jigs and cramping equipment ranging from the simple male and female jig plus hand cramps and cold setting glue to the sophisticated and expensive heated jig and press, and even (best in my view) the vacuum presses. But, failing such industrial volume and sophistication, for the occasional one-off there is a way of making the shape that requires only the convex half of a simple jig and no cramps at all.

The method is rather unorthodox and may cause the raising of an eyebrow or two, but I can assure you it works if it is done correctly. Only concave or convex shapes are possible; strangely enough you can get a much larger arc with this method than with the male and female jig, where not much more than a quarter circle is practical because beyond that side pressure (or rather lack of it) becomes a limiting factor.

You need to make the simple jig shown in fig. 5, which consists of two long former pieces held apart at the depth of the drawer by crosspieces; the separate tops to the two ends should be thicker (say 1½in, 38mm) than the rest of the components, for which 1in (25mm) is quite adequate. The tops of the end pieces should also show long grain to the top. Dimensions, obviously, are to suit the drawer in question, allowing for trimming.

Pin together then cut and trim the two long former pieces for accurate and identical shaping, mark them as a pair before you separate them and assemble the jig – or, more rightly, saddle – on a baseboard. I'd recommend screwing everything, particularly the tops to the end crosspieces, which will need replacing after a couple or three lamination pro-

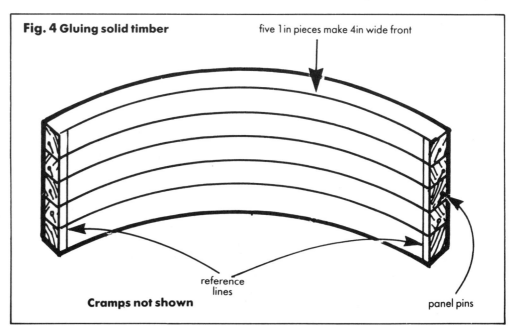

Fig. 4 Gluing solid timber   five 1in pieces make 4in wide front

reference lines

Cramps not shown   panel pins

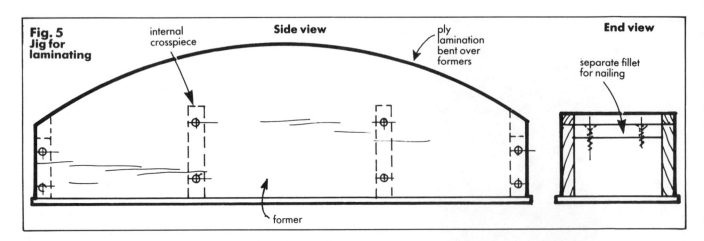

**Fig. 5
Jig for
laminating**

internal crosspiece

Side view

ply lamination bent over formers

End view

separate fillet for nailing

former

cesses.

The best material for laminating is, in my view, 4mm Finnish birch ply. Anything thinner may not shape correctly, thicker will not bend easily and the grain could crack and open up, a fatal result. Use a synthetic glue, preferably a gap-filling one, although PVA will do a splendid job. The laminations should be cut 'cross-grain', i.e. with the grain following the shortest dimension, and around ¼in (6mm) oversize in the short direction and about 2in (50mm) in the longer. Select the two best pieces, free of open or patched knots, for the outer laminations. Check also that the ply itself is not delaminating, very rare with Finnish birch, but not unheard of.

Firmly fix the saddle down to the work surface, with paper below it to prevent glue fouling. Put several layers of paper across the top of the saddle with plenty of overhang, which will not only help to keep it clean but also even out any slight variations in the top edge.

Lay the first lamination on the saddle *dry*. Keep one edge of the ply lined up with the face of the former, and equalise the length as near as possible. Partly drive a panel pin into one end of the lamination and through into the thick crosspiece, avoiding fixing screws of course! Firmly smooth the ply with the palm of your hand across to the opposite end, making sure that the edge is level, and partly drive a pin into the other thick crosspiece. Satisfy yourself that it's lying correctly (if not, remove one of the pins and adjust), and hammer the pins *right in*, or bend and hammer them flat. Drive in two more at each end about ½in (12mm) in from the long edge, and hammer them flat too.

The ply should now lay snugly across the top. Do *not* pin into the top edges of the formers. The ply laminations *must* be allowed to find their own curve, which should follow the formers if they have been correctly made, but don't worry if slight gaps are seen between this first layer and the formers.

The rest of the laminations will be applied with glue, which could make them slide and so more difficult to fix. To overcome this problem, hammer a pin into each end, so that the points just project, *before* gluing the surfaces. Turn the lamination over, raised if need be because of the pins, and brush glue on to this first, then on to the surface of the lamination on the saddle. Bring the two surfaces together, pin one end, and as before smooth across to the other side and pin. Keep the edge level. Adjust if need be and drive in

two more pins at each end. Continue in this way until the final lamination is in place. It may be necessary to use longer pins for the upper layers, since it's best if all the pins go into the saddle ends. Now it comes clear why you need thick crosspieces and extra length on the laminations.

When the whole assembly has been put together, tear away the surplus paper and check the joins after washing off the excess glue. The glue line may be a little thicker than with pressure methods, and it may require extra time to set. About 24 hours at 70°F (21°C) should do it – longer in cold or damp conditions.

All being well, prise the shape from the saddle. It will have lots of pins sticking out at each end, and it may be possible to pull them out by the sharp end, but if not, then just clench

them firmly into the ply. The waste will take care of them.

Don't be tempted to cramp any part of the assembly, or to drive pins anywhere except into the end crosspieces, it will do more harm than good. Extra pressure in the wrong places could cause 'flats' as well as separation either side. The secret of success with this method is in the smoothing of the lamination across the saddle with the palm or heel of your hand. It must be done with a pushing action, as if trying to stretch the ply, and held until the panel pin is driven in. It's worth doing one or two dry runs just to get the feel of it.

Finally, whatever method you've used to make your shaped drawer-front, this is really just the beginning of the matter. The real work starts from here if you're going to make a drawer! ∎

POWER PLANTING

Textures and colours in assorted
combinations set the tone for this
natural-looking plant holder by
Ivan Phillips

A plant holder like this should not be confined to a conservatory; its contrasting woods and cork-tiled texture will go very well in a hall or living room. The box is removable from the stand, which is made of ⅞in finished solid mahogany; you can choose a native hardwood if you like, but the idea is a tonal contrast between that and the lighter cork of the box. You will also find that the cork blends very well with the foliage of indoor plants.

The construction consists of a simple frame with two parallel long rails, and two slightly deeper cross rails at each end. The box sits on these rails without any fixing. There are no stretchers below the height of the box rails, but haunched tenons provide the necessary strength.

Frame

The legs of the frame are tapered top and bottom (fig. 1), and on all four sides at the top (fig. 3). Cut them to length, mark and cut the mortises for the haunched tenons on the cross rails, and then plane the tapers. Be very careful with your marking out; the taper starts 4¼in from the top of the legs.

A look at fig. 1 will tell you that the shoulders of the cross rails are cut at an angle to fit the taper of the legs. Obviously it's best to mark these shoulders off the legs themselves, matching each joint individually, after the tapers have been worked. The cross rails are 9¼in wide at their narrowest; the tenons should be at least 1¼in deep, not including the haunch. The

two long rails are through-mortised to the cross rails; you can wedge them if you like, even using a contrasting wood for decorative effect. If you decide to do this, remember to relieve the mortise from outside to allow for expansion of the tenons.

Box

The best material for the box, which is certain to get wet during its life, is ¾in marine ply. Failing that – and remembering you are cladding it – you can use cheaper plywood. Best birch or

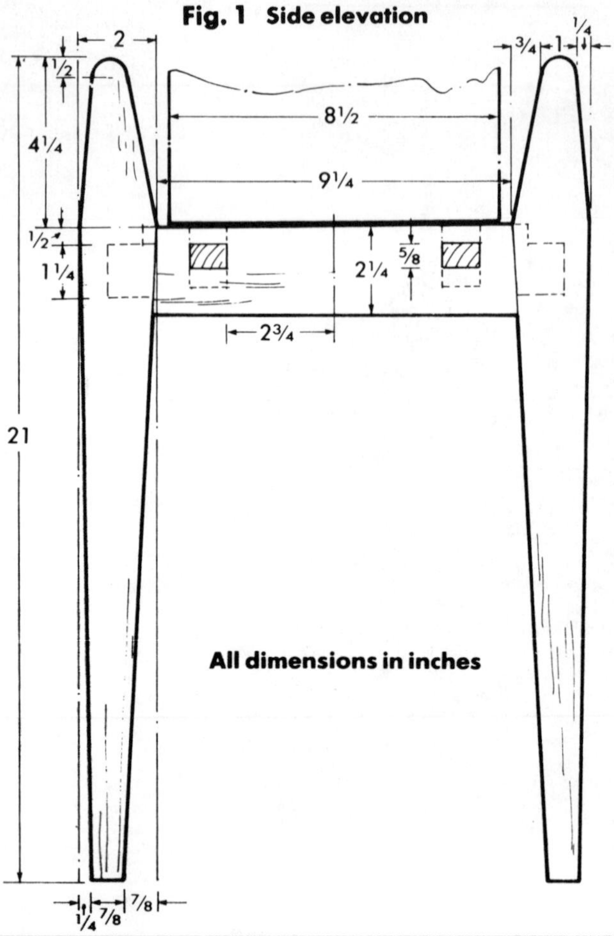
2
3/4
1
1/4
1/2
4 1/4
8 1/2
9 1/4
1/2
1 1/4
2 1/4
5/8
2 3/4
21
All dimensions in inches
1/4
7/8
7/8
Fig. 1 Side elevation

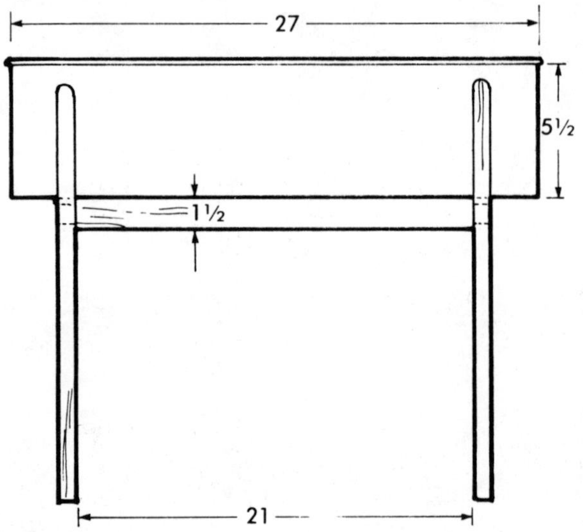
27
5 1/2
1 1/2
21
Fig. 2 Front elevation

even the lower quality Malaysian would do. Blockboard is also an alternative, but it must be well sealed, unless you are planning to take the plants out every time you water them.

The ends of the box before cladding are 8½in wide, which gives adequate clearance between the legs when the cork is applied – another ¼in or thereabouts in total. It's worth choosing your cork tiles before you cut these components to make sure of the final dimension. Cut a rebate ¾×½in in the ends to take the sides (fig. 4), and one the same size all the way round the base for the sides and ends to sit in. Glue with Cascamite or another good waterproof glue, and screw, dowel or dovetail-nail the joints.

A wide range of cork tiles can be found at most big DIY stores. Try to get ones of the average ⅛in thickness; I chose light-coloured pre-sanded tiles with a fairly variegated pattern. Avoid the sealed variety – I think the plastic gloss looks quite wrong in combination with solid wood and plants. Fix them with impact adhesive, preferably the kind that allows a bit of slideability, and give them two coats of matt polyurethane to seal them.

The exposed top edges of tiles and box will need covering; I used ramin hockey-stick moulding, mitred at all corners, which is easy to come by and goes well with the cork in both colour and texture.

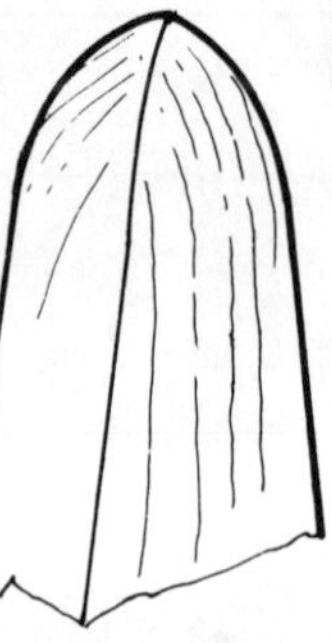
Fig. 3 Top of leg

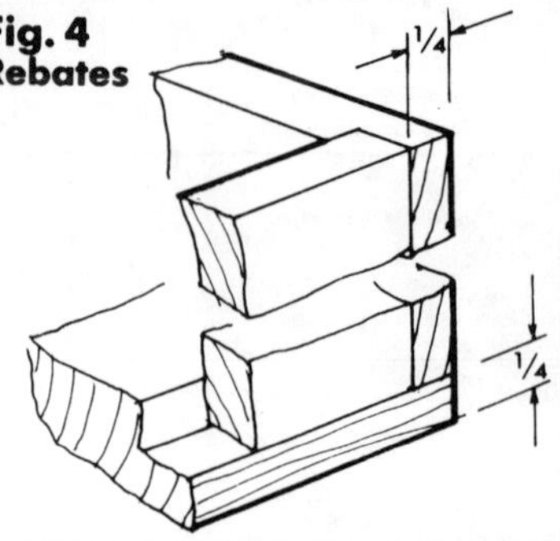
1/4
1/4
Fig. 4 Rebates

Finish

When all the outside surfaces are sealed and finished – I used Ronseal Satincoat for the frame, still keeping away from high gloss – give the inside of the box a full paint system of primer, undercoat and gloss, or several coats of exterior varnish. A good waterproof and sealing alternative, which sinks nicely into the wood, is a microporous stain/varnish. You might want to make up a metal tray for the plant pots if you have the ability and the equipment, but you can get flower pots these days with draining trays, and I have found they work fine. Now all you've got to do is keep the plants alive. ■

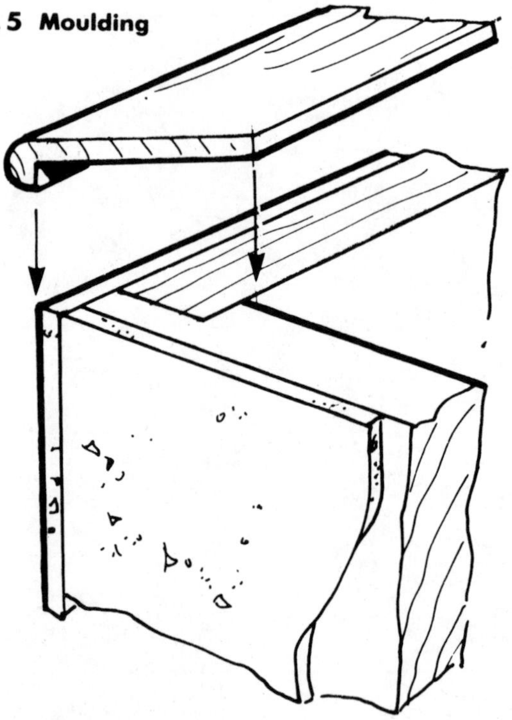
Fig. 5 Moulding

Cutting list

Frame				
Legs	4	21in ×	2in ×	⅞in
Cross rails	2	11¾	2¼	⅞
Long rails	2	23	1½	⅞
Box				
18mm (¾in) plywood or blockboard:				
Ends	2	8½	5¼	
Sides	2	26½	5¼	
Base	1	27	8½	

Cork tiles
76×1in ramin hockey stick moulding

HANGING AROUND

Jim Robinson produces a wall-mounted cupboard that is an open and shut case for storage problems

The door frame is assembled separately, then attached to the cupboard

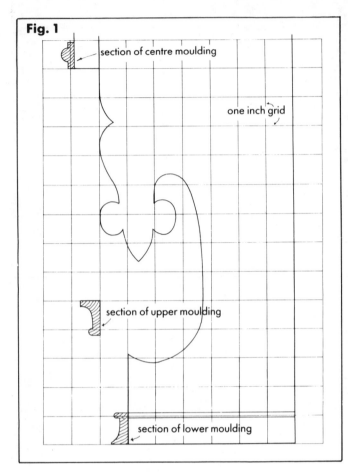

Fig. 1

section of centre moulding

one inch grid

section of upper moulding

section of lower moulding

When my daughter moved house recently she asked me if I could make a wall cupboard to provide extra kitchen storage space. There was already a fitted pine cupboard, but not wanting to work in a softwood I choose olive ash to coordinate.

As the dark heart streaks of large English ash trees, olive ash is beautiful in appearance and being strong and sound it is easy to work. It glues well and is simple to stain and finish, though the interesting grain and colour can make staining unnecessary.

The open shelf adds character to an almost square (36in wide × 35⅝in high) front elevation. It is of course possible to adapt the measurements, though beware bowing if the cupboard is much larger.

Construction

The first stage is to select and plane material for the two sides, top and two cupboard shelves to a thickness of ⅞in. To give extra weight to the lowest moulding and have depth for the plate groove, the bottom, open shelf is planed to 1in.

Using the best grain for the sides, cut and plane the top and sides to a width of 7in. Transfer the decorative shapes at the bottom of the side pieces, from fig. 2, with grid squares and cut out with a band saw or coping saw. File and sand smooth.

The two shelves are finished to 6in wide, allowing the ⅜in back to be rebated into the inner face of the sides and top. The bottom shelf, which is also rebated to take the back, is cut to the same width as the sides below the decorative feature. To perch plates safely on this shelf make a groove along the shelf with a router, plough plane or circular saw, but a stopped groove looks best so use the most suitable method: routing, if possible. Experiment to find the optimum position for your plates to stand in the groove.

Cut a recess at the middle of the centre shelf to provide clearance for the catches that are attached to the rear of the doors and lock on to the upright.

The top and bottom, shelves and sides are joined by means of simple housing joints, worked preferably with a router. This type of joint is adequate because

after gluing and cramping the top and bottom can be reinforced with dowels, which will be hidden by the applied mouldings.

The rear of the cabinet is clad with ⅜in ash of random widths rebated to form an overlap. Chamfer the edges to create a feature, not an unsightly gap if shrinkage occurs. Glue and pin the planking into the rebates and to the back of the shelves.

The frame that takes the doors is another stress member and is constructed with mortise and tenon joints (fig. 4). Cut these joints very accurately: olive ash is hard and you do not

have the room for manoeuvre that softer woods offer.

Along the top and bottom of the frame drill countersunk holes for 1½in × 8 screws which I hid with the mouldings. To supplement the screws, the frame is attached to the sides with 6 × 30mm preformed dowels. Drill 6 × 20mm holes in the leading face of the sides (15mm deep holes do not leave space for excess glue). Locate corresponding holes in the frame using dowel centre markers, and drill taking care not to break through the outside.

Glue, screw and lightly cramp the frame in position, and once

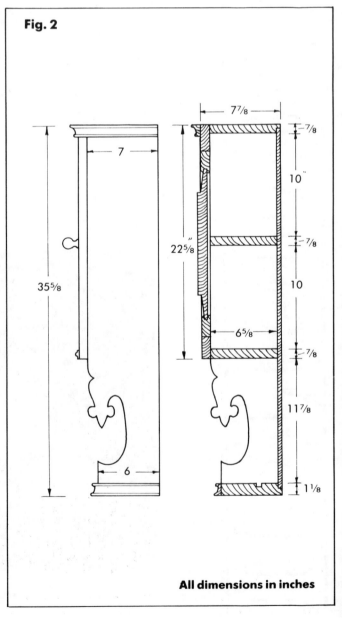

Fig. 2

7⅞

7

⅞

10"

22⅝"

⅞

35⅝

10

6⅝

⅞

11⅞

6

1⅛

All dimensions in inches

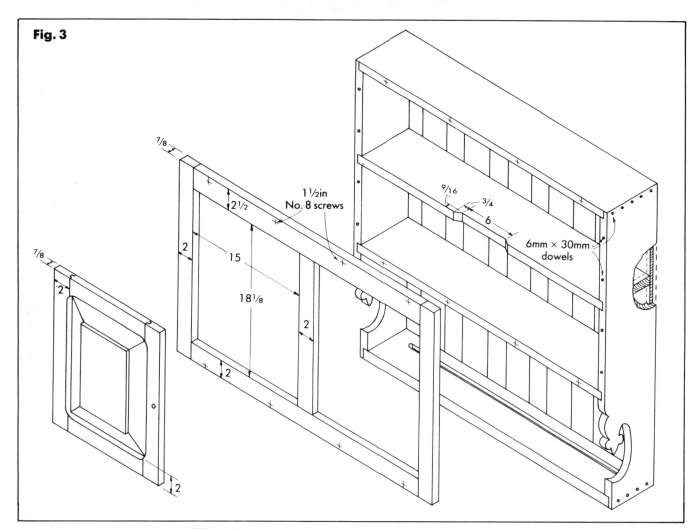

Fig. 3

7/8

7/8

2

2

2½

2

15

18⅛

2

2

1½in
No. 8 screws

9/16

3/4

6

6mm × 30mm
dowels

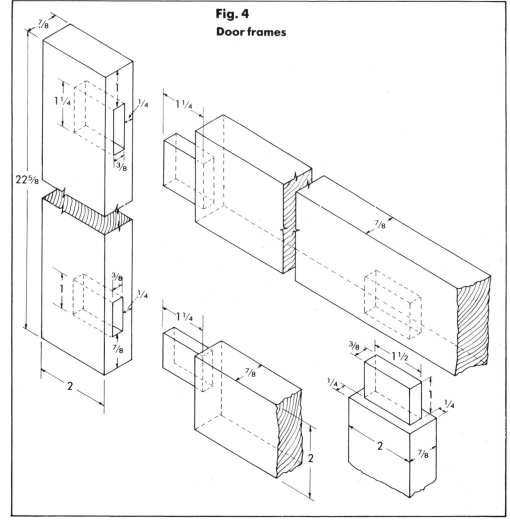

Fig. 4
Door frames

7/8

1

1¼

1/4

3/8

22⅝

1

3/8

1/4

7/8

2

1¼

1¼

7/8

7/8

1¼

7/8

2

1/4

3/8

1½

1

2

7/8

1/4

dry, clean up the cabinet before applying the mouldings. The shape of the mouldings is dependent on taste and available tools. I made three different mouldings (fig. 2), using a router and coving bit and a small rebate plane for the upper and lower ones, and a corner rounding bit for the central moulding. In the latter case I could have used a circular saw to rebate the edges of the moulding and round over the middle with a small plane, or a scratch stock.

To apply the mouldings use a strong glue because you should avoid using pins or nails which inevitably leave marks. If you use Cascamite on one face and wipe the other face with formic acid the drying time is greatly decreased and you only need to temporarily attach with sticky tape. Remember to make enough of the upper and lower mouldings to go round the corners, where mitres are used. Trim the centre moulding flush with the sides.

Cut out the components for the door frames and cut or rout out a ⅜in square groove along the inner edges for the panel. Unless you are lucky enough to have timber sufficiently wide for the panel you will have to glue up widths of ash. Ensure that the edges are square and straight, and that when you glue up the panels there is no bowing or sliding in the cramps.

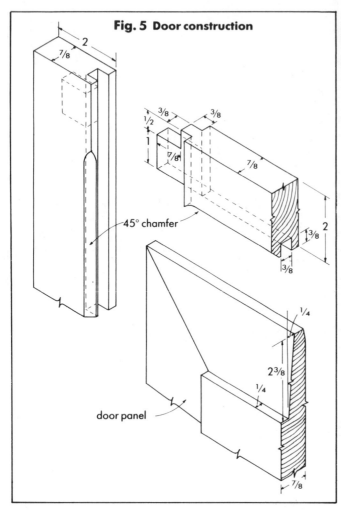

Fig. 5 Door construction

2

7/8

45° chamfer

3/8   3/8

1/2

7/8

7/8

1

2

1 3/8

3/8

1/4

2 3/8

1/4

door panel

7/8

Drill a ½in hole in each door for the knob and catch, and hang the doors on brass flush hinges. Turn two knobs, drill ½in holes into each and glue in ½in dowel (fig. 6). Push through each door, for a loose fit, and attach a shaped catch at the other end with a small brass screw.

To hang the cupboard, brass fittings screwed to the back, at points of strength, are sufficient for good walls, but for cavity walls or for those liable to break up you may have to take further

Supporting batons under shelves attach the cupboard to the wall

measures. Cut 4in batons from ¾in square olive ash and screw to the underside of the centre shelf and the cupboard top to take long screws.

This is a versatile cupboard, providing valuable storage space in dining room or sitting room as well as a kitchen. ∎

Field the panels with a circular saw and angled jig, fence or blade, or use a router and plane. Having cut the joints of the frame (fig. 5) and chamfered the inner edges for effect, glue up the doors. Avoid getting glue on the panels as shrinkage is bound to occur, and the panels must be able to move.

As shrinkage is likely, apply the chosen finish to the panels before assembly of the doors to avoid any unfinished wood showing later.

Detail of fielded panels and cambered door

**Fig. 6
Latch fitting**

¾in
No. 6 screw

hole left loose
for ½in shaft

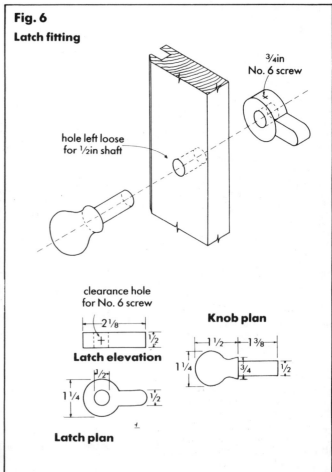

clearance hole
for No. 6 screw

2 1/8

1/2

Latch elevation

1/2

1 1/4

1/2

Latch plan

Knob plan

1 1/2   1 3/8

1 1/4

3/4

1/2

BACK NUMBERS

Good design puts comfort and posture first, says Dr. Waring Robinson

Man, it seems, has finally learnt to stand on his (and her!) own two feet – at least as far as his posture's concerned. Some might disagree, claiming the human skeleton is more at home – and under less strain – walking on all fours. In fact, homo sapiens' adaptation to an upright position has been slow but sure, with our spinal structure gradually taking on a remarkable dual function of weight bearing and movement.

But problems often start when we tire of this bipedal stance and change position. We assume many different positions, of which the semi-foetal is perhaps the most restful. But what happens when we sit? Many people are employed in sedentary work; most of us sit down for long periods. Back pain seems mainly a problem of the sedentary, and this is supported by experimental evidence.

Here lies the challenge for the furniture industry, and for chairmakers in particular: using this knowledge to create designs which make comfort and good posture a priority. A badly designed chair is not only uncomfortable to sit on for a man or woman: it may also gradually change the finely balanced physique of a child into the poor posture so common in adults. This is where anthropometrics (study of measurement of the human body) and ergonomics (study of human performance at work) come in. It's obviously not realistic to try and design one chair to suit everyone: but using a mean set of measurements, it's possible to create a design basis that can be adapted for individual needs.

To understand this, consider the function of the cartilagenous discs which lie between the bony vertebrae. These change shape to accommodate body movement, and act as shock absorbers. This function causes a change of pressure within the disc. Experiments have shown that intradiscal pressure is lowest when lying down, increases on standing, and is highest when sitting.

It's also important to maintain the natural S-shaped curves of the spine, as this reduces intradiscal pressure and means less strain for the ligaments and muscles. It also keeps the chest and abdominal cavities free, unlike in the slouched position. All this may seem like obvious good sense; but how do we go about meeting these needs, as far as furniture's concerned?

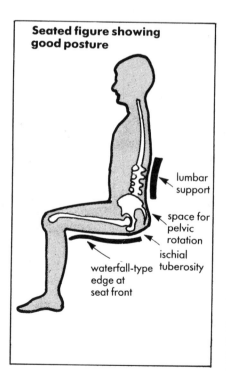

Seated figure showing good posture

lumbar support

space for pelvic rotation

ischial tuberosity

waterfall-type edge at seat front

Firstly, the back rest must give correct lumbar support in the appropriate area. Secondly, the pelvis must be able to rotate backwards to its maximum, with flexion at the hip joint rather than at the expense of the lumbar spine. Many chairs fail here, as the back of the chair doesn't free the sacral area. Finally, rotation of the pelvis is eased when the legs can be occasionally tucked under the seat. Bending the knees relaxes the hamstring muscles: when contracted these oppose the backward rotation of the pelvis.

Let's now look at things from a design point of view, in particular chair dimensions.

● Seat height: this must be sufficient for the body weight to be taken on the skin, fat and muscle over the ischial tuberosity – the bony mass felt in either buttock which becomes more apparent when sitting down. This has a richer blood supply than other buttock areas, and is well adapted to supporting body wight. At the same time, the height must not be so great that much of the weight will be taken by the distal posterior part of the thigh: this leads to compression of the arteries, veins and nerves, producing a tourniquet effect. When the knees are at right angles and the feet flat on the ground, there should be hanging space at the lower part of the thigh. Limb measurements vary considerably, and for this reason an adjustable chair is best for work. The average seat height is about 17-18in for a man, and about 15¼in for a woman. The overall average works out to about 16½in, though this becomes 17-17½in when sitting at a table.

● Seat width: this only matters if you're considering a minimum allowance for hip width and spread of the buttocks, or for a shift of posture. A comfortable width would be 18in; 17in is the minimum.

● Seat depth: the minimum back-of-knee-to-buttock measurement in a woman is 16in, while the maximum for a man is 20in. Taking the smallest measurement as a guide, 15 inches is a suitable depth.

● Back rest: in an upright chair, this should be angled backwards at about 95° to the seat surface, which itself may tilt backwards from 3-5°. This tilt combines with forces of gravity to settle the body into the chair in a position where lumbar support is used to the full; it also helps prevent the body gradually slipping forward. A back rest should allow freedom for the back to be arched occasionally to improve the extent of the lumbar curve. The lumbar region should be supported over a distance of 6-8in, and should be convex in cross-section; it should be raised free of the sacral area or its effect will be lost. A good height from the seat surface to the lower border of the back is 6-7in. This space may be formed by shaping wood, the hammocking effect (ie the 'give') of soft furnishings, or by simply leaving a space, as in office furniture.

● Seat composition: generally speaking, a soft surface is best, but it must provide a counter-pressure for the ischial tuberosity and not submit to body weight. A ½in depression in a padded seat is enough; if it's too soft, the surrounding tissues get compressed. A waterfall-type edge to the seat front also helps reduce compression.

Even with these guidelines, there are still problems – for they only take one upright body position into account. As soon as the sitter moves into a forward position, such as when working at a desk, intradiscal pressure increases and the advantages of the chair diminish. Discomfort may then make the sitter move forward to the edge of seat, so that all planning for the back is lost. One answer – though not always a practicable one – to this is to slope the work surface slightly, setting it at a distance to suit one's own focal length.

But is there an alternative to the traditional upright seat, one that will ensure good posture and reduce intradiscal pressure? Before answering, I'd like to give a couple of examples where good posture occurs. Looking at the position adopted by a horse rider, the back always seems upright and comfortable with the right spinal curve, achieved by a forward tilt of the saddle. The trunk is prevented from slipping forward by crutch support and having the feet in stirrups. Then again, a child sitting on an adult chair often tilts the seat forward, achieving a stable position while drawing at a table. We often seem to be much more concerned about a chair's mortise-and-tenon joints than any possible effect on the child's posture!

These and other examples have led to experiments, where chair rigs were set up which had variable tilts to the seat from a maximum backward tilt of −25° to a maximum forward tilt of +25°. This tilt was altered at 5° increments, and at each position the knees were flexed from 10° to 110°. The shape of the spine was then measured. Throughout the experiment, the subject was asked to sit upright, with feet supported on an adjustable platform. When the seat was at +15°, +20° and +25°, with knees flexed at 110° and 90°, body weight was partially supported by a knee-pad. Results clearly showed the relationship between pelvic rotation and the effect of hamstring muscles on the lumbar curve. The best position was found to be when the seat was tilted forwards at +15° and the knees flexed at 70°.

One outcome of all this research was the development of the Balans Aktiv style of chair or kneeling stool. This only needs a pelvic angle of about 60° for a good spinal position. As its name implies, it's designed for the workplace; it's really an activity chair, as opposed to the traditional upright chair which is passive in function. But despite widespread enthusiasm for it, unfortunately it does have some disadvantages. The forward tilting seat may rub the skin, setting up shear forces and reducing blood flow to and drainage from the area. In people with poor circulation, such as the elderly, this may cause tissue damage with obvious consequences. For this reason, it's best used as a working chair for the young.

Some argue that ergonomics is ineffectual because it doesn't take account of people's natural inclination to change posture and slouch in a chair. I think this is a rather negative view, and not necessarily true. If children's chairs were ergonomically designed to suit their various phases of growth and development, perhaps they wouldn't become adults with posture problems.

Over the last nine years in Denmark, 6,000 pupils have been using furniture with a sloping desk top and a positive tilt to the seat, so that body weight is taken partially by the feet. In this way, good posture is maintained. I think such an initiative sets an example to us all: let's hope we can act on it. ∎

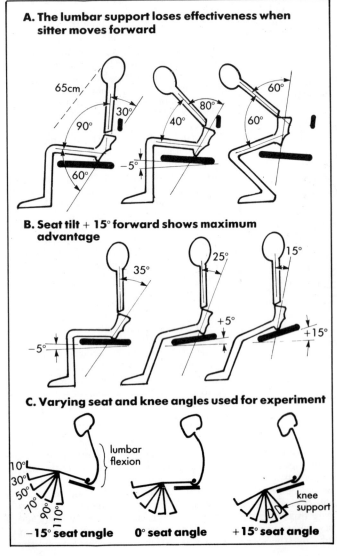

A. The lumbar support loses effectiveness when sitter moves forward

B. Seat tilt + 15° forward shows maximum advantage

C. Varying seat and knee angles used for experiment

lumbar flexion

knee support

−15° seat angle   **0° seat angle**   **+15° seat angle**

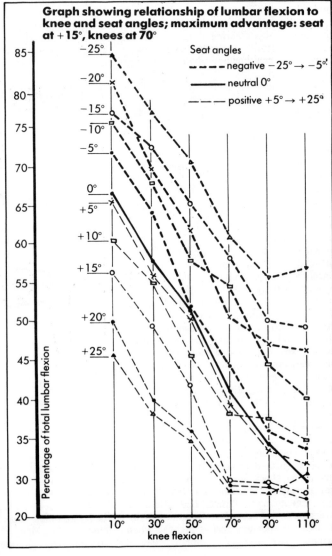

Graph showing relationship of lumbar flexion to knee and seat angles; maximum advantage: seat at +15°, knees at 70°

Seat angles
- – – – negative −25° → −5°
- —— neutral 0°
- — — positive +5° → +25°

Percentage of total lumbar flexion

knee flexion

A SEAT IN THE SUN

Peter Anstey re-created a family heirloom; this unusual curved garden bench could be a centre-piece of your garden this summer

When I was a boy, we had in our country garden a craftsman-built teak bench designed in the shape of a gentle curve, which was a positive invitation to companionable relaxation. It always drew admiring comments from our visitors, and today, more than 50 years later, it still adorns my present home, the wood, apart from minor repairs to the back rail, as sound as when it was made. My father, a retired naval officer, used to tell us that its material was timber salvaged from one of 'the wooden walls of England': nice to think that we could have been relaxing on summer afternoons on a survivor from the Battle of Trafalgar!

Recently I was asked to make a similar bench in a slightly updated form, and I accepted the commission without immediately realising the problems involved. Curves in a three-dimensional context are subtle things, and the practical geometry of reproducing them in wood, though not all that difficult, is quite complex. For example, consider the vertical slats of the finished bench in the photograph. They may appear to be parallel, but in actuality they aren't. The distance along the inner curve of the top rail is in fact nearly ¾in more than that along the inner curve of the bottom rail. This is because the seat back slopes approximately 5° from the vertical, so that the top rail curve is marginally wider and more gentle than the lower. Accurately getting the differing mean distances between centres of adjacent slats at top and bottom is by no means easy if you want visual symmetry.

The solution lies in appreciating that all the curves in the design of the piece are of necessity *concentric* – they are parallel segments of circumferences, all having a common centre. The two back rails with the sloping curve of their connecting slats, the horizontal seat slats, and the front seat rail all have a common centre, though with varying radii. The radius which I chose as the basis for all the others is 13ft 11in, which is the radial distance from the common centre to the inner curve of the lower back rail (there is nothing magical about this figure: it simply represents a suitable degree of curvature, which could be greater or less, depending on your requirements).

Thus it follows that a simple and practical method of measuring and marking out the curved components of the bench, obviously, is to take a light lath a little over 14ft long (say, 1 × ½in profile) and lay it on a large enough area of flat ground (fig. 1). Pin one end loosely with a nail to a piece of timber heavy enough to resist movement, to provide the centre for all the concentric curves. At the other end of the lath mark off respective distances for inner and outer circumferences of each curved component, and drill centred holes at each distance for a pencil to project through slightly. Place underneath the lath a piece (or pieces) of white card or white-painted hardboard large enough to include all the curved dimensions and, using the lath as a compass, carefully scribe through at all measurement points the shape of each curved component. When you cut them out, these shapes will provide accurate templates, particularly for the horizontal seat slats, which involve 12 curves (six inner and six outer) of

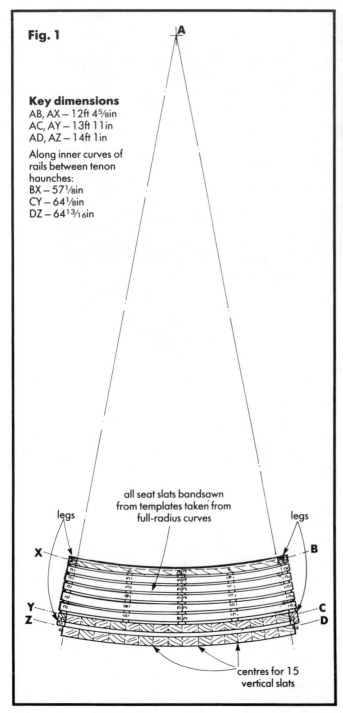

Fig. 1

Key dimensions
AB, AX – 12ft 4⅝in
AC, AY – 13ft 11in
AD, AZ – 14ft 1in

Along inner curves of rails between tenon haunches:
BX – 57⅛in
CY – 64⅛in
DZ – 64¹³⁄₁₆in

all seat slats bandsawn from templates taken from full-radius curves

legs   legs

centres for 15 vertical slats

reducing radii. For the three main curved rails, you may find it easier to pencil the outline curves direct on to previously prepared surfaces of the timbers for the rails.

Construction

You'll see from the photograph that the essential structural elements of the design are the three curved rails, two at the back and one at the front, which support the side members and provide essential rigidity. Roughly bandsaw the rails to the required curvature and thickness and then finish to the previously marked dimensions with a spokeshave. The curves involve considerable wastage, of course, but some of the surplus could later be used for the vertical back slats. Allow for substantial 1¼in tenons at both ends of each rail which at the assembly stage will be housed in mortises

cut in the sides of the front and rear leg members. Complete the back rail assembly by cutting equally spaced mortises for the 15 vertical slats, plus ¼in tenons, which will connect the upper and lower rails. You'll get accurate marking of back and front mortise centres using the lath method already described; lay each rail on the ground on its respective circumference (approximately ⅝in apart), then project from the common centre to the outer rail the radii formed by the previously marked mortise centres on the inner rail. This will ensure that the very slight radial relationship of each slat to its neighbour is visually maintained.

The next slightly awkward problem is the assembly of the back rails and their connecting slats, complicated by the need to accommodate the 5° slope back of the upper half of each rear leg member. You'll see (fig. 2) that the lower rail mortises

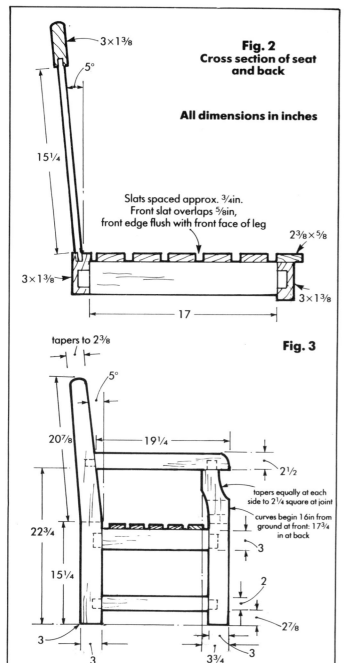

Fig. 2
Cross section of seat and back

All dimensions in inches

3×1⅜

5°

15¼

Slats spaced approx. ¾in.
Front slat overlaps ⅝in,
front edge flush with front face of leg

2⅜×⅝

3×1⅜

3×1⅜

17

tapers to 2⅜

Fig. 3

5°

20⅞

19¼

2½

tapers equally at each
side to 2¼ square at joint

curves begin 16in from
ground at front: 17¾
in at back

22¾

3

15¼

2

3

2⅞

3

3

3¾

3

are cut at the same 5° angle to the vertical. Gluing and clamping is best done in two stages, the slats first being glued to the lower rail mortises at the 5° angle, the upper rail at this stage merely providing a guide for clamps to hold the slats in their correct lateral and angular positions. Once the lower joints are firm, the upper rail can in turn be glued and clamped without fear of disturbing the angle of the slats.

Now complete the whole back and seat frame by mortise-and-tenon jointing the three intermediary seat stretchers between the lower back rail and the front rail. Use the lath method again to set out the positions of the stretchers by projecting radii from the common centre. While each stretcher is flush with the top of the front rail, it is vertically offset ⅝in lower against the back rail, so as to allow for horizontal alignment of all the seat slats with the top of the back rail. Slightly taper each stretcher at its bottom rear corner to line up with the base of the back rail (fig. 2).

Shape the legs from 4×3in wood so the bases are 3in square and the upper portions profiled as indicated in fig. 3. The rear leg top halves slope back at 5° to correspond to the seat back. The front legs curve backwards, beginning at 16in (back of leg) and 17¾in and then taper to 2¼in square at the top. Each front and rear leg member is connected by two stretchers, upper and lower, and by the side arm rest with mortise-and-tenon joints as shown. The upper stretcher at each side should be at the same height from the ground as the intermediate stretchers joining the two curved seat rails, thus completing the base for the curved seat slats. Glue up the side assemblies.

The final stage is cutting the key mortises for the 1¼in tenons of the three curved seat and back rails and provide rigidity and strength to the finished structure. Lay one side assembly on the ground and roughly position the rail structure vertically above it so that the rail tenons are resting on their mortise positions. Then mark and cut the mortises. It will be found that any slight inaccuracies, for example in the slope of the seat back, can be compensated at this stage by the flexibility of the rail structure, which will permit the upper rail tenons to be adjusted to their correct mortise positions. Glue each side separately, and if you do not have a long enough clamp, use the weight of the rail structure to hold each group of three joints in position while the glue is setting. Reinforce the finished assembly by through-drilling, pinning, and gluing each joint with two ⅜in dowels. Treat all other main structural joints similarly.

The curved seat slats are best constructed using card templates marked out as before with the lath. Each slat is made in two identical halves to be butt-jointed over the central seat stretcher and dowel-pinned over all the stretchers (fig. 1). Halving the slats in this way allows you to cut them economically from appropriate lengths of 4×4in timber sawn into ⅝in thick strips. Bandsaw or jig-saw the curved shapes well outside the marked dimensions and finish with a spokeshave. For good looks of the finished bench it is important that the curves are properly concentric and accurately radiused. Finally insert two shaped corner pieces between each front leg member and the front rail to reinforce the structure at these inherently weak points.

Conclusion

Green or partially air-dried wood is a practical proposition since this is an outdoor piece of furniture intended to withstand the rigours of a British winter. All the main structural elements are fairly massive, and possible movement of the timbers is well controlled by the positions of the various joints. Fortunately I was able to get excellent quality heartwood oak from my local timber yard at about £10 per cu ft, so that the total cost of all raw materials was around £75.

With its high tannin content, green oak reacts strongly with ferrous metal, so if you choose oak, use dowels throughout rather than screws to add strength to the joints. Obviously, you'll need a completely waterproof resin glue such as Aerolite to ensure that water doesn't get into the joints, particularly the seat dowels and the bottom mortises of the vertical seat slats.

I treated the wood with a mid-oak stain and then rubbed over with teak oil to give an attractive finish and at the same time provide protection against weather. It is a good idea to treat every piece of wood in this way before gluing, since the oil finish will help to inhibit glue staining of surfaces adjacent to each joint.

Once your bench is complete, sit down, relax and enjoy it! ∎

Cutting guide

Back curved rails	2 from 72in ×	6in ×	3in	
Front curved rail	1 from 60	6	3	
Front legs	2 from 24	4	3	
Rear legs	2 from 36	4	3	
Arms	2 from 24	3	3	
Centre seat stretcher	1	18¾	1⅞	2½ *
Intermediate seat stretchers	2	18¾	1⅜	2½ *
Upper side stretchers	2	17½	1⅜	3 *
Lower side stretchers	2	17½	1⅜	2 *
Vertical back slats	15	16	1⅞	⅜ *
Curved seat slats	12 from		2⅜	⅝

* Finished sizes including tenons

THE GREAT CRAFTSMAN

▲ Arts and Crafts simplicity in the lines of this oak library chair, 1955

His quest for excellence and beauty – Alan Peters

E arly in December our leading national newspapers carried long obituaries of a furniture maker, a man whose reputation and standing in society was recognised by those outside the narrow confines of the woodworking and craft world.

Edward Barnsley, who died on 2 December 1987 after a long illness, ran his Hampshire workshop at Froxfield for over 60 years from 1923 until his health failed in 1985, and during much of that time he set those standards of excellence and integrity by which all other work was judged. He was not responsible for the introduction of the concept of the creative furniture maker, the search for quality, the merits of handwork, or indeed the many other ideals that sustained him in his long working life. Rather, he inherited much of this from his father, Sidney, who was a member of the Cotswold Group of craftsmen and a direct disciple of William Morris and the British Arts and Crafts Movement of the late 19th century.

Edward Barnsley's important contribution was that he saved their ideals and skills from near-extinction in the lean years of the 1930s and 1940s, and from 1945 onwards in particular, that he provided the training facilities and inspiration for a post-war generation of craftsmen. There are few woodwork teachers over 40 years of age who were not influenced by him through his long involvement with Loughborough Teacher Training College, and few furniture makers practising before 1970 who were not inspired by his example to do better.

It is perhaps typical of the man and his 60 years of service to the crafts that, despite so much that has been written about him and his workshop, I can find nothing that he has written of himself and his achievements. The work simply had to speak for itself, and it spoke to us warmly as the work of caring human hands, work that came from the heart rather than coldly from the drawing board.

Design is a contentious subject, and in many ways the least important aspect of his work – in fact, he detested the very word. His was a world that revolved around his clients, the workshops, his makers and his materials, and his furniture was a gradual development from his father's thinking to a style that was so distinctively his. He could not understand the impatience for change and the idolisation of innovation which has

more recently motivated the craft world. His thinking was more in line with the craftsmen of the East, who build slowly on tradition rather than strive perpetually to change it.

For those of us who were fortunate enough to pass through his workshop, this is a time for reflection and we have much to dwell on. For me personally, the experience is now over 30 years old and many other influences have come my way. I am delighted that there is a much greater diversity in craft furniture now than there was when the Barnsley tradition reigned supreme. However, I also know the great debt I owe this man, and I am grateful to have been just a small part of his life's quest for excellence and beauty. I know too, how much so many others also owe, some of them without even being aware of it.

▲ Early Edward Barnsley: bureau on stand with burr oak panels, 1928

▲ Another early piece

▲ This lady's walnut wardrobe with dressing glass, trays etc, originally cost £63

Edward Barnsley, who died in December 1987, pursued the ideals of the Arts and Crafts Movement for 60 years. Here Alan Peters gives a personal appreciation of the craftsman he worked with, and John Hemsley surveys the background of a unique woodworker who continues to inspire

Idealism in a living tradition – John Hemsley

The importance of Edward Barnsley is three-fold – as a direct link with the founding fathers of the English Crafts Furniture Movement, as an individual craftsman of the very highest calibre, and as a teacher.

Edward Barnsley was the son of Sidney Barnsley, one part of that famous threesome, Gimson and the Barnsley brothers, young London architects and designers who moved to the Cotswolds in 1893 to form what later became known as the Cotswold School of Furniture Making.

They had been fired by the ideals of John Ruskin and William Morris, who were profoundly disillusioned by the results of the Industrial Revolution; they emphasised the need for a man to have pride and satisfaction in his work, and the relationship between good design and simplicity.

Bombay rosewood dining table, 1973

THE GREAT CRAFTSMAN

Display cabinet in Bombay rosewood, 1958

Ernest Gimson and Edward and Sidney Barnsley took these ideas on board and believed strongly in a return to handwork as a means of achieving fulfilment for the maker and quality for the customer. Honesty to materials and construction; functionalism; simplicity of line with the minimum of decoration: these were their tenets. They preferred English timber, rather than the mahogany and rosewood which had been the cabinetmaker's materials for 200 years, and kept their finishing as natural as possible, rejecting the fashionable staining and french polishing.

For their design inspiration they went back to the Middle Ages, as Morris had done, and drew largely on country traditions – the jointing constructions of mediaeval houses and barns, the techniques of the wheelwright, the green woodworking of the country chairmaker. The result was a freshness and honesty that was missing in mainstream Victorian furniture, occupied with superficial appearance and decoration.

The Arts and Crafts Movement, with its emphasis on creativity at every stage, led Gimson and the Barnsley brothers, in their individual ways, to be involved from concept to finished item. Sidney took the idea to one extreme; he was a designer and sole maker, working independently and keeping even the most tedious parts of making to himself. Gimson had a small team of makers, but directed them so closely that his personality was on every piece.

In this country setting a 'crafts colony' developed, and Edward Barnsley had a stimulating beginning to his life. At the age of six he was already making small items in wood in his father's workshop. Later he was sent to the progressive Bedales School, founded in 1893 in Sussex and following the philosophy of Rousseau, who insisted that education should be close to nature and children should learn by doing wherever possible. Arts and crafts were a central feature of the school, which attracted many followers of Ruskin and Morris.

Close by the school, which was near Petersfield, Geoffrey Lupton – an ex-pupil of Bedales and of Ernest Gimson – had established a workshop in a picturesque setting, trying to repeat what Gimson had done in the Cotswolds. The Froxfield workshop, with its timber store, adjoining cottage and nearby cottages for workmen, became the centre of a little colony engaged in quality building and furniture making.

Edward Barnsley, who wanted to learn his father's craft after leaving Bedales, became a pupil of Lupton; he learnt furniture making and helped with the construction of the Gimson-designed Great Hall at Bedales School. After three years he left to study furniture design and making under Charles Spooner at the London Central School of Arts and Crafts. Spooner quickly acknowledged his talents. 'You know, Barnsley, you know more about this than I do – I can't teach you anything,' he said once.

He had only been in London a few months when he faced the turning point in his life. Lupton had decided to give up the workshop and take up farming in Southern Africa. At the age of 23 years, Edward Barnsley took over the Froxfield workshops lock, stock and barrel, including the staff. At first he rigorously upheld all the Cotswold School traditions: handtools and bench work were central, with the only power equipment a treadle circular saw (there was to be no electricity at Froxfield for another 30 years). Work was solely in solid timber, chiefly walnut, oak and chestnut. Huge 4in oak boards were converted by hand ripsaw and hand planing. The ideals of the Craft Furniture Movement were lived out and worked out to produce hand-made furniture that literally was hand-made.

By the mid-1940s Edward Barnsley was beginning to question certain features of the Cotswold tradition and to develop a quite distinctive personal style. His work was to become more sophisticated, and he looked for inspiration to the great cabinetmaking era of the 18th century and Regency period. The starkly simple lines were to give way to curves and serpentines, and the native woods, becoming more difficult to obtain, were to be supplanted by rich Cuban mahogany, Australian blackbean and Indian rosewood, with fine lines of holly or sycamore inlay.

In retrospect Edward Barnsley described his development: 'What I like to think I've done is in some measure to improve on two backgrounds or traditions. One is the Gimson/Barnsley with which I started, on to which I like to think I've added something new; the other is the 18th century from which I derive most of my plans and thoughts.'

In the early 1950s the way of work changed, too. Edward Barnsley lifted his earlier objections to powered machinery (other Arts and Crafts Movement workshops had accepted the necessity of power-driven machinery as early as 1902), electricity was installed in 1953 and a large planing machine completed what had been a day's work by hand in less than an hour.

Although power was there, machinery played only a very lowly but important role at Froxfield. It was used to avoid time-consuming chores such as sawing and planing large pieces of wood – power tools regarded as the servant of the skilled craftsman – but handwork remained the fundamental method.

The idealism and honesty of the Arts and Crafts Movement lived on his careful choice of wood for each item of furniture, his attention to detail at every stage, and his never-ceasing quest for perfection.

He recognised craft as a living tradition by taking on a succession of pupil/trainees. Several of Britain's independent designer/makers spent some of their formative years at Froxfield: Robert Townshend, Oliver Morel, Kenneth Marshall, Alex McCurdy, Sandy Mackilligan and Alan Peters are just a few of the names.

In the post-war period he was Design Adviser at Loughborough Training College, where young woodwork teachers soaked up his very practical approach to furniture making. 'If you can't see the thing that is being asked for in your mind's eye fairly quickly, then maybe you won't produce the thing to its best advantage,' he told them. This interest in training will continue with the Edward Barnsley Educational Trust that funds apprenticeships at Froxfield.

His influence has been far wider, however. There are over 7,000 individual Barnsley pieces, many of them in the United States where he had a strong reputation. These pieces are his memorial. ∎

● Acknowledgements to *Gimson and the Barnsleys*, Mary Comino (Evans Brothers, 1980, £13.50), and *Cabinetmaking, the professional approach*, Alan Peters (Stobart & Son, 1985, £17.50). Also grateful thanks to *Woodworking International* magazine.

COMPUTER CONSOLATION

Struggling to get your computer equipment into efficient order? Here's three ideas to choose from

Box it in — Bob Grant

This piece was designed to carry the BBC Micro unit, comprising keyboard, VDU, disc drive and/or tape recorder, with a shallow drawer underneath for spare tapes and discs. The keyboard unit is set at the right height to use with a standard chair.

The construction is straightforward, with stopped housings for the carcase (a power router with a guide will be a great help), mortise and tenons for the stretcher rail and dovetails for the drawer. The carcase is made from ¾in veneered blockboard; it's worth seeking out a matching decorative veneer on both sides. Ideally, all the carcase components should be cut from one sheet for continuity of grain and colour.

Start by cutting out the ends as a handed pair. Mark and cut the housings at one-third depth, noting that they are stopped at different widths for the top shelf

▲
A Rolls-Royce of computer desks: Whitehead and Lightfoot's design in grey bolivar veneer with banded lippings and ebony details boasts a touch-button rising table for the VDU, a hideaway keyboard, and — among other things — a drinks cabinet. . . .

◄
At a less ambitious level, Bob Grant's no-frills design for a veneered cabinet would be just the thing for a small study or office.

and lower shelf drawer-stop. The housings run out at the back and, apart from the top shelf, are later covered by the vanity panel which is set into a rebate that exactly matches the housing depth.

Hold the three pieces together in a vice and mark out the lengths along the ends. The shelves vary in width, and the top and bottom shelves, which don't come flush to the front, must be lipped before final assembly of the carcase. At the rear the top shelf is rebated, while the middle shelf is reduced in width by the thickness of the

Photo Ray Clayton

back and butts against it when assembled.

The stretcher rail also has a ¼x¼in rebate at the back to carry the vanity panel. Tenons at either end fit into ¼in mortises set in about ½in deep. The rail is set flush to the back. The tenons are dowelled through the back edge of the carcase and the front edges are worked with a decorative cavetto moulding.

The feet bars are held in a ¼in groove worked on the bottoms of the sides and will prevent the face veneers splitting as the piece is moved. The bottom edges of the bars are slightly relieved with a spokeshave to provide a 'four foot' bearing on the floor. The carcase ends should be polished before gluing the feet on, otherwise it will be difficult to get an even finish.

The vanity panel acts to firm up the entire construction. It's screwed, not glued, at intervals around the edge and is only fixed after the drawer has been made and fitted, so that you can check the fit on the back of the drawer.

When you assemble the carcase for gluing, the drawer bearers must be screwed into position; it will be a tight operation if you have to do it afterwards.

When you've cut all the joints: lip the top and lower shelves; seal and polish all the carcase components; fix the drawer bearers; and glue up, making the usual checks for square and winding. Dowel the stretcher-bar tenons and flush off the front edges. Fix the (previously polished) feet — you'll need substantial cramp bars to span the cut-off corners at the top front edges. Then apply the veneer lippings in one length each side from the front foot to the top back. You can buy iron-on edgings, but it's no great problem to cut slightly over-width strips of veneer, fix them with an impact adhesive and trim them with a sharp knife afterwards. Polish the lippings when fixed. The back edges remain in their raw state and are best stained and polished to match the rest of the piece.

The drawer has standard lap dovetails at the front, and through dovetails at the back, with the sides and front grooved on their inner faces to take the ¼in ply bottom. A central divider, housed at the back and front, serves as a muntin with the bottom screwed up to it, and also screwed at intervals along the underneath of the back.

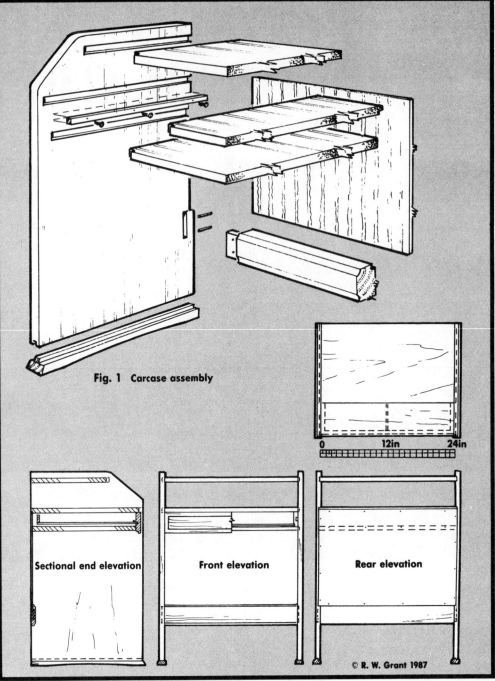

Fig. 1 Carcase assembly

0   12in   24in

Sectional end elevation

Front elevation

Rear elevation

© R. W. Grant 1987

The drawer front, which is set back under the middle shelf by ¼in, is also made to cover the front edge of the lower shelf. The shelf acts a drawer-stop and a cavetto finger-grip is worked on the inner under-edge of the front. The drawer back is set down about ¼in lower than the sides, preventing crumpled paper or whatever from jamming the drawer. That's why the back vanity panel is made so it can be removed. With the drawer glued up, work the grooves on the sides to fit the bearer bars on the carcase (a power router will help at this stage) and the final squaring of the end at the front can be cleaned out with a chisel. Rub some candle wax in the grooves to help the smooth running of the drawer. The ⅛in ebony inlay lines are positioned ¹¹⁄₁₆in in from the drawer edges and are mitred in to prepared scratchstock grooves. After they're glued in, clean and polish the whole drawer-front.

As the console was built for the home, not the office, I finished it with two coats of sanding sealer and then wax-polished it. Presanded faced blockboards will take most finishes, but avoid oversanding — the decorative facing veneers are paper-thin and bare patches 'grinning through' won't look very attractive. ▶

Cutting list

Carcase

Ends	2	33¾in	x	20in	x	¾in	sapele faced board
Top shelf	1	24		14		¾	,,
Middle shelf	1	24		20		¾	,,
Lower shelf	1	24		19		¾	,,
Stretcher rail	1	23½		3½		¾	solid sapele
Vanity panel	1	18½		24		¼	sapele faced ply
Drawer bearers	2	18		½		³⁄₁₆	solid beech
Lippings	all front edges ¾						sapele veneer
Feet	2	20¼		1⅛		¾	solid sapele

Drawer

Drawer front	1	23½		3½		⅞	solid sapele
Drawer back	1	23½		2		⅜	,,
Drawer sides	2	18		2¾		⅜	,,
Drawer divider	1	18		2		⅜	,,
Inlay lines	to 'frame'						ebony or black
	drawer			⅛		¹⁄₁₆	stained lines
Drawer bottom	1	23		18		¼	ply

70

Photo Ray Clayton

Pile it up —
Bob Grant

This piece of equipment is designed to accommodate home computing hardware based on the popular makes of micro-computers — the computer and its keyboard; a disc drive or tape recorder unit; a printer; and a portable television (or VDU). Before embarking on the project check the sizes of equipment and make modifications as necessary. The work station heights (chair seat to middle shelf and operator's eye level to screen), are based on the average human sizes. At 6ft 3in I'm above average so these sizes would be too small for me.

The structure is simple, based on mortise and tenon frameworks. The drawings show the necessary details and you can check against the cutting list for finished sizes.

I used pine, but any straight-grained wood is suitable. Make the two end frames first; glue up the cross rails first, with the leg ends dry-fitted into the foot bars. Shape the foot bars underneath with a spokeshave to provide four bearing points before gluing. Check for square and wind before leaving the cramped structure to dry. The tenons on the front ends of the frame rails (fig. 2) are modified to allow for the meeting with the shelf support rail tenons, which are slightly offset to gain a longer length.

Flush off the frames when the glue is dry and mark and cut the mortises for the middle shelf support-rails and the stretcher bar tenons.

Now you can glue the whole structure together; shoot the two shelves to dead length and then button or bracket them on. Wedge the stretcher-bar through tenons from the outsides.

Apply what finish you like, avoiding high-gloss slippery polish to the shelf surfaces.

Cutting list
(includes 1½in tenons)

Front legs	2	27¼in	x	2⅛in	x ⅞in
Back legs	2	35½		2⅛	⅞
Top brackets	2	8½		2½	⅞
End rails	2	9½		2½	⅞
Foot bars	2	20		2½	⅞
Top shelf	1	33¼		9	⅞
Middle shelf	1	33¼		10½	⅞
Middle shelf support rails	2	34¼		1¼	⅞
Stretcher bar	1	35		3½	⅞

Fig. 2 Joint details

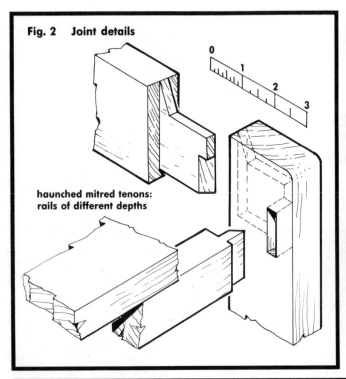

haunched mitred tenons:
rails of different depths

Spread it out — Alan Cranston

The vital element for housing your computer equipment is a sturdy worktop — long, wide and thick. It needs to be long to carry all the different pieces of equipment; I recommend a length of 12ft, a depth of about 27in, and 1½in thick so you need fewer supports underneath.

On the left-hand side of the top I've added an extra piece I call an 'elbow board', on which you can rest your forearms; computer keyboards are easier to use if they are set back about 9in from the front edge. This board is also handy for holding copy paper, pens and pencils and to use the 'mouse'. My board is 4ft long, 9in wide and 1⅜in thick, adjoins the front edge of the worktop and is fixed by two or three 2x1in battens screwed under the worktop and extending them forward about 8in.

This is how I've laid out equipment on my worktop: computer, disc drive, monitor and keyboard clustered around the elbow board; dot matrix printer and tape drive to the left; daisy wheel printer to the right with a couple of video recorders further to the right. With this amount of equipment I've got three 13 amp double socket outlets lined up on the wall at the back of the worktop about 3in above the surface.

You could also use trestles, pedestals or a purpose-made fitment to support the worktop. You could use a piece of furniture to support one end and an adjustable tripod at the other. Keep the height about 31in, with a batten along the wall to support the back. Keep it simple and flexible, for computers are an ever-changing scene.

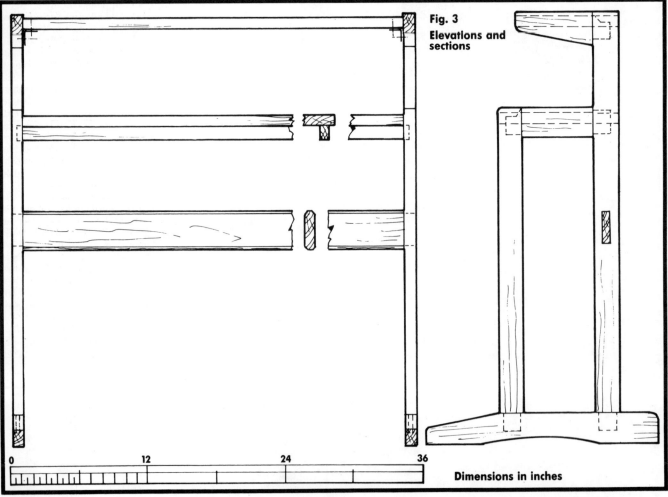

**Fig. 3
Elevations and
sections**

Dimensions in inches

THREE-QUARTER TIMES TABLE

Jim Robinson adds a Victorian table to his range of children's furniture

Makers of the child-size smoker's bow chair in *WW/Dec. '88* may have been asked to complement the piece. So for the benefit of long-suffering parents and grand-parents, and their fortunate protégé, this Victorian table is three-quarter size, as was the chair. The sturdy design matches the stocky bow chair, and the dimensions were kept to reasonable size as a space-saving consideration.

I chose olive ash, which is hard and durable with the brown mottled markings found in large ash trees. The table would, originally, have been made in pine but when making furniture for children durability is more important than historical authenticity.

The legs

Cut the blanks for the legs from 3in thick board on the bandsaw. If 3in timber is hard to find glue together 1½in boards with a urea formaldehyde adhesive, like Cascamite, taking care to match the grain where possible. Cut the ends square and mark where the pommel (square section) meets the top bead. Gently cut a 'V' to each side of the mark using the long point of a skew chisel.

It is worth practising this V-cutting on a piece of scrap wood. Always take gentle shallow cuts to avoid breakout. When the required depth is reached, round the rest of the blank using a large square-ended gouge and smooth with a skew, before marking on the leg. If turning a

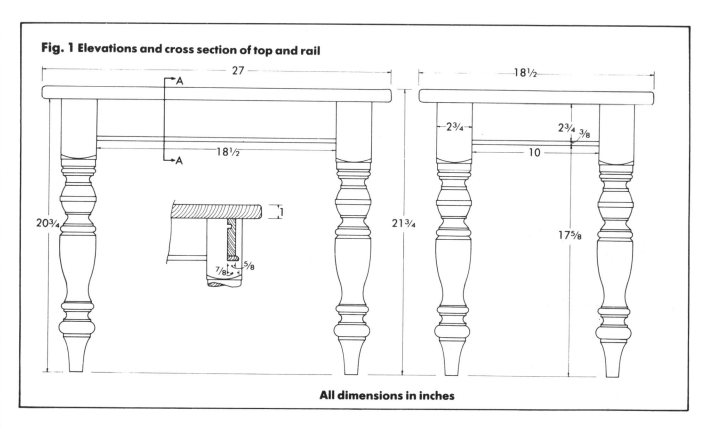

Fig. 1 Elevations and cross section of top and rail

All dimensions in inches

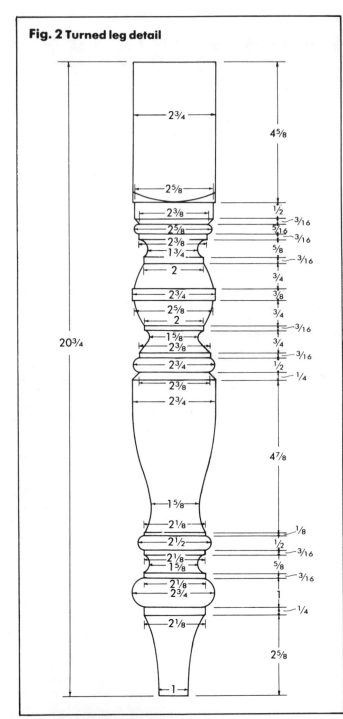

Fig. 2 Turned leg detail

Underside showing turnbuttons and corner blocks

Top and rails

Plane the timber for the top and four rails. Finish the top to 1in thick, or ⅞in if using 1in timber. For the rails use ¾in wood, planed to ⅝in. Rub joint the planks together producing a top 27×18½in, with the grain alternated to minimise the tendency to warp. Vertical grain, as in quarter-sawn timber, is best.

When the glue is hard plane and scrape level and sand down to 320-grit garnet, having rounded the edges which can later be planed down to hide the dents created by over-zealous children.

Cut the side rails to 21in and 12½in long, and form a groove along the inside edges to take the top fittings (figs 1 and 3). Cut the tenons 1¾×1¼×⅜in (fig. 3). Plane a rounded moulding on one edge of four pieces of ⅞×⅜in strip and pin these strips underside the rails.

Glue up the legs and rails, remembering to put softwood blocks between the sash-cramp jaws and the timber. Strengthen the joint further by gluing blocks into the corners, and join the top to the rails with small blocks along the top edge of the rails allowing room for movement, to prevent splitting.

Before fixing the top to the rails I applied three coats of Danish oil at one-hour intervals. Brush it on and remove any surplus after a few minutes with a lint-free cloth. Rub down the final coat after 24 hours with 0000 wire-wool and wax, to remove any roughness caused by dust particles. Danish oil produces a fine finish, but will show up any defects. So to avoid criticism from the discerning child or grandchild don't stint on the finishing. ∎

number of identical pieces put the important measurements on a piece of wood and then transfer to the blank. Use a fingernail gouge for the hollows and a skew for the rounds, measuring diameters frequently with callipers. Sharp tools are essential as ash can be very hard and rough areas are difficult to sand out. Smooth with garnet paper from 150-grit to 320.

Take the legs from the lathe and cut the rail mortises before finishing. Cut the mortises on the legs as deep as is possible using a ⅜in router cutter. Increase the depth to a little over 1¼in by hand, also squaring off the ends.

Fig. 3 Leg and rail assembly

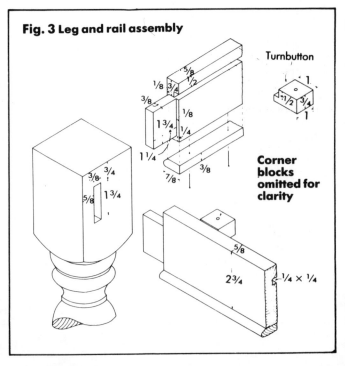

Turnbutton

Corner blocks omitted for clarity

Brolly folly

If you need a stand for those hard-worked umbrellas, and fancy giving yourself a course in unusual coopering, try Tim Kidman's technique for built-up octagons

● *Spiralling oak leaves encircle the unusual coopered cylinder, faired in to form a 'squashed' circle*

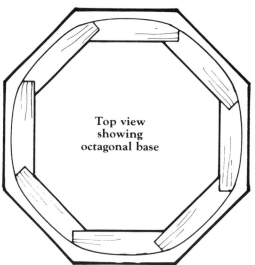

Top view showing octagonal base

I made the plank-back stool described by Alan and Gill Bridgewater in the August 1985 *Woodworker*, and almost before I'd had time to stand back and admire it, I was asked to make a matching umbrella stand.

About the same time, I saw through my 'nautical eyes' an article describing the construction of a hollow wooden spar, made by cutting right-angled rebates at 45° into the long edges of eight pieces of wood. When it was glued and pulled together, the angles and corners were self-aligning, and formed a circular wooden spar. I decided to try this technique out.

I needed a height of 16in to match the stool, and so cut eight pieces of oak 15x3x¾in; I cut the rebates into the long edges of the pieces by setting up a 45° fence — a bandsawn and planed bit of softwood — on the router table, then with a straight two-flute ¾in cutter projecting between the 45° fence and the vertical fence, all I needed to do was get the angle-fence side of the cutter to the right depth and plumb in the middle of the long edge. Once it was set up, cutting the 90° rebate was easy. The rebates are effectively 90° vee-grooves in the timber edges.

I glued the eight pieces of rebated oak together, pulling them into position with 24in plastic wire ties, for which I was lucky enough to have a tie gun. You could also use a string windlass, or 24in Jubilee clips, or extra-strong ratchet band cramps.

I made the base from an 8in square piece of oak, 1⅝in thick. While the cylinder was still square-surfaced, I marked off its outside shape on to the base piece, and then cut that out on the bandsaw. I cleaned up each side with a plane, then marked semi-circular shapes out on each face. I found the centre on the underside, and scribed a 2in circle, then drew lines from the bottoms of the semi-circles on the faces to the 2in circumference. That gave me eight triangular shapes, which I cut out with chisel and gouge, finishing off with a good woodcarving gouge. I cut a ¼in rebate round the outside of the top to fit the cylinder exactly on to the base.

I planed the cylinder not quite circular to keep the maximum gluing area and minimise the joint lines, then drew eight oak leaves in a spiral pattern, and carved them

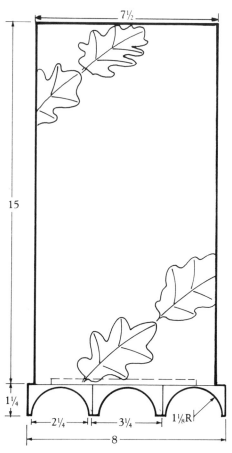

All dimensions in inches

● *Long plastic wire ties used to pull together the eight pieces of oak*

with my woodcarving chisels, gouges and a Swann-Morton scalpel.

The inside of the stand needed a drip-tray, which I made from galvanised steel, cut into octagonal shape from an 8in square. I cut the corners to give a 1in lip when they were bent at 90°, and soldered them with aluminium/zinc solder.

Finally, the cylinder and base were stained, glued together and polished, and the drip-tray placed inside. The stand now graces our hall along with the stool, giving a traditional country air to our umbrellas.■

UPSTAND

When he was set the challenge of making a plant-pot stand with a limited range of tools, Mike Rate came up with this solution

When asked to make a plant-pot stand with a difference, I had to design something that could be made without a lathe or router. The design then evolved, and the result is certainly different.

Select a close-grained red wood, if necessary cut roughly to size at the woodyard. After planing the stem square, mark the design on all four sides using a mortise gauge, shading the parts to be removed to save confusion later. To make a stand 23in high overall, the stem starts at 21¾in long.

Once the marking out has been checked, drill the ¾in diameter holes halfway through from each side, to avoid splitting the stem. Then the slots should be sawn and roughly chiselled out, for trimming later.

Leave the stem aside to

The stand on the left has rounded links and is fitted with adjustable plant pot holders on the stem

settle and cut out the top with a jigsaw, finishing with a file. On one face cut out a hole 1¾in square, ½in deep, making sure the sides are square as it is to fit over the top of the stem, then finish the top with grades of glasspaper and a sanding block, sanding with the grain of course.

The feet proved to be quite a problem as they all have to be the same shape and the centre of gravity should be kept low. Draw one on thick paper, then cut it out and use it as a template. The jigsaw was used to cut out the shape of the legs, then the tenons were cut to size. The feet are filed and sanded to their finished size, making sure all four are identical.

Return to the stem, and if it is still straight, use a mallet and chisel to reduce the thickness of the 'links' to size and to make the holes square. At this point, an alternative would be to leave the holes round and put a large radius on the outer corners and

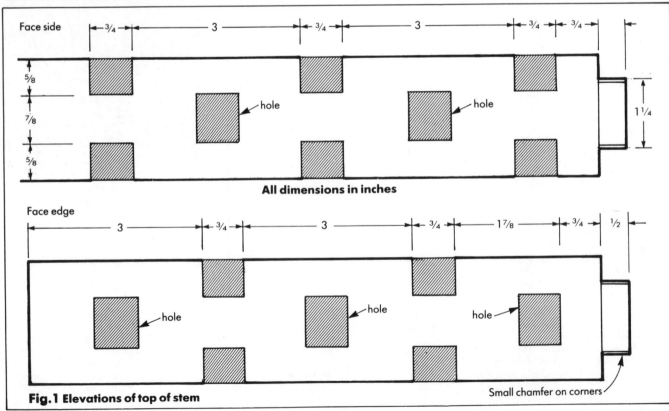

Face side

All dimensions in inches

Face edge

Small chamfer on corners

Fig. 1 Elevations of top of stem

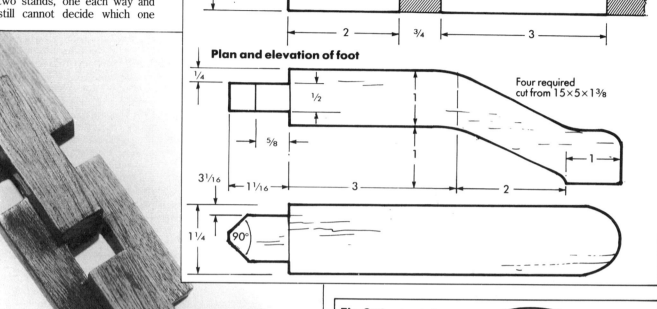

Fig.2 Bottom of stem

Plan and elevation of foot

Four required
cut from 15×5×1⅜

90°

edges of the links to make a round chain. I have now made two stands, one each way and still cannot decide which one

The square link stem, the holes are drilled then squared with a chisel

The holes in the round link stem are cut square so that the plant pot rings cannot rotate

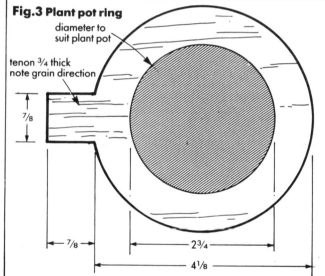

Fig.3 Plant pot ring

diameter to
suit plant pot

tenon ¾ thick
note grain direction

looks better.

Before finishing the stem it is necessary to cut the tenon at the top, making sure it is square and a good fit into the stand top. When the tenon fits, chamfer the corners to allow easier entry into the mortise when gluing. At the other end of the stem, drill through for the mortises to receive the feet. Take care with the chisel to make sure that the mortises are square, not forgetting that all four feet will meet in the centre. Finish the stem with a chisel, file and sandpaper. When all the parts are finished dry assemble them to check that the stand is upright.

The top is glued on first, and when the glue is dry go over the stand with fine glasspaper again. After dusting down apply the first coat of varnish, paying particular attention to the end-grain.

To make the stand more interesting and give it a greater capacity for plants make two plant pot rings, with spigots to fit the holes in the centre of the links. The spigots should be an easy push fit into the stem, making them movable for repositioning as the plants grow.

The height of this 'different stand' can be changed by adding or subtracting links to suit. ∎

Doubled up

When space is at a premium dual-purpose units are the answer. Leslie Stuttle's ingenious desk converts into a dressing table

Living in a small bungalow, I am always looking for space-saving ideas. My wife wanted some library shelves on which to keep her books and I was looking for somewhere to do some paperwork without having to clear it all away after each session.

The obvious solution was to use our spare room — but how to do this when it was so small and would be needed on occasions for a short-stay visitor?

My idea was a desk unit which would easily convert into a dressing table. The basic idea consists of an 'open' stand with its own drawers, into which fits a reversible top surface which carries its own double-ended drawer sections. One way up, the top presents dressing-table drawers and a backboard; the other way, you get a higher flat surface with drawers below it.

For all large panels I used $\frac{3}{4}$in blockboard veneered both sides, with matching solid timber for the remainder and for edging strips.

Making the stand

Start by making the stand, followed by the top section and then the drawers. Cut and prepare to size all the pieces for the stand except the drawer-runners and guides and the shaped corner blocks.

Then cut the 1x$\frac{7}{8}$in shoulders on the top side rails before setting out all the mortises and tenons, being careful to mark the correct mortises on front and back legs.

The stub tenons on the short rails forming the bottom of the drawer openings shouldn't be more than $\frac{5}{8}$in long, so their mortises don't run into those of the side rails; this avoids glue getting into them

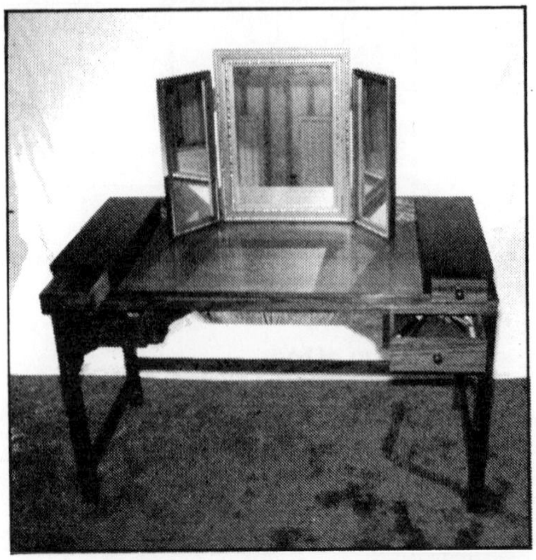

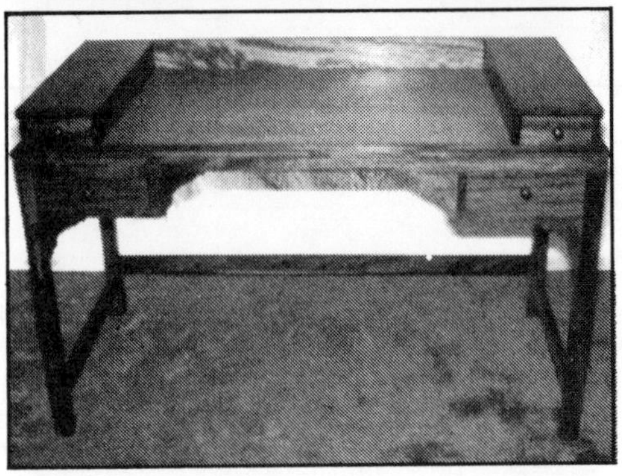

● *As a dressing table, the piece already has a certain charm. The mirror stores in the space created when the top flips over*

when fitting the side rails and also stops side rail wedges wandering. Don't cut the middle back rail mortises too deep either, as the same applies.

When gauging mortises and tenons, note they are not all the same. Further, the bottom side rails and back rails are set in the middle of 1$\frac{3}{8}$in square legs, whereas the rails are only $\frac{3}{4}$in thick, so you must reset the gauge.

Gauge the middle back rail tenons from its inside edge and the matching mortises from the inside of the legs as the rail is $\frac{3}{16}$in narrower than the legs to fit the plywood panel.

When you've completed setting out and doubled checked, cut the tenons and chop out the mortises. Check all joints fit and then try a dry run assembly.

To do this, fit the two centre rails into the front and back top rails, then the top and bottom side rails into the legs, followed by the middle and bottom back rails. You should now be able to stand the unit up so that the front and back top rails can be fitted on to the stub tenons on the legs.

Fit the two short rails which form the bottom of the drawer openings, then slip into place the two wide pieces which form the sides of the drawer carcases. These side pieces are $\frac{7}{16}$in shorter than the overall width of the frame to allow a $\frac{1}{4}$in strip to be glued to the front end to cover the endgrain and leave $\frac{3}{16}$in at the back for the ply panel. Test everything for squareness, and when you're satisfied dismantle. Number all joints to make gluing up easy.

Before you glue, cut enough wedges for all joints and make cuts in the tenon ends to accept the wedges. As you glue, check that each section is square.

Leave the short drawer-opening rails until the other joints have set and meanwhile cut the four corner-blocks from 1$\frac{1}{8}$in thick timber.

Now fit the short rails, drawer carcasing sides and the $\frac{1}{4}$in strips to cover the endgrain, followed by the corner-blocks. These blocks are glued and screwed but those fitted under the top rails can't easily be screwed to the side of the drawer carcasing as there is already a screw passing through the bottom rail into the side piece. A strong glue like Cascamite should do, or screw the blocks on by placing the two screws off centre.

Now clean up the whole job so far, before preparing the four $\frac{1}{2}$x$\frac{3}{8}$in pieces which are glued and pinned to the top surface of the top rails with mitred corners and $\frac{1}{8}$in overhang. Finish by fitting the drawer-runners and guides plus $\frac{1}{2}$x$\frac{1}{2}$in softwood

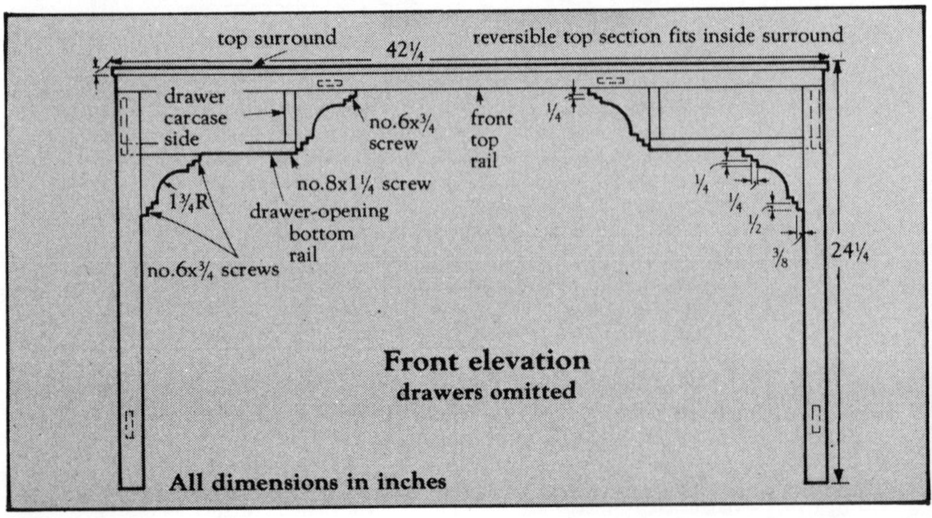
top surround
42¼
reversible top section fits inside surround
drawer carcase side
no.6x¾ screw
front top rail
¼
no.8x1¼ screw
1¾R
drawer-opening bottom rail
no.6x¾ screws
¼
¼
½
⅜
24¼
Front elevation
drawers omitted
All dimensions in inches

● *In desk form, the top has flipped over and the drawers at the back become the drawers at the front!*

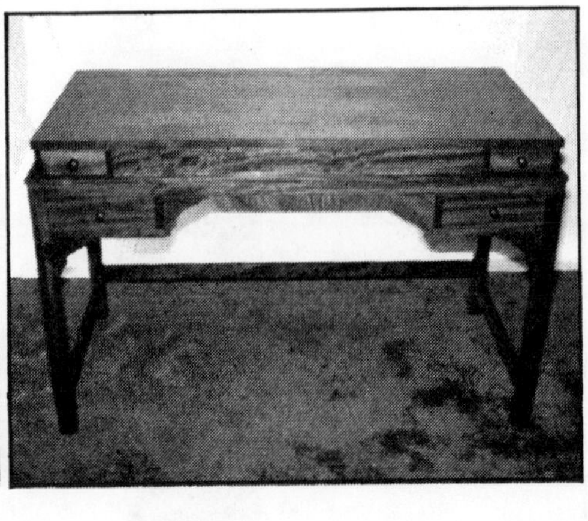

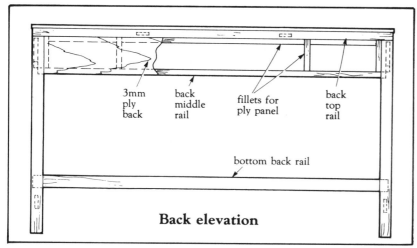

3mm ply back | back middle rail | fillets for ply panel | back top rail

bottom back rail

Back elevation

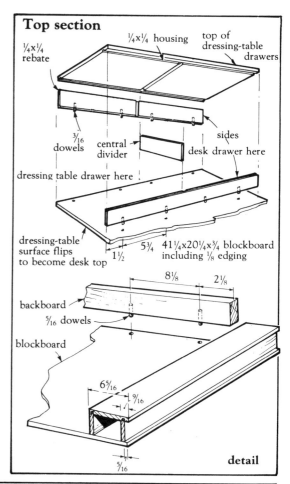

Top section

¼x¼ housing | top of dressing-table drawers
¼x¼ rebate
³⁄₁₆ dowels | central divider | sides | desk drawer here
dressing table drawer here
dressing-table surface flips to become desk top | 5¾ | 1½ | 41¼x20¼x¾ blockboard including ⅛ edging

backboard | 8⅛ | 2⅛
⁵⁄₁₆ dowels
blockboard
6⁵⁄₁₆ | ⁹⁄₁₆
⁵⁄₁₆

detail

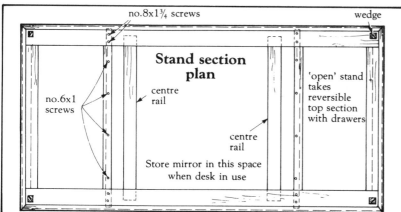

no.8x1¾ screws | wedge

Stand section plan

no.6x1 screws | centre rail | centre rail | 'open' stand takes reversible top section with drawers

Store mirror in this space when desk in use

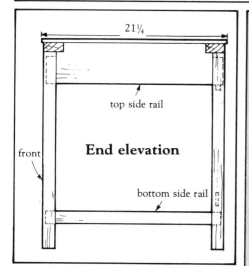

21¼

top side rail

front | **End elevation**

bottom side rail

strips to the back legs and the underside of the back top rail. Cut and fit the 3mm ply panel.

Now carefully measure the opening formed by the ½x⅜in strips fitted to the top rails and cut a piece of blockboard to finish ⁵⁄₁₆in smaller. Glue and pin ⅛in edging strip all round it. Lay the board on the frame and check that it fits; there should be roughly ¹⁄₃₂in clearance on all sides. If it looks good turn the board over, front to back, and provided everything is square it should still fit.

Cutting list

Stand

4 legs	23¾in x	1⅜in x	1⅜in
2 front and back top rails	42	2¼	1
2 top side rails	20½	4⅝	1
1 back middle rail	40½	1³⁄₁₆	¾
1 back bottom rail	41¼	1½	¾
2 bottom side rails	20¼	1½	¾
2 drawer carcase sides	20⁹⁄₁₆	3⅝	⅜
2 facing strips for above	3	⅝	¼
2 drawer-opening bottom rails	9⅝	1⅜	⅝
2 centre rails	18½	1½	½
4 corner-blocks	3½	3½	1⅛
4 drawer sides	20	3	½
2 drawer-fronts	8⅜	3	¾
2 drawer backs	8⅜	2⅜	⅜
4 drawer runners	18⅝	⅝	⅝
2 drawer side guides	18¼	1¾	⅜
2 drawer top guides	16¾	1	⅝
2 drawer top guides	16¾	1¼	⅝
2 top surrounds	42¼	½	⅜
2 top surrounds	21¼	½	⅜

Top section

2 edging strips	41¼	¾	⅛
2 edging strips	20¼	¾	⅛
2 drawer carcase tops	20¼	6⁵⁄₁₆	½
4 drawer carcase sides	20¼	2¼	½
2 drawer carcase central dividers	5½	2¼	¼
1 back board	28⅝	2½	1
4 drawer fronts	5	2	⅝
8 drawer sides	10	2	⅜
4 drawer backs	5	1⅝	¼
1 top	¾in blockboard to fit		

Doubled up

Top section

Now you can make the box-like sections for the drawers. Get accurate sizes from the blockboard top you have just fitted; these boxes must be dead accurate, because the drawers have to work both ways up!

Form ¼x¼in rebates on one edge of each side piece and plough two ¼x¼in grooves in the top panels, remembering that one groove is ¼in from the edge whilst the other is set in ⁹⁄₁₆in. Lay one pair of sides and one top on the bench and mark the ¼x¼in housing for the centre piece. The housing on the side pieces is worked on opposite sides to the rebates and on the top pieces it does not extend past the ploughed grooves. Try a dry run and then glue up.

The boxes and blockboard top can now be drilled ready for the dowels; don't go more than ⅝in deep into the blockboard as dowels shouldn't show through. The boxes are fitted so that the ⁵⁄₁₆in overhang faces outwards and should be in line with edge of blockboard. When fitting the dowels insert them into the boxes first and then check that only ⅝in is left protruding to fit into the top.

To finish off cut a piece of 2½x1in to fit snugly between the boxes along the back edge and fix it to the top with dowels.

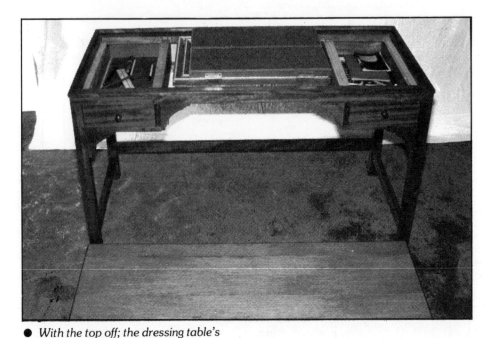

● *With the top off; the dressing table's backboard between the drawers is a 'frontboard' when it's a desk*

Stand — Joints and components

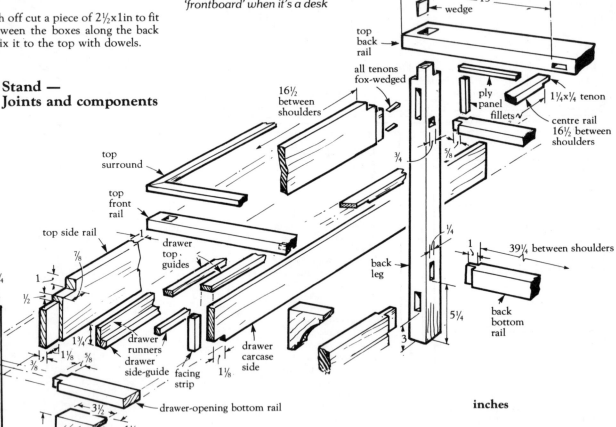

inches

Drawers

The last stage is to make and fit the six drawers. The two large drawers will require stops, whereas the small drawers can stop against the central divider, if their overall length is made to match the length of their respective carcases. You need four drawers 10x5x2in, and two of 20½x8⅜x3in.

After fitting drawer pulls of your choice

— I turned some small knobs with spigot ends, drilled the drawer fronts and glued the knobs in — the whole unit can be rubbed down and finished to your taste.

If you buy a free-standing winged mirror the job is complete. Remember when turning the top over to convert the function to remove the small drawers and put them back in the other way up! ∎

Table-top seat

When is a table not a table? When it's a settle — one you can make with the help of Vic Taylor's splendid drawings

The 'Monk's bench' is unusual as an early example of dual-purpose furniture. In one guise it acts as a side-table for serving food, and by re-arranging and re-fixing the top it becomes a settle.

We can tell that it is intended as a side-table because of the following two features; first, the back edge of the top lines up with the back edge of the cross-piece (fig. 2), whereas there is an overhang at the front edge; and second, there is a slot cut through each cross-piece and a peg can be pushed through to engage in a hole in the arm at each end. This allows you to slide the top towards you when sitting at the table and gives you more leg-room — quite a normal characteristic of this kind of table.

The individuality of the design, however, lies in the fact that you can withdraw the pegs, take the top off and re-position it as a settle-back by inserting each peg through its slot into a second hole bored through the back end of each arm, as shown in the end elevation, fig. 2. The result is a settle with a wooden seat and back which will need some cushions to make it comfortable.

The piece was probably made in the early or mid-17th century; it's difficult to be precise as furniture of this type was usually locally made by the village carpenter and the woodturner, and popular designs continued to be made for many years after their inception. Settles of this style are often called 'monks' benches', but there's no evidence that they were particularly favoured by monks; anyway, most monasteries had been dissolved by Henry VIII and the monks disbanded by the end of the 16th century, many years before our design came into existence.

Construction

The top couldn't be simpler. It consists of three pieces of oak, laid alongside each other and nailed to the two cross-pieces. The inevitable has happened, of course, and the pieces have shrunk across their widths with resulting gaps and splits.

If you are concerned with authenticity you can do the same, but shrinkage plates (fig. 5A) would be better. Fig. 5B shows how the plate is first screwed to the cross-piece, sunk slightly below the surface (say 1/32in or so) which means that the cross-piece and the top will be in close contact. Use a round-head screw to fix the plate to the underside of the top; the slot will allow movement without the top splitting.

Fig. 1 shows the various joints used. You will see the framing uses mortise-and-tenon joints, all pegged; the joints on the seat rails are double tenons.

The wedged tenons on the tops and

● Having it both ways; a flick of the wrist and the table becomes a settle – and not just for monks!

Methods of construction

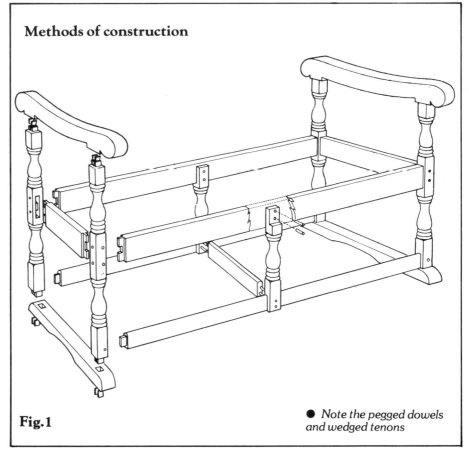

Fig.1

● Note the pegged dowels and wedged tenons

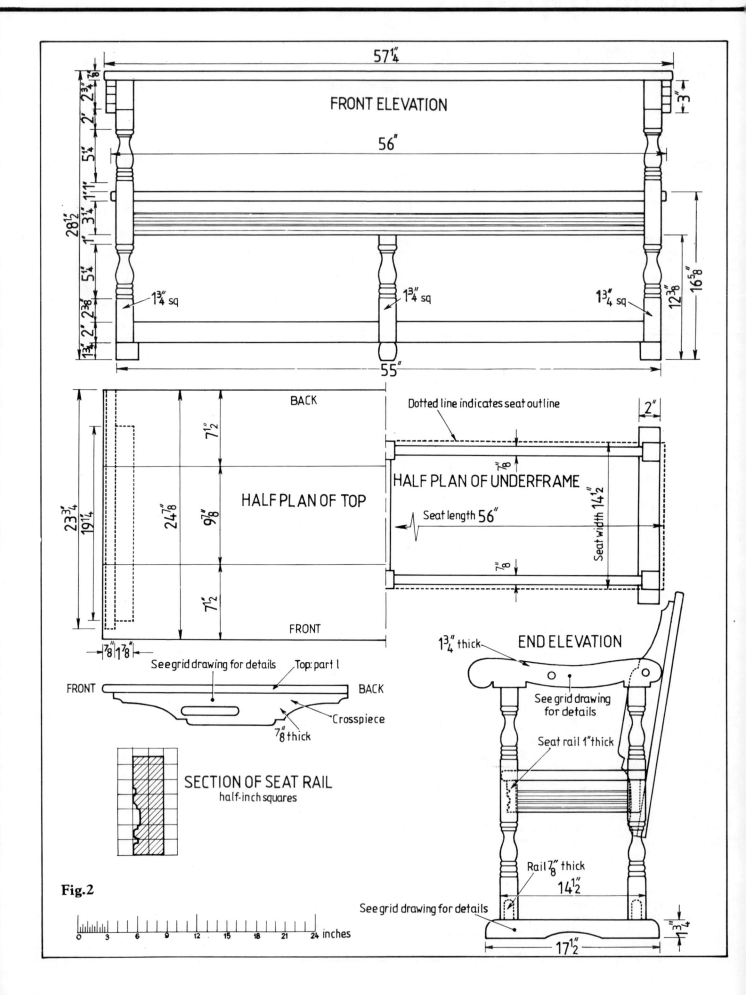

FRONT ELEVATION

57¼"

56"

3"

28½"

2" 2⅜"
2¾ 7/8
5¼
1½"
3¼
1"
5¼
2" 2⅜
1¼

1¾" sq

1¾" sq

1¾" sq

16⅝"

12⅜"

55"

HALF PLAN OF TOP

BACK

FRONT

7½"
9⅞"
7½"

24⅞"

23¾"
19¼"

⅞" ⅞"

Dotted line indicates seat outline

2"

HALF PLAN OF UNDERFRAME

Seat length 56"

⅞"
⅞"

Seat width 14½"

See grid drawing for details   Top: part 1

FRONT

BACK

Crosspiece

⅞" thick

SECTION OF SEAT RAIL
half-inch squares

END ELEVATION

1¾" thick

See grid drawing
for details

Seat rail 1" thick

Rail ⅞" thick

14½"

See grid drawing for details

17½"

1¾"

Fig.2

0 3 6 9 12 15 18 21 24 inches

Table-top seat

bottoms of the legs need cutting carefully. The tenons at the top ends are blind and call for a slightly different treatment from the bottom ones which are through tenons; fig. 4 shows both kinds, B at the bottom and C at the top of the leg. Points to note are:

● The saw-cuts to accept the wedges should only extend two-thirds of the tenon length.

● The mortise should be slightly splayed as shown to allow for the expansion of the tenon when the wedges are driven home, but the splay only extends for two-thirds of the mortise depth, the same as the length of the saw cuts.

● Judge the size of the wedges nicely. They mustn't be too thin to expand the tenon properly, nor should they be too thick so they force the tenon apart prematurely and jam it before it's fully home.

The tops of the intermediate legs are cut away to accept the seat-rails, and the joints are pegged right through (fig. 1). At the bottom they are bridle-jointed over the underframe rails as shown at fig.4A, and the joints are pegged right through with dowels, which also fix the intermediate cross-rail.

Like the top, the seat consists of two pieces nailed to the end seat-rails and notched round the legs. This is obviously another case for using shrinkage plates along the end seat-rails; fixing to the front and back seat-rail can be by pocket-screwing (fig. 5C), if you don't mind a gap opening up in the middle of the seat. If you prefer comfort to authenticity, pocket-screw at the front and use shrinkage plates everywhere else.

All the seat-rails had moulded faces, the profile of which is shown in fig. 2. This would probably have been worked with a combination of moulding planes and scratch-stocks, but life is easier for us, and we can use a spindle moulder or a router to speed things up.

The only other components are the two pegs (detail, fig. 3) which call for straight-forward wood turning.

Furniture like this almost always began its life 'in the white' — free from any kind of polish. Hundreds of years' worth of wax polish would have been applied, of course, and you can do the same thing; use any good quality proprietary wax polish.

You can see from the main drawing that the piece has had some heavy wear, particularly on the front under-frame rails where the wood has been worn away to about half the original size. If you want to give your reproduction the same appearance you can use a rasp to simulate the wear, restricting it to the front under-frame rail and the edges of the legs, where feet would normally scuff the wood. The edges of the arms were also notched and bruised, and so were all the edges of the top.

● The design is reproduced by kind permission of Mrs Lyle, Barrington Court, near Ilminster, Somerset. ∎

Fig.3

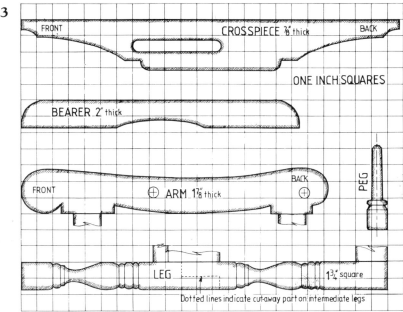

Fig.4

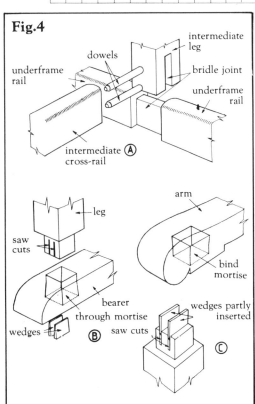

Fig.5

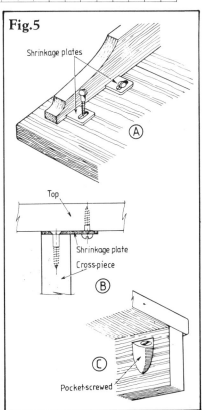

Cutting list
All components in oak: all dimensions are finished sizes

Top	1	57¼in x	24⅞in x	⅞in	1454mm x	632mm x	23mm
Crosspieces	2	23¾	3⅛	⅞	603	80	23
Seat	1	56	14½	1	1423	369	25
Arms	2	19¼	2¾	1⅞	489	70	48
Legs	4	23	1¾	1¾	584	45	45
Intermediate legs	2	13	1¾	1¾	330	45	45
Long seat-rails	2	53¼	3¼	1	1353	83	25
End seat-rails	2	13⅛	3¼	1	333	83	25
Under-frame rails	2	53¼	2	⅞	1353	51	23
Bearers	2	17½	1¾	2	445	45	51
Intermediate cross-rail	1	11	2	⅞	280	51	23

Crossing the bar

Jim Corcoran describes how he planned his breakthrough into the specialist joinery trade — and how it turned out in practice

● **Above:** Jim's bar looks a treat, but it learnt him a few lessons - like the difference between solid oak and blockboard! **Below left,** snapping a line on a stout piece of waney-edged oak; **below right,** the basic construction on site

Until September 1984 I was a Royal Naval shipwright artificer. That meant I'd trained and gained experience in a whole range of different skills, from carpentry to plumbing — so, when I decided to move over into Civvy Street, cabinetmaking and joinery seemed a natural field.

To start the business off, I'd lined up one big job: a new 30x10ft bar for the Park Gate British Legion Club in Hampshire. I was operating out of a newly acquired 650sq ft industrial unit in nearby Stubbington, where my only piece of fixed equipment was (and is) a Lurem C260N universal machine which I bought from SAF Power Tools at Fareham.

I'd done similar jobs before, but nothing on this scale, and I was determined to get it right. So I did a lot of local research on small but important points such as the correct height for optics, the width and height of stock shelves, the lighting, the height and width of the counter, etc. I was well aware that only the right combination would make a bar that was comfortable for the customer, efficient and stress-free for the staff, and generally pleasing to the eye.

I bought no less than £5400-worth of sawn joinery-quality English oak from J. & S. Agates of Horsham, Sussex. I'd never used timber in such volume before, and my estimate of the cost eventually proved 20% short. That, however, was nothing to the 40% shortfall in my estimate of labour. If there was a failure in the job, under-estimating was it. I should have charged an awful lot more.

What's more, the timber was air-dried, and when I got it on site it shrank by a frightening amount. It was winter and the club's central heating was going full pelt, with the result that the canopy warped and actually split once it was up. I hadn't given the timber enough time to acclimatise. I know now that I'd have been commercially better off using oak-faced blockboard instead of all that solid material. If I did the job again, that's the main change I'd make — apart, of course, from a major adjustment to the price!

My first job was panelling about 60x9ft of wall, for which I used the Lurem to get out pieces up to 10in wide. I tongued, grooved and rebated them to make panels about 24x⅜x108in.

Then I made the stock bar, whose components varied from 18x1in for shelf uprights to 15x¾in for the shelves. I made up the sizeable upright widths by tonguing and grooving narrower boards on the Lurem's spindle-moulder. The bar top — 22ft long, 1½in thick and 18in wide — was cut from one piece. Bottle display units sit on top of it, and incorporate two overhead light-boxes.

As for the main bar, its principal features are a 26ft top, again 1½in thick but 22in wide. There's a small handbag shelf right along the front beneath it. The front fascia is fabricated from six tongued-and-grooved panels, screwed to the uprights and then embellished with mouldings.

The canopy consists of ½in-thick tongued-and-grooved panels secured to five hanging frames, each panel measuring about 54x24in. Its main features are internal overhead lights and the ability to fit security shutters as required.

Finally came the finishing touches — covering all the butt joints with mouldings of various sections, and giving the whole construction a protective coat of two-part polyurethane varnish.

The project had taken some three and a half months of hard work. I was single-handed (I did all the drawings and estimating) except for the occasional bit of help when it was essential in order to move something. The job was made rather more difficult by lack of co-ordination among my clients; and, although I built it to a good standard (apart from a few small sins of the kind which yield to examination on any large job), and the result looks very nice, it did not work as a promotional exercise. That kind of specialist joinery has largely been cornered by better-known firms, and I was soon forced to get down to 'grubbing': doors, windows and general carpentry.

However, since then I've also built a racing dinghy which has carried a world champion to victory, and I'm currently laying down another boat. Ideally, that will be where my future now lies . . . ∎

Hand-made and handsome

Mark Ripley's small tall
cabinet embodies a
modern approach to
traditional craft. He
shows how it's made

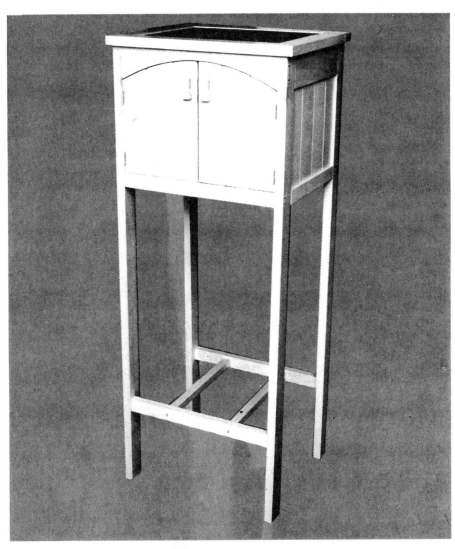

● *Straight from the saw; sycamore au naturel is used in this well-balanced small cabinet*

My training is in contemporary furniture design aimed at mass production, but the bulk of my work now is in cottage style, with strong emphasis on traditional forms and techniques. The transition to a traditional approach occurred when I took several commissions, all of which had to be made in my very basic workshop with only a small bandsaw and hand-tools.

I looked to the time before machines for my inspiration and methods and found the results exciting and satisfying. I was also working (I still am) as a woodwork instructor with handicapped adults and was thinking in simple terms when designing projects for them, again to be made with hand-tools. I do use machines — not to is inefficient and often boring — but I do so with care and now that I'm considering full-time making, I want to maintain a modest workshop with an emphasis on bench work.

One reason for this is that high-tech accuracy is simply inappropriate for this type of work. Perfection needs to be measured in human terms, not engineering ones. I am not advocating rough work, indeed this piece requires some careful making just to get it together. It is more a case of creating something that looks and feels carefully hand-made, something that people want to use and will enjoy living with.

Construction

Sycamore is a sweet-smelling, easily worked wood which requires some careful selection because of the grey/blue streaks which you sometimes find. They aren't easily detectable in a sawn board, so if possible, plane the boards first. The overall appearance of a piece will be governed by timber-selection decisions at this stage; aim for a balance. The grain is not very pronounced in sycamore, but the colour varies a lot and I used lighter wood in the panels and doors than in the framework. The cutting list should be prepared accurately with the exception of the side-panels, which should be left slightly oversize for final thicknessing and fitting later. The rails that receive through tenons should be allowed 1/16in at each end for finishing after assembly. All the mortises and tenons should be marked out; note that the ones in the sides are 1/16in wider than those in the front and back.

However you cut the mortises, it's advisable to do them before the tenons,

because the slots from a slot-mortiser or router are sometimes slightly wider than their cutter. Now is also the time to cut the stopped grooves in the vertical rails into which the side-panels fit. I cut the grooves in the horizontal rails on a small table-saw, but if you use a router it would be advisable to cut the grooves before ripping the rails from the blank board. The bigger workpiece makes it easier because there's better support for both work and router. When you are squaring up the through mortises, cut halfway from each side of the rail to avoid break-out. These mortises will also require tapering to take the wedges in the tenons (fig. 7).

The tenons on this job are small and sycamore is not very forgiving about gaps so they do need to be accurate. A well-tuned bandsaw will cut straight and true and it's quick and accurate for many jobs in terms of setting up and machining time. The slots for the wedges can also be cut with a bandsaw.

The tenons will ideally fit straight from the saw with a firm push-fit. This is an ideal

time for trial assembly to check that all those grooves line up before fitting the panels.

The side-panels may now be thicknessed to fit their grooves, I suggest by hand. The finish straight from a perfectly sharp smoothing-plane is incomparable and something that no machine can reproduce. It will also give a subtle contrast between the panel and the frame. If you don't have a table-saw to cut the tongues and grooves you can use a router, but a circular saw-blade is the right width and it's probably easier to work with considering the size of the pieces.

I like the finish straight from a circular saw and it's sometimes appropriate to use it, especially in furniture of this style. It does need to be used sensitively and whilst the blade-marks on the frame members inside the cabinet may be left, those visible from the outside will need scraping clean with a sharp chisel. The same effect may be employed on the fixing-battens for the doors and the buttons, with the edges lightly chamfered. The ply panels for top, bottom and back are veneered in a complementary veneer, or you can use good-quality ply and stain it. All the panels should be fitted dry, but before any gluing, all frame members should be lightly sanded, and every edge, including the tenon shoulders, slightly chamfered. All the wedges should be sawn from a slat of mahogany the same thickness as the tenons, after which the stretcher assembly may be glued up. The side-panels and frames can also be assembled, using a light coating of PVA glue. The curve on the top front rail can be drawn by flexing a piece of steel or plastic between three pins tapped into a piece of waste ply or hardwood (fig. 6). Cut this out and use it as a template for the rail itself.

Once this piece is cut and finished, complete the assembly by joining the two side-frames by the front and back rails and stretcher-rails, not forgetting to insert the back and bottom. Allow any excess glue to go off before removing it with a chisel, rather than trying to remove it wet.

The top is a straightforward framework with a ply panel inserted. The doors are constructed in a similar way to the side-panels, but they have staggered tongue-and-groove joints. They are simply assembled with battens. The bottom and sides of the doors should be fitted in the cabinet first, so the precise curve of the top rail can be scribed directly on to the backs to ensure a good fit. The brass hinges are set into the doors; I fit a small magnetic catch to a block behind the top rail.

The buttons to fix the top are best made in a strip to make marking out and drilling easier. Cut the notch out with a bandsaw before removing the button from the strip.

Each handle is bandsawn from a single block (fig. 5), keeping the workpiece as big as possible for as long as possible, and using two specially-designed push-sticks when it gets too small. Use a small fine blade and take great care of your fingers! Each piece should be sanded smooth and reassembled in its former relative position, using contact adhesive for a clean and easy joint. The handles are fixed with screws through the back of the doors.

Fit the dark cork tiles for the top and bottom, ready for gluing with contact adhesive after finishing.

In Denmark some years ago, I was impressed to see furniture totally unfinished, just bare wood, which looked superb. I haven't got that much courage but have left the interior unfinished. The rest is covered with two coats of gloss polyurethane, matt-finished with fine-grade wire wool and dressed with 50/50 boiled linseed oil/white spirit, applied with a cloth and rubbed dry. The cork tiles will also look better with an oil dressing to bring the colour out.

I made this cabinet two years ago on spec as a promotional piece, and after an occasional oiling every few months, it has darkened slightly and is developing a fine silky appearance. ∎

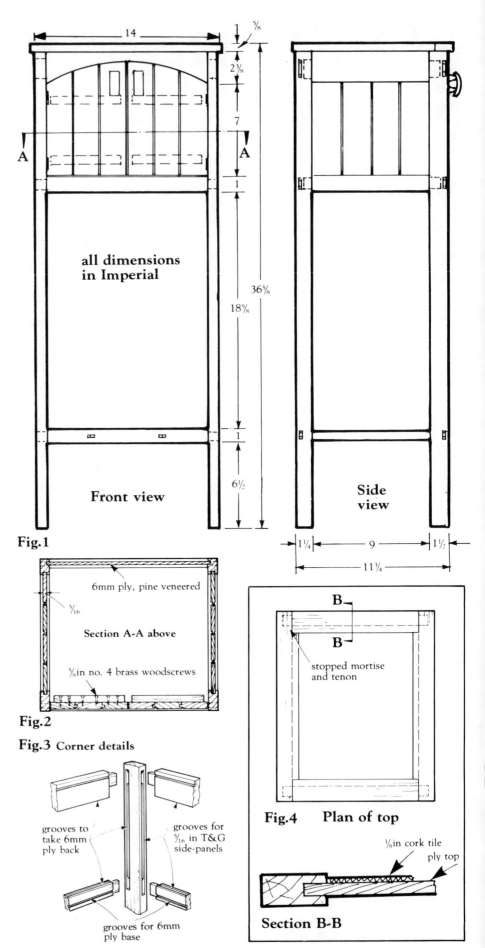

all dimensions in Imperial

Front view

Side view

Fig.1

6mm ply, pine veneered

Section A-A above

⅜ in no. 4 brass woodscrews

Fig.2

Fig.3 Corner details

grooves to take 6mm ply back

grooves for ⁵⁄₁₆ in T&G side-panels

grooves for 6mm ply base

stopped mortise and tenon

Fig.4 Plan of top

⅛ in cork tile

ply top

Section B-B

The quiet American

A transatlantic transplant is making his name in fine English furniture. Aidan Walker went to see him

Peter Kuh, an ex-architecture student from the University of Kansas, stands fair in the middle of a strong tradition of English furniture-making. An afternoon in his workshop at Otterton Mill, which houses several practising craftspeople near the south Devon coast, revealed that behind his shy, slow-talking manner there lurk a sharp wit and some very firm ideas on the one-man furniture business.

He didn't finish his architecture training. Unhappy about the evident communication problem between the originator of a design and its builder, and impatient with the latest in a long line of silly projects (an elephant house), he decided to quit. Since he was leaving anyway, he reasoned with his mentors, could he build a chair instead of design an elephant house?

'It was a total write-off,' recalls Peter, ' a totally academic chair.' He had no machines, almost no hand-tools, and even less woodworking knowledge; he bought a waney-edge lump of oak and set to with a will. No great exponent of machine woodworking, he claims this experience taught him a lesson on what machines can do. 'Everyone should make at least one piece of furniture totally by hand.'

Peter worked for a builder in 1971-2, and later in a Boston furniture factory doing mainly unskilled work. He used a timely inheritance to pay for a year's training with Simon Watts, a cabinetmaker in Vermont. The year was particularly useful in providing time for him to develop hand skills and to get acquainted with the running of a small workshop. Having had some difficulties with his own apprentices, he sees both sides of the argument over paying for a 'practising' training. Why pay someone for the privilege of producing for them? 'I think workshop training is the best possible situation to learn the trade in,' he says. 'Unfortunately, there are far too few places for apprentices. If you're paying the boss, he can't put pressure on you to produce — and he can't fire you. I don't really want to take pupils, because I want to give the orders. I *want* to pay anyone that works here.'

Peter moved to England in 1975 to work with Alan Peters ('The hardest-working human being I think I've ever met'), initially on a provisional offer of six weeks' training. He stayed for two years.

'You must have impressed him.'

'I think I depressed him. When I arrived I thought I knew what I was doing. I feel dwarfed by Alan's commitment to his work.' He started his own business in 1977, well-positioned for the designer-craftsman network that seems strongest in that part of the country. He's been at Otterton Mill ever since.

His workshop is public, by an unwritten agreement with the Mill that in return for very favourable rent he will leave his doors open for visitors to walk round. It's 'not altogether an easy trade-off'; he reckons he gets about 10% of his orders from people who just walk in, but he has also given up counting the number of people 'whose only reaction is that my work is very expensive — compared to G-plan or MFI. Occasionally I find people are actually helping me with designs.' He was working on the height-adjusting mechanism for his music-stand, possibly his most publicised piece, and pays tribute to an engineer who walked in, got talking and ended up sending him a long letter and a detailed drawing. 'The ones I don't enjoy are the ones who come in, hold up a hand with missing fingers, and say: "I'm a woodworker too!"'

Apart from Peters, whose insistence on quality of workmanship and honesty of design he holds in extremely high regard, Peter also cites Edward Barnsley's work as an influence. 'I like curves much better than straight lines. Here we are trying to make something as beautiful as the tree which the wood originally came from; I like the elegance afforded by small-section components, I like inlay. People consider my work strongly traditional, but I'm not interested in fashion. I tend to ignore it, I don't look at exhibitions that much. I tend to work in a vacuum, which has its good and bad points.' He does, however, have a taste for the extreme — 'the over-the-top quality' which some regard as typically American.

The fact that his work undoubtedly stands in a high English tradition is a problem when it comes to acceptance in exhibitions. 'Modern galleries refuse to acknowledge the usefulness or worth of traditionally based work. Some won't even have it if it looks traditional.' As any craft

● Peter's chair designs blend ergonomics and style

worker should be, he is aware of the assistance available through local and national grants, and has made several unsuccessful applications. 'The Crafts Council and the regional arms of the Arts Council can really influence the way things go; it'd be a shame if they put all their money behind space-age stuff.' His latest application for a grant is currently under assessment.

Peter is excited, on the other hand, about 'my own contribution to space-age furniture', a bathroom chair in ash whose laminated components curve in three dimensions. Other chairs, the music-stand — indeed much of his work — curves in two, but this is a first attempt at compound shapes. The back-rest comes round to form the front legs. It is experimental, and Peter is highly appreciative of the client's willingness to pay the design development costs. With any batch work (he does sets of dining-chairs and machines 10 music-stands at a time), he will produce one piece to finished standard so the clients can see what they're getting before he makes the whole lot; he uses mock-ups and prototypes, but still sees the design side as 'the intimidating side. I might do two weeks' work and end up with nothing'. It's obviously a great advantage — almost a luxury — to have a client who is prepared to subsidise something like the bathroom chair; it eventually took 160 hours to produce.

Comfort and ergonomics, thankfully, are strict parameters for Peter's chair designs. For this one, he started with templates of an average human back-shape, made up from

● Meticulous stringing and elegant shaping of the drop-leaf table-legs confer quiet distinction

standardised data, and worked out dimensions accordingly; then he had to devise a jigging system to hold springy laminates in place in their compound curves. ('Alan Peters calls it "torturing wood"!') Try-outs at laminating the main, single back/legs member exposed gluing problems. The solution uses a three-dimensional jig on a gridded piece of block-board, which consists of triangulated former-posts standing out to the precise positions where most clamping stress is taken. Peter had to measure out into the air to the positions where aesthetic and practical factors determined the key points of the structure, the grid ensuring symmetry. ⅛in ash laminates were glued and bound together with bicycle inner tubes, a cramping system that evolved to eliminate separation at the twistiest bits. The single piece was held in the middle and bent either way to clamp to the former-posts; the seat and vertical lumbar support 'stile' were comparatively simple laminating jobs. For 160 hours' work, £600 doesn't seem so expensive.

Which brings us to the old chestnut of sales and marketing. How does a one-man business make money? Committed as he is to impeccable craftsmanship and finish, Peter has found selling bulk orders to shops difficult because he can't make it pay if he works on it himself, and can't in all conscience pass the work that apprentices turn out. A bread-board deal has faded away because the profit margins were too low,

although he had a CoSIRA trainee with him long enough to produce 300 in a year. 'I don't think I made a penny on them, apart from the few I sold through the workshop.' Similarly, a batch-production scheme for stools has died the death because 'young people come unstuck with my fussy insistence on precision.'

I suspect that Peter would rather not bother with selling as such at all. 'I was never brought up as a businessman. I'm basically anti-capitalist, but here I am running a business. When I set up in 1977 I didn't have a clue about how to sell a piece of furniture, and I had absolutely no business training. My approach was basically to copy Alan Peters' most visible selling method. I got into as many exhibitions as I could with various galleries and the Devon Guild of Craftsmen. On average I showed work in four or five exhibitions a year with usually one in a prestigious place like the Crafts Council gallery or the Prescote Gallery; in retrospect this is a wise marketing method since these exhibitions tend to attract people who are seriously interested in the work shown and who can often afford it. Another advantage of exhibitions is that the mark-up is usually low compared to that in exotic shops. I've always preferred to sell where the mark-up is low for the simple reason that if I discount my prices too much I end up losing money on the things I've made . . . I've done enough of that to know how soul-destroying it is.

'Once I had a foot-hold after a few years of exhibiting as extensively as possible, I had accumulated a small clientele; four to six customers who liked my work, trusted me not to overcharge and came back almost every year for something else.

'Aside from putting work in front of people either in my workshop or at exhibitions, the way that I market is really to discuss the qualities of design and construction which I put into the piece in which they are interested . . . in other words, I try to convince them I have a con-siderable amount of expertise and that they can trust me with their commission. For those who are only partially converted, this sometimes sways them my way. I am uncertain that I lose some customers by not having a line of chat to bring them on to my side; my social skills fail me here.

'Marketing, I believe, also includes selling work at the right price. Estimating is tricky and it can only be done reliably after some experience. I always keep time-sheets, and refer to them for estimates. If you don't price work correctly you end up working long hours just to keep your bank balance up to zero. You must be brave enough to quote prices which seem absurdly high at times, but of course you mustn't price yourself out of work. You have to apply intuition here as well — you can't simply apply a hard-and-fast rule of, say, £10 an hour or nothing. You might lose an important job that way that will pay off in other areas — good photos, publicity,

● 'The bathroom chair represents what I love and hate most about this crazy job.' Peter's contribution to 'space-age furniture'

opportunities to do experimental work.

He is adamant that 'the best part and also the worst' of the one-man set-up is that you're totally in command of the entire process. 'This is what attracted me to design/ making — you constantly hear architects complain that the builder has screwed up their design. I do think co-operatives are a good idea — a proper co-op — because all the overheads are shared. Being on your own all the time can also drive you crazy, which is another good reason for a good co-op.' But then, setting up and keeping a co-op running demands commitment to the idea, and time that a solitary furniture-maker will never have. Just a few orders, and Peter will be working flat-out for months to fill them.

He makes no bones of the fact that the last two years have been hard. 'I sat down and evaluated the whole thing last winter,' he says: 'and decided that, despite the financial difficulties, the rewards were sufficient. All I want to do in my life is make half a dozen pieces with a timeless quality — I'd feel I was a lucky human being if I achieved that.'

'What struck me about Peter,' says Alan Peters, 'was that he has a great, dogged per-severance. I've seen many people with a great desire to be designer-craftsmen, but so few survive. Peter persists. He's still there, and there are lots of high-flyers who've fallen by the wayside.

'If there's one word to describe what I aim to achieve in design, workmanship and my dealings with customers,' says Peter, 'it's integrity.' If compliments were paid in cash, and a craftsman's honesty were bankable, Peter Kuh would be a very rich man. ∎

The Mill is a working museum, open from 10.30 to 5.30 daily, and shorter hours in the winter.

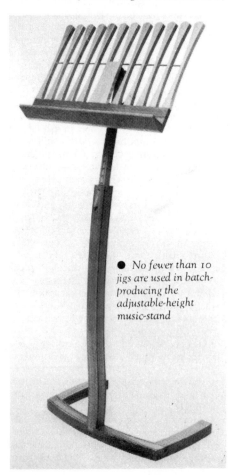

● No fewer than 10 jigs are used in batch-producing the adjustable-height music-stand

The Morris men

Towards the end of last century, something happened in English furniture – something whose effects continue today. This is the tale of a man, his ideas, his work, and some of his successors

Max Burrough offers an appreciation of the most famous Arts and Crafts genius of them all

William Morris was gifted in many ways apart from the practical. By the time he was seven, in 1841, he had read all Scott's novels, and wrote both poetry and prose with apparent ease. Despite his academic leanings, though, his school-companions noted his restless fingers, and that he got relief by making nets for hours on end! He originally intended to take holy orders when he left school, but abandoned the idea and signed articles with the well-known Oxford architect G. E. Street.

During this time he practised many crafts — wood-engraving, clay-moulding, carving in wood and stone, and illuminating, among others. He always considered what he later called 'the noble craft of house-building' to be man's finest employment but he found working at a drawing-board tedious in the extreme, and left the office to pursue an art career in London. While living with his friend Burne-Jones in Red Lion Square, Morris sketched, and had a local firm make, some furniture described as 'intensely mediaeval'. According to the diary of the man now believed to have been responsible for the actual making, oak, walnut, pitch pine, lime and mahogany were all to be used. Besides at least one large cabinet, the pieces included high-backed chairs and a round table.

In 1857 Morris and a few friends returned to Oxford to paint the upper walls and roof of the new debating hall of the Union Society. Morris stayed on in Oxford with the ailing Burne-Jones, and during this time experimented with various handicrafts; he carved a block of freestone, drew and coloured designs for stained-glass windows, modelled from life in clay and began his first experiments in embroidery.

He married in 1859 and had his friend Philip Webb draw up plans for a house to be built in an apple orchard in Kent; in 1860 the young couple moved into Red House — determined, as one friend said, 'to make it the most beautiful place on earth'. This task gave Morris the opportunity to discard any thought of current Victorian furnishing, and he and his friends set to designing and making everything for the house. Here, apparently, Morris practised what he subsequently preached in his lecture 'The Lesser Arts of Life'.

A great settle from Red Lion Square was taken and set up in the drawing-room, and Webb and others designed plainer pieces,

including an oak dining-table and other tables and chairs, so that from the beginning the furniture was of two distinct kinds. Here is an extract from that famous lecture:

'So I say that our furniture should be good citizen's furniture, solid and well made in workmanship, and in design should have nothing about it that is not easily defensible, no monstrosities or extravagances, not even of beauty, lest we weary of it. As to matters of construction, it should not depend on the special skill of a picked workman, or the super-excellence of his glue, but be made on the proper principles of the art of joinery. Also I think that except for very removable things like chairs, it should not be so very light as to be nearly imponderable, it should be made of timber rather than walking sticks. Moreover, I must need think of furniture as of two kinds: one part of it being chairs, dining and working tables and the like, the necessary workaday furniture in short, which should be, of course, both well-made and well-proportioned, but simple to the last degree . . .

'But besides this kind of furniture, there is the other kind, of what I should call state-

furniture, which I think is proper even for a citizen; I mean sideboards, cabinets, and the like, which we have quite as much for beauty's sake as for use. We need not spare ornament on these, but may make them as elegant and elaborate as we can with carving, inlaying or painting . . . **"**

It was during busy weekends, when the house was full of friends, happy and working, that the idea of the firm Morris and Company surfaced. It was possibly inspired by the Great Exhibitions, planned for 1862. Soon a dozen men and boys (who came from a London boys' home) were employed. Webb designed most of the important furniture, and large schemes of decoration were carried out for rich clients. But at the same time the Sussex chairs (5/- each) and cheaper furniture and wallpapers were produced, so the artist Walter Crane could well write: 'The great advantage and charm of the Morrisian method is that it lends itself to either simplicity or splendour. You might be almost as plain as Thoreau, with a rush-bottomed chair, a piece of matting, or an oaken trestle table; or you might have gold and lustre gleaming from the sideboard, jewelled light in the windows, and the walls hung with arras tapestry.' The expensive pieces designed by Webb (later by George Jack) display the

● *One movement – many faces. The mahogany cabinet (left), designed by C.R. Ashbee and made by the Guild of Handicraft in 1898-9, has a holly interior. The mahogany secretaire (above) and escritoire (right) were designed by George Jack (photos Sotheby's, Cheltenham Art Gallery, The National Trust)*

best of Victorian cabinet-making; the firm also made and sold furniture 'of the best forms of the Chippendale and Queen Anne period, especially in regard to carved drawing-room and dining-room chairs'.

In 1875 the original parners disbanded and Morris became sole owner of the firm. In 1877 a showroom was opened in Oxford Street, and many records survive of Morris's autocratic attitude to customers. William Rosetti wrote: 'Mr Morris laid down the law and all his clients had to

comply willy-nilly with his dictates. The products were first class, the artistic quality of the handicraft excellent, and the prices high. There were no concessions to other types of taste, and of course, none at all to bad taste. Reduction in prices was out of the question.' Well might Morris, in a lecture delivered in 1880, say: 'Have nothing in your house that you do not know to be useful or believe to be beautiful'.

William Morris died in 1890, when W. A. S. Benson took over the dictatorship of the firm, which closed in 1939/40. Unfortunately it was not until 1890 that the firm's furniture was stamped with the name and number. Undoubtedly, Morris's furniture, and his philosophy of life influenced many people, notable C. R. Ashbee, Ernest Gimson and the Barnsleys and Ambrose Heal, all of whose work and influence can

be traced to the present day.

A little-known impression of Morris was given by a woman who worked for him as a carpet weaver. He was a short man with a big red and brown beard; he always had a walking stick — you could hear him coming! He was a peculiar man but I think he was good at heart. He jumped about — it was very irritating for the man who had to follow him. Dealing with a rug or a piece of glass he used to dance around like a cat on hot bricks. When I used to see them going down to Merton Abbey station — (Morris, Burne-Jones and William de Morgan) they were always screaming with laughter. They were all talked about quite a bit, but I don't think Morris was really liked by the upper ten, because he was a Socialist.'

For all his dream of Utopia, his prose, poetry and romances, Morris was essentially a practical person who never lost touch with humanity. 'He was not ashamed of being a tradesman; he gloried in it. That was a new thing in his day.' As W. R. Lethaby, the first Principal of the Central School of Arts and Crafts said, 'he was a workmaster — Morris the maker'.

● The William Morris Gallery is at the Water House, Lloyd Park, Forest Rd, London E17.

Books

J. W. Mackall, *The Life of William Morris*, Longmans, Green & Co, London 1899

P. Henderson, *William Morris, His Life, Work and Friends* Thames and Hudson, London 1967

R. Watkinson, *William Morris as Designer* Studio Vista, London 1967

T. Bradley, *William Morris and His World* Thames and Hudson 1978

The Morris men

Idris Cleaver introduces some lesser-known Arts-and-Craftsmen who are only now getting the recognition they deserve

● *This 'swan' chair was made by Eric Sharpe in 1943*

During the past 20 years or so, we have been seeing and hearing a great deal of the work of the Cotswold school of designer-craftsmen led by Ernest Gimson and the Barnsleys, but little is mentioned about some of the lesser-known craftspeople originally inspired by William Morris and the Arts and Crafts movement. They worked quietly and unobtrusively to produce handmade furniture of the highest quality in various parts of the country, in single-person workshops or with the help of a few apprentices and assistants.

Three such men were originally A. Romney Green's assistants (WW/June 83). They all left to set up their own workshops and produce furniture which is only now beginning to be fully recognised as a contribution to the Arts and Crafts movement. **W. Stanley Davies** moved into a purpose-built workshop in Windermere; **Eric Sharpe** set up on his own in Martyr Worthy, Winchester, and **Robin Nance** moved to St Ives, Cornwall.

Stanley W. Davies

Stanley Davies was an Oxford history graduate until he came under the influence of A. Romney Green. During the first world war he served with the Friends' War Victims' Relief Unit in France, an experience which fundamentally affected his whole attitude to life. He decided to move away from the academic career which his parents had persuaded him to follow, and devote himself to making beautiful things that would bring joy and happiness to maker and owner. In order to do this he entered Romney Green's workshops in Hampshire.

He soon revealed his gift. One example of his craftsmanship is a parabolic wheatsheaf-back chair which he made and Green designed, on permanent display at the Cheltenham Art Gallery and Museum.

His early designs were naturally influenced to some extent by Romney Green, but he soon developed his own personal and distinctive style. There is little doubt that his small walnut cabinet, with its specially selected matching panels and exposed joints at the corners of the carcase, showed Davies' familiarity with the work of the Gimson/Barnsley Cotswold school, although it is doubtful whether Davies ever met either Gimson or Barnsley.

After two years with Green he left in 1922 to start his own workshop, which he had specially built in Windermere in the Lake District. It took Davies some time to develop his own design style, and it was not until after the second world war that his work was in greatest demand. The total

output from his workshop exceeded 2000 pieces; each with a distinctive style that came from keeping close to the basic principles of woodwork and developing from sound tradition.

The desire was to import a timeless value to the work rather than follow fashion. The lightness and apparent simplicity of his pieces reveal the beauty of the wood, the skill of the workmanship, and the structural emphasis of the design. The woods he used were mainly English oak, chestnut, cherry and cedar, with some imported timbers such as mahogany. Unless the customer specifically requested it he always gave a natural finish to the wood; he considered this to be the only 'true' finish for his English oak and chestnut cabinets. It did indeed allow him to express his genius through original and ingenious chamfering. He put chamfers on existing chamfers and worked twisted chamfers on the octagonal feet of some of his sideboards and desks. He did not altogether approve of pieces of wood (such as inlay) used solely for decoration, considering that the decorative effect should only be achieved by what he called 'structural design'. The character of the design should be governed by the construction and not by structurally unnecessary applied decoration.

He enunciated his whole philosophy of craftwork in a series of radio talks and articles. In a radio talk in 1933 he spoke of 'the truth in construction and finish which is true to the nature of wood; careful joints which can hold together without glue; careful selection of timber because of its natural strengths and weaknesses; a careful finish which does not alter the natural colour of the wood, and sensible simple design. Good art is not laboured in appearance; rather it should give a feeling of ease and simplicity. Sparing use of thoughtful

and sensitive decoration can be very effective, specially when the craftsman has put into it something of himself.'

He thought it was sensible to use machines for first sawing logs into boards, but he saw 'no sense in getting machines to do work which men enjoy doing by hand, and not only enjoy, but find great opportunity for their skill, inventiveness and artistic ability in the doing of it'. He was always fearful that the machine might influence the design and reduce the individual responsibility of the craftsman. Towards the end of his life, though, he was forced to introduce a few small machines in an attempt to reduce costs. He felt strongly that furniture should not be called 'handmade' if machines were used for anything other than sawing or planing; also that the craftsman should see his work through from start to finish, true to the Arts and Crafts principles. Despite the increased demand for his work in the post-war years, Davies would never employ more than seven assistants as he felt that was the maximum number he could control.

Eric Sharpe

From 1921 to 1929 Eric Sharpe was a pupil of and assistant to A. Romney Green, first in London and later when he moved to Christchurch, Hampshire. At the end of this period he set up his own workshops in Martyr Worthy, Winchester, where I first met him, when I visited his workshop with Edward Barnsley. Sharpe and Barnsley were close friends, and both had been pupils at Bedales School.

Sharpe, also greatly influenced by Romney Green, first became acquainted with the work of the Cotswold school after he had set up on his own. It was through the now almost forgotten designer-craftsman Malcolm Powell that he first came across the work of Gimson and the Barnsleys, and there is little doubt that they had a profound influence on him thereafter.

His work soon attracted the attention of architects who commissioned him to make domestic furniture, a number of church works, and special ceremonial and memorial pieces. These included the cabinet to

● *A stationery cabinet designed by Stanley Davis*

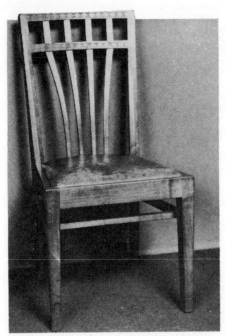

● *This chair is probably by Romney Green (photos Cheltenham Art Gallery)*

house Winchester Cathedral's book of names of the fallen in the second world war; the Bidder Memorial chair (the Mistress' Chair for Girton College, Cambridge); the high table of Newnham College, Cambridge, in 1940; and the casket for the freedom of the City of London presented to Winston Churchill in 1943.

Perhaps the most prestigious of his pieces was the presidential chair presented to the Pharmaceutical Society of Great Britain by the Australian Societies in 1933. At the presentation meeting Sharpe gave a description of the chair, explaining its design and the woods of which it was made; he used a sample species from every one of the colonies in Australia and New Zealand, the top rail carrying a map in which each colony was represented by a piece of its own native wood.

Unlike Davies, he was very fond of incised lettering in wood, and used a great deal of carving in his work for churches. His essay on 'Woodwork' in *Fifteen Craftsmen on their Crafts*, edited by Jon Farleigh, gives an appraisal of Gimson's work which shows his obvious admiration for it.

Robin Nance

Nance was also trained by Romney Green until he started his own workshop in 1933 in St Ives, Cornwall. Most of his work is handmade, well designed, of good material and of sound workmanship, as is to be expected after such training. He uses machines only in the early stages of his work, which is aimed at producing furniture mainly for customers of limited means; his pieces are much sought after by tourists in the area. Although he rarely employs more than four craftsmen, he does not limit himself to furniture, and whenever required he undertakes work commissioned and designed by architects.

THE CONTINUING STORY

The work of the Barnsleys and Gimson changed the course of modern furniture not only in Britain but also in Europe and America, **writes Idris Cleaver** — and Edward Barnsley (now 85) has been continuing and refining that tradition since 1923, when he set up his own workshops in Froxfield, Hampshire.

For some of those 62 years I had the privilege of working there. So I was especially pleased and excited to be able to attend the workshops' recent open day.

It was because the financing of five-year apprenticeships proved too much, even for Barnsley, that the Edward Barnsley Educational Trust was set up five years ago, so that apprentices could continue to train at Froxfield. During the visit we saw them at work, together with the older craftsmen, and is was good to see them continuing the workshop's superlative standards.

Overall administration continues to be the responsibility of Edward Barnsley; his architect son Jon Barnsley supervises the work, and has adapted many of his father's drawings without in any way departing from their personal and distinctive style. The high standard of work produced, and still expected of the apprentices, is assured by the presence and guidance of George Taylor, a master-craftsman by any standard. Still actively making the magnificent pieces which one has come to expect from him, he is the last remaining man originally apprenticed to Barnsley over 50 years ago — and soon to retire. Oscar Dawson, the other remaining craftsman, died sadly and unexpectedly some months ago.

The first three apprentices were taken on in 1981, and new ones will be appointed each year from now on. Applications are, as expected, heavily over-subscribed. This year the trustees decided that the next apprentice should be chosen from local candidates, if a promising one were available — and last year Darren Harvey, a 16-year-old from Cowplain who was

● *Edward Barnsley and two apprentices watch George Taylor at work*

● *A writing-table by apprentice Colin Eden-Eadon*

● *More apprentice work – a box for timber specimens*

working for the Youth Opportunities Scheme, was selected by interview after a two-week trial period in the workshop. His apprenticeship was confirmed subject to a satisfactory six-month probationary period, and he has proved a very promising craftsman. New applications are currently being considered; four candidates have been selected for interview, and are to be given a week's trial in the workshop before the final choices are made. Richard Elderton remains in charge of the apprentices' training, in collaboration with George Taylor and Jon Barnsley.

In spite of the progress already made, the trustees have plans for very necessary extensions, and are appealing for funds. The first priority is a display and archive room with a dry timber store beneath it. Thanks to a grant and gifts of books a fairly good reference library has been started, but many more books are needed (and would be greatly appreciated).

The trust has obviously learnt from past experience with Gimson's workshop drawings, which have only now (about 65 years after his death) been filed and catalogued for Cheltenham Museum and Art Gallery. A research assistant has been busy at Froxfield, evolving a definitive system of classifying and cataloguing Barnsley's drawings, numbering them, and filing them in order. The trust hopes they will be available for inspection by scholars, students, historians and craftsmen some time in 1986. ∎

The watertight case

A box made from two pieces of wood? The North-west American Indians did it, so why shouldn't you — guided by Alan and Gill Bridgewater

● *The painted designs on four sides of a Kwakiutl Indian food tray – before bending!*

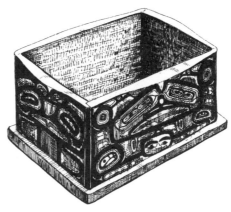

● *Your finished project. Motifs, of course, are up to you*

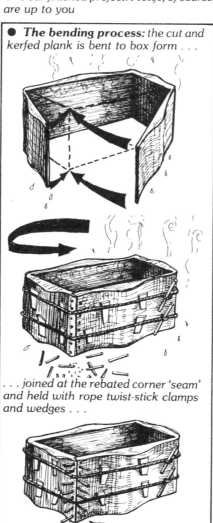

● **The bending process:** *the cut and kerfed plank is bent to box form . . .*

. . . joined at the rebated corner 'seam' and held with rope twist-stick clamps and wedges . . .

. . . drilled at the corner and fixed with glued hand-whittled wedge-pegs

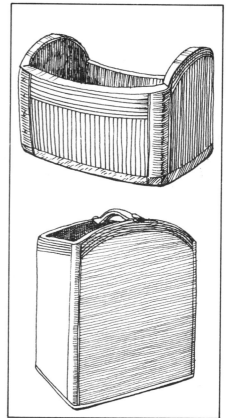

● *A Kwakiutl food-tray and water-box, with characteristic curved-rim profile*

How was this possible? It was clear enough: 'The Kwakiutl Indians were superb carpenters. They made boxes, the sides constructed from a single piece of wood . . . . The craftsmanship was of such perfection that they were watertight and used by the women for cooking . . .'

I knew the Indian tribes that live on the north-west coast of British Columbia were uniquely skilled in wood crafts — building, carving and painting, everything from gigantic totem poles to masks, bowls and canoes. But watertight boxes and chests? I wonder. The *Encyclopedia Britannica* rumbles on about the Canadian Indians for page after page, until you come to this little gem: 'The even-grained cedar was split into planks with which the larger communal, rectangular houses were built; smaller boards were steamed and bent into service-able watertight boxes . . . ' Aha! Our scratchings about in libraries, museums and old book shops led to the British Museum in London, The Pitt Rivers Museum in Oxford, a museum in Cambridge, and to the books of Franz Boas. We eventually saw some 19th century Indian boxes and trays, and sure enough, the sides of the boxes appeared to be made from a single plank bent three times along its length, rebated, pegged, sometimes sewn at one corner, then let into and fixed to a massive slab-cut base. I would have liked to have pulled the boxes apart and discover just how they had been made . . . but you know museums. Thanks to Franz Boas' books, and some Canadian sources, we soon had the answers.

The original method

The Indian craftsmen consulted the spirits when it was decided that a box was needed, and then set about selecting a suitable standing tree. The lower branches and spurs were lopped off flush with the trunk, then the tree was felled. Then the Indians drove lines of wedges along the length of the trunk, converting it into planks. The centre plank was checked for flaws, and then worked with an elbow-adze, crooked knife and gouge until it was 1½-2in thick.

The smooth tool-textured plank was then measured for width, adze-trimmed to size, and marked out for the box required. Knife-cuts were made across the grain and width of the plank at the inside corner positions, then worked until they became crisp-sided V- or U-trenches. Next the plank was turned over, and the wood pared and thinned opposite each of the kerf-cut trenches. The ends of the plank were then rebated and cut so that when it was steamed and bent, they would come together and form the fourth corner of the box. A shallow trench was dug on the waterlogged beach, a fire lit, and then the plank was soaked, heated, and steamed using hot stones, with sea-grass as insulation. The box maker would put rope stick-twist clamps across the width of the board, place the plank face-down, then, standing on the plank and the clamp, heave the sides of the box over and in. The rebated ends were brought together when the box corners were all at 90°, the whole box held true with more rope stick-twist clamps. Then the 'seam' corner was drilled, glued and pegged. When the whole clamped and pegged box was cool, the bottom edge was thinned and then let into a slab-cut and rebated base-board. Finally, the corners were trimmed and the box carved and painted.

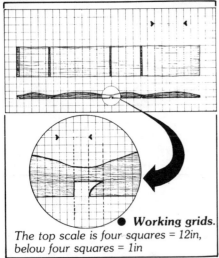

● **Working grids.**
The top scale is four squares = 12in, below four squares = 1in.

Making a kerf-cut steam bent chest

You will see we used a 2in-thick plank of rough-sawn seasoned cedar, and made a box about 12in wide, 24in long and 12in deep; also see from the drawing above how we marked out and measured the kerf-cuts.

You can (up to a point) change the overall size of the box, but **you must adjust the size of the kerf-cuts to fit.** For example, if you look at our kerf details top far right, you will see we reduced the 2in plank thickness to about 1in; see how the depth and width of the kerf and the depth of the kerf undercut all relate. It might also be a good idea to have a trial run on a piece of scrap wood, and see if you can successfully work a couple of corners. Our researches have come up with a dozen or so kerf types (above right); everthing from a simple V-cut, almost like a folded mitre, to a very complicated, deeply worked and undercut double 'swallow-tail' type. There is room for experiment! The Northwest Coast Indians usually made their boxes out of straight-grained, knot-free cedar, but no doubt you could try woods like maple, pine or even parana pine.

Look for a piece of rough-sawn straight-grained wood that seems sound and a good colour. Avoid stains, twists, knots, splits and all the other nasties that might cause problems, and most important of all, go for a piece of 'tree centre' wood that has its grain at 90° to the plank face. Set it out along its length (above). Allow 1in for the fourth corner rebate, 12in for the first side, ½in for the first kerf, 24in for the second side, ½in for the second kerf, 12in for the third side, ½in for the third kerf, and finally 24in for the fourth side. The board should come to a blunt end finish. Mark the inside

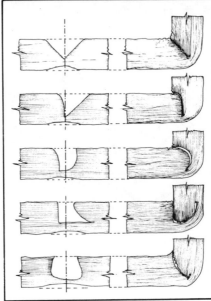

● A selection of kerf types the Indians used. The fibres are stressed and compressed at the joint

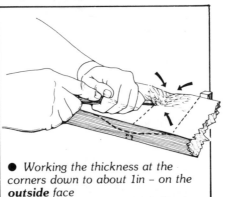

● Working the thickness at the corners down to about 1in – on the **outside** face

and outside of the board and all the kerf channels.

Place your marked-out wood outside up, then work with an adze or gouge along its length so the wood comes to a series of 2in hills — the box sides — and 1in hollows — the kerf corners (above).

Flip your plank over so that it's inside up, then cut in the ½in-wide corner kerf channels with saw and chisel to a depth of ½in. Chop out and rebate the channels, leaving them straight-sided and crisply worked. Work away at the channel sides with a sharp long-bladed knife and a ½in chisel; the side undercuts should go ½in into the wood. Cut a 1in-wide, ½in-deep rebate at one end of the plank, then work the other end of the plank to fit.

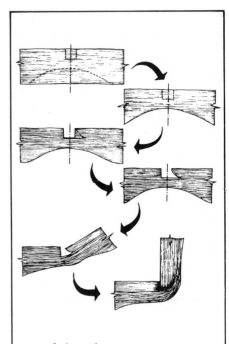

Kerf details
● The order of working the kerf-cut and steam-bent corners

● Support the plank on a sandbag to work the corner rebate and ½x½ kerfs

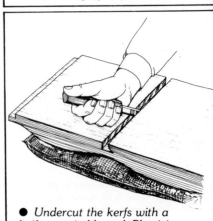

● Undercut the kerfs with a knife or suitable tool. Plasticine models help visualisation!

94

The watertight case

Steaming and Bending

The equipment options go from a sophisticated steamer with a long plywood steam-box and a purpose-built gas or electric boiler, through an Indian-style metal tank and raw fuel fire, to a knocked-up electric-kettle-hose-and-plastic-bag! This part of the project is tremendously exciting, so all the more reason to be completely organised. Set yourself up with heat/fire-proof gloves, non-inflammable protective clothing and a tidy work area, together with someone to give a hand. It may be worth having a trial run with a scrap of wood.

Steam the plank for 45-70 minutes, or until you can flex and bend it at the kerfs. Now work with what I would describe as considered and controlled haste. Take the steamed wood, make sure the stick-clamp is in place, and bend the wood a corner at a time. Hold the box sides down with the weight of your feet, then heave the wood up, so that the box angles are at 90°. Work the corner kerfs in order 1 — 3 — 2. The wood should eventually wrap round so the blunt end of the plank comes to rest in the 1x½in rebate. When this stage is reached, quickly get the strap or rope twist-stick clamps in place, then quickly drill, glue and peg the rebated corner seam. Drill from both faces, and vary the peg angles for more strength. Wait at least 48 hours for the glue and wood to rest, then take the knife and gouge and trim back the fourth pegged corner so that it matches the other three.

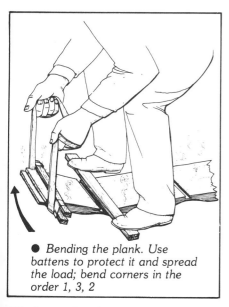

● *Bending the plank. Use battens to protect it and spread the load; bend corners in the order 1, 3, 2*

Fixing the bottom

Place your steam-bent box on the base so there's an all-round base-to-box lip of 1½in, then mark each of the box/base sides and the position of the base/slab trench. Then trim back the outside bottom edge of the box with a knife to 1in thick all round. Put the box back on its base, mark out the revised trench width, then clean out the trench with a chisel to a depth of about ½in. Go easy on this channel or trench —

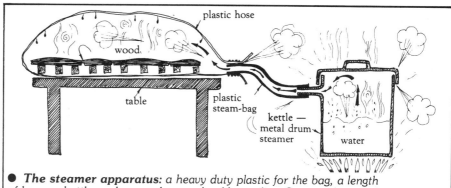

● *The steamer apparatus: a heavy duty plastic for the bag, a length of hose, a kettle or drum and a couple of hose clips. Support the wood off the surface of the table, and steam it until the kerfs are pliable – about an hour*

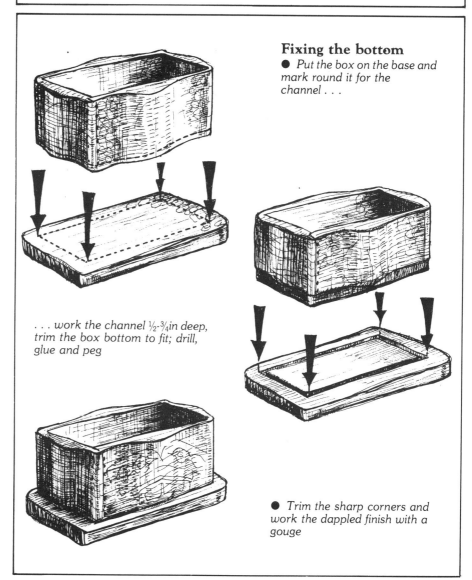

Fixing the bottom
● *Put the box on the base and mark round it for the channel . . .*

. . . work the channel ½-¾in deep, trim the box bottom to fit; drill, glue and peg

● *Trim the sharp corners and work the dappled finish with a gouge*

especially when you come to the round corners, where you might have to use a knife and gouge. When the box-to-base is a good fit, drill, glue and peg, as with the box corner-seam. Finally take a sharp knife, trim off the kerf-bend whiskers or sprung wood fibres, and go over the whole box giving it a nicely scalloped and tooled finish.

Painting the Motifs

Look at our design ideas, then decide just how you want your motifs. Make a good master design of how the motifs will fit the box sides, then take a tracing and press-transfer the lines of the design on to the wood with a pencil — you could use carbon

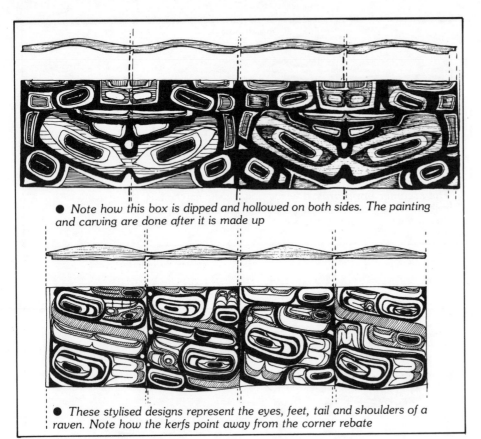

● *Note how this box is dipped and hollowed on both sides. The painting and carving are done after it is made up*

● *These stylised designs represent the eyes, feet, tail and shoulders of a raven. Note how the kerfs point away from the corner rebate*

paper. Now lightly cut in the drawn lines with a craft knife, which will stop the colours bleeding. Block in the design areas with watercolours — don't try to work solid, heavy, vibrant colours, but rather limit your palette to basic earth colours like red ochre, black, and yellow ochre, with maybe just a touch of blue and green. When the paint has dried go over the whole box with a scrap of sandpaper and just break the colours at box corners, edges and pattern high-spots. Finally, give the box a couple of coats of wax inside and out — and the job's done!

Afterthoughts

If you like the idea of this project, but consider our methods and techniques just too primitive, there's no reason at all why you shouldn't, say, work the end-plank rebate and the initial kerf-cut with a power tool. Shape the project to suit your own needs and aims.

It really needs to be approached with as few preconceived ideas as possible. You might ruin a length or two of wood, but along the way you will extend your wood-working skills — and have a lot of fun! ■

Cutting list *All rough sawn cedar*
Sides	74½in	x 12in	x 2in
Bottom	27	15	2

12 ¼in cedar pegs; PVA glue; watercolours.

Past defence

Peter Howlett looks at
College work and the
High Street, and bemoans
the lack of intelligent
reference to past mastery
in furniture design

Clever stuff, some of those latest
college designs. But how eminently
forgettable. It's my belief that the
insular nature of degree courses, with their
narrow vision of the way forward, en-
courages these superficial results.

Of course, there is a place for experiment
and innovation, and further education
should be fun, a time away from home
when students become 'themselves'. But
colleges have a duty to direct the studies so
they point students towards a vision of a
better way of life. I firmly believe that this
direction must pay some attention to the
past, getting tradition into perspective as
well as pushing the contemporary scene
forward with vigour and enthusiasm. What
happened yesterday is equally important as
what will happen tomorrow.

'There must be a better way of doing
this,' a craftsman once said to me, referring
to some repetitive hand operation. And he
meant it! As an apprentice sweeping the
floor, then keeping the glue-pots going and
working his way up to be a journeyman
cabinetmaker of consummate skill, he saw
the sense in seeking to improve, of building
upon tradition, not forsaking it entirely or
sacrificing it for speed and immediacy.

What has happened to this spirit of craft?
Our vision appears to be radically impaired
by a violent reaction to the materials which
we now have at our fingertips. No thanks to
the top designers and entrepreneurs, we
now see more MDF and — in reaction to it
— solid wood abused by college students,
and veneered surfaces bastardised by High
Street furniture chains.

We are set to drown in a sea of pseudo-
Georgian elegance and Jacobean stained oak
at one end of the market and bored to tears
with joke effects at the other. It seems to me
we're missing out on the adventure and are
either indulging ourselves in gaudy
eclecticism, or bowing low to bad taste.

Designers and college tutors who structure degree courses have a responsibility to
make good design and art less of a novelty
and more accessible to the buying public. In
accord with their role and status, tutors
ought to show us clearly what the true
potential of their protegés is.

Joe Public deserves more than the trivial
offerings that owe more to a straight-line
edger and speed-sander than to human
need. Unfortunately, the public are largely
unaware of designer/craftspeople and what
they have to offer, because they're provided
with bland and insubstantial offerings

● *Boxing clever – **above**, detachable intersecting boxes; **below**, burr maple integrated squares. Peter's own work shows strong design concepts!*

whose only virtue is quality of finish. It's
equally unfortunate that our top designer/
craftsmen seem to delight in the bizarre and
extreme.

In a spoof radio programme, the script
writers sent up Terence Conran in a
sketch entitled 'Conran the Barbarian'. I
felt the satirists had captured the fundamental elements of 'Conranology' — making
money, marketing, empire building and
profit margins — and they confirmed the
disgust I had felt when I heard that he
wanted to rip out the beautiful curved
windows of Heal's store. They may not be
particularly efficient from a display point of
view but they are a surviving testimony to
all that Ambrose Heal and his company
stood for — quality and style.

My heart sank at the shoddiness of the
furniture inside the store; some items were
reproductions of Heal's classic 'cottage'
furniture, originally made in chestnut. Oak
was now being used; doors were badly
hung, latches didn't work, some lower
drawers were sloppy and melamine lacquer
was sprayed inside and out. Such work is a
travesty, not a tribute, to one of the great
pioneers of the machine age who found a
way of mass-producing quality designs to a
high standard of craftsmanship and finish.

And yet the influence of Conran is so
great that much of what comes out of the

colleges could well be from, or destined for,
a Habitat catalogue. Certainly some
students ought to have a place in such a
team designing contemporary furniture.
Visually, most of it is quite pleasing, if not
innocuous, but does it have to be made so
badly, finished in such severe and awful
colours, marketed in a crass and pseudo-
precious way and made ultimately to pack
into a flat box? Who has decided that this is
what the public will have? It is as awful as
the current range of Ercol furniture which
seems to have abandoned the purity of line
developed in the 60s for a pseudo-repro-
duction style that has no affinity with any
specific historical period.

At the other end of the spectrum stands
the giant influential figure of John Makepeace. Unfortunately, much of Makepeace's work which reaches the public eye
— through his own promotion work — is
the result of a fertile yet wandering
imagination. It's hard to know which
direction the man will take next! What we
tend not to see is his formal work, the traditional, almost conservative, pieces which
owe much to a tradition kept alive by
Barnsley and Davies, and show the other
side of Makepeace's 'whole log' approach.
It's also hard to reconcile, in an age of
shrinking resources, the use of so much
solid timber, and even harder for us lowly

mortals to see where the justification for such a high price-tag lies.

Sadly, the colleges seem to be bowing down to these mighty men, encouraging students to cream off all that is superficial in such work. If this is what's happening, and the evidence of another round of degree shows would seem to suggest it is, they can't be acting in a responsible way.

I wonder how many students have had to discover for themselves the work of Mackintosh and the Shakers, or under their own steam badger the curator of furniture at the V&A to open the 20th-century gallery during the week so they can see in the flesh that superb chair by Ponti (incidentally an interpretation of a traditional Italian design) or the subtle laminated work of Alvar Aalto? How many know the work of Jacques Ruhlmann or the superb lacquer-work of the architect and designer Eileen Grey? These past masters still have something to teach us today.

It really is time we saw something better coming out of our colleges, something which owes its form to a wider sphere of influence than the tarty clichés prevalent in the current design scene. It's time we recognised there is a great ocean of influence, past and present, to swim in.

I am as much moved by the superb quality of the late 40s joinery in the refurbished Hunterian Museum as the beautiful veneer work of Martin Grierson. And I'm equally influenced by both. I marvel at the work of Gaudi, with its sinuous and plastic forms and frequently refer to the burial furniture catalogued by Carter when he raided the tomb of Tutankhamun. I continually thirst for knowledge about how such pieces were made, what materials were used and what these discoveries can offer me and my work.

Surely we have reached a point beyond painting MDF in bright colours or bolting together rough hewn billets of elm? There has to be a greater sensitivity to and learning from the past, a definite break with the art-dominated ethos of furniture studies and its severely restricted counterpart — industrial design. It's hard to recognise any of the great historical wealth of work in the degree shows. There are faint glimmers of acknowledgement but in their preciousness, they often miss the point.

I used to think, rather arrogantly, that my pieces had some intrinsic value and would become 'antiques of the future'. Now I've climbed off that ego-trip I'm aiming for a soundness of design which simply says 'that piece is right'. I still have my frivolous moments, and there is a place for such work alongside the rational and pleasing.

But just because we live in a throw-away society we shouldn't allow this to debase our sense of the past — not worship of it — with its timeless pieces and glimpses of genius. Colour, modern materials and an efficient technology are all means to an end and not an end in themselves. We're worshipping false gods if we try to immortalise the past, just as we are if we only look back a few years; there is so much in the 6,000 years of surviving furniture to learn from.

It's also effete to say 'I looked at the log and saw what it wanted to be.' Such an approach is either pure mysticism or an absurd pretension. The true craftsman is searching for honesty, and he/she does it with integrity. The work reflects the true value of the price-tag. There's no need for a philosophical explanation because we can see the person in the work; it has, in James Krenov's words, the 'personal thumbprint'. Ultimately it has style and is superbly made.

I recognise that these qualities, which are born of years of working the material and exploring its possibilities, can't be taught in our colleges overnight. But if we are exposed to it at an early enough stage it will have an effect on us. It might divert us from using materials simply because they exist towards using them because they provide a better solution to old problems. More than ever we have the resources to see first-hand what has been done and what is being done. It would be a shame if lack of direction led to a squandering of these experiences. ∎

TIMBER SUPPORT

Designers and therapists together produce equipment to enhance mobility in disabled people. Brian Boothby, Director of Postgraduate Studies at the London College of Furniture describes a unique course

D esign challenges don't come much harder than this one; can you design a special wooden frame to safely support a severely handicapped child? A difficult problem, certainly, but it was brilliantly solved by an unlikely partnership of crafts people and therapists at the London College of Furniture's Disability Design Research Unit. The students worked closely together, liaising with the disabled child, her parents and the special care unit that she attended.

After working through numerous sketch proposals, chipboard mock-up was made to try out with the child. The finished product was intended not only to support a floppy spastic child, but also to bring her gradually from a lying position into a more vertical posture to allow for weight bearing through the child's feet. This therapeutic procedure would allow the therapist to develop head and neck control, and ultimately hand and eye coordination for the child. At the planning stage, it was important for the group to get their designs into three dimensions as quickly as possible; a full-size mock-up would soon tell them if the model's dimensions were correct and if it was likely to function well. They could then return to the drawing board and redesign and develop as they saw fit.

Timber was chosen for this project, since the team could make amendments easily without involving the whole design. The unit needed to be able to fold flat for transportation, hence the simple hinged support. The group achieved the graduated angle of support necessary for therapeutic reasons by means of a routed groove within the base frame which allowed pins on the supporting brace to lock into fail-safe slots. Upholstered supports, wrap-around velcro pads, foot platform and foot supports are all adjustable, which allows accurate positioning of a patient. Getting these adjusting details right for physiotherapists working with children of various sizes can occupy a good deal of the designer's time.

A final prototype was then delivered to the child's therapist with a request for comments against given headings. This feedback to the research unit is essential to the growing data base on design for disability. Interest in this particular piece of equipment was expressed by overseas therapists working with children, and this generated further requests to the college and an opportunity for more extensive testing. A batch of six of these Talia Prone Boards was produced and in due course put into use in a number of countries.

At this point the college's registered charity DEMAND (Design and Manufac-

The Talia Prone Board in action, solidly supporting a severely handicapped child

99

ture for Disability) took on design development work based on the accumulated evidence of the early models in field trials. Ultimately Nottingham Rehabilitation, a company specialising in the marketing of medical rehabilitation aids, was invited to take on the prone support as a marketable product. The prone board has sold well, and has now been developed by DEMAND to include a table attachment, thus allowing the unit to be used in teaching sessions with disabled children.

Very often a one-off design for a specific patient can be turned into a more generic design that will function well for a number of users.

Wood is frequently used when making products for use by disabled people. It lends itself well to making one-off individually tailored pieces for specific functional needs. Even when a design has been well developed, for batch-production, wood may be the appropriate medium. After all, the market for equipment for disabled people is not a large one, and neither does it generate large profits. Often equipment has to be made in quite a variety of dimensions to suit the sizes of people; batch production, with wood as the material can be the most versatile.

There are some items where metal or plastics are entirely appropriate, but wood does have a warmer appearance and helps to diminish the clinical appearance so often found in rehabilitation equipment. And when

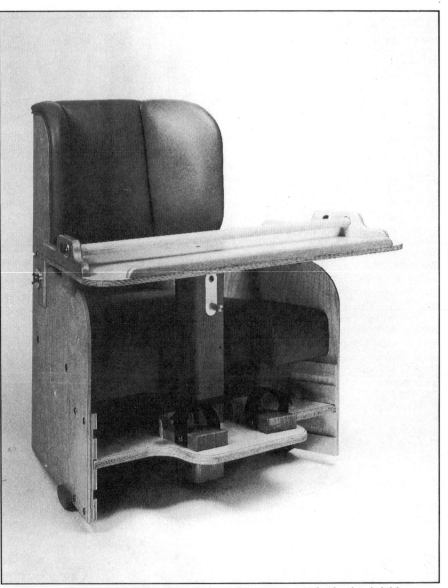

This preformed plywood chair gives good postural support to cerebral palsied children

Information gathered using this posture-measuring chair rig resulted in a new seating range for disabled children

it's treated with a suitable finish, it can withstand the hard use to which some equipment is subjected rather better than some other materials.

Wood has been used for example to build a chair rig to accurately measure the posture of cerebral palsied children, in a research project by design student Kanwal Sharma. Made from ply, with routed slots to hold adjustable measuring blocks, the rig yielded information which eventually led to the design of a seating range, now in production for disabled children.

Pre-formed ply has been used to give a warm appearance to another chair for cerebral palsied children, who need good postural support.

Sometimes solid wood is used, as in an ash chair for a girl with juvenile arthritis and artificial knees and hip joints in both legs; this chair gives good support, with a spring-assisted seat riser.

Pre-formed beech laminates have been used in an indoor wheelchair being developed by DEMAND; it is fully adjustable to give good anthropomorphic support. The

beech-laminated main chassis gives a strong, sprung, shock-absorbing structure.

A standing frame is designed by a physiotherapist and a furniture designer together uses laminated veneers to provide a support that flexes. This frame is for cerebral palsied children with standing problems, helping to develop good posture; the design is now in production by Nottingham Rehabilitation.

We've also used wood for an educational 'toy' – a wooden truck with battery powered motors that young disabled children can learn to steer; 'playing' with the controls help children develop hand/eye coordination and movement patterns for when they eventually use an electric chair.

The London College of Furniture has been running its Design for Disability course, a one year post-graduate course, for six years now. This unique course brings together graduates from the paramedic professions on the one hand and the designing and making professions on the other.

Therapists are knowledgeable about

medical conditions and the needs of disabled people, but may not be so familiar with the manufacturing process necessary to bring about a particular piece of supportive equipment. Designers and craftspeople, on the other hand, may be skilled at producing good-looking articles but not know the complexities within the subject of human anatomy, physiology and pathology. The course specifically sets out to bring these two professional disciplines together to solve problems for disabled members of the community.

Stimulated by the Chronically Sick and Disabled Persons Act (1970), much has been done to provide equipment that diminishes handicaps. There are often complaints, however, that many products for disabled people lack sophistication and are aesthetically unattractive – sometimes resembling surgical appliances.

I believe design for disabled people has lagged far behind what could be done. But that design gap is capable of being filled by well-trained designers, craftsmen and technologists working with medical practitioners and therapists, by including disability as a factor in their working brief.

Our post-graduate course started in 1981 after a number of LCF student projects for disabled people had been successfully completed as part of project programmes within many different college courses. The college raised finance for this

An ash chair designed for a girl with juvenile arthritis and artificial knee and hip joints in both legs

by establishing the charity DEMAND, and this organisation now has its own suite of workshops close to the college in East London. The charity not only provides bursaries for students, but offers workshop facilities for working in wood, metal and plastics. You can quite often see a therapist turning his or her hand to work at a bench with a good deal of skill. We hope these therapists will return to their professions able to brief craftspeople and technicians to produce good-looking pieces of equipment for their patients.

DEMAND receives requests from hospitals and special care units for equipment development, and is also able to review the designs and benefit from the general research carried out elsewhere within the LCF; taking proven prototypes, the charity can develop these into production models.

There are also gains for those manufacturers producing articles for rehabilitation. Often they don't have teams of designers, makers, technicians and therapists who can research and develop equipment for their disabled purchasers. These manufacturers are willing to look at well-researched and developed designs in the form of prototypes with working drawings.

I believe the unit is making a valuable contribution to provide equipment that disabled people need, and to introduce much needed design qualities into the articles they use in their daily lives. ∎

WICKER'S WORLD

Osiery is the ancient craft of willow basket-making — and this century it almost breathed its last. Master craftsman John Taylor brought it new life and profitability with his Yorkshire business, as Leonard Markham discovered

Yorkshire's Wharfe Valley has been a home of traditional osiery since Viking times. One of its last surviving craftsmen is John Taylor of Ulleskelf, near York, whose basket-making ancestry goes back to the 16th century. But in the early 1950s bankruptcy loomed when industrial and agricultural demand for wicker products ceased. John was the only basket maker in Ulleskelf to survive the change to synthetic wares, by adapting his osiery production for the domestic and commercial display market — and expanding into cane-furniture manufacture.

The frequently flooded scrubland flanking the River Wharfe provides the four best types of willow for osiery, including the varieties Champion Rod and Black Mole, which are principally for basket-making. Blue Bud, a hardier, more resilient variety, is used for woven fencing; the fast-growing Longskin is preferred for hampers and mill-type skeps or baskets.

The willows are grown mainly on owned land which has been in the family for generations, spaced 18in apart in rows: competition for light promotes rapidly-growing straight stems that can reach 15ft in one season. No fertiliser is needed as regular flooding deposits a natural mulch, enriched with waste from the local brewery!

Cutting, with a traditional willow knife, begins in spring, before the sap rises. Stems ▶

▲
Cutting rods in the spring with a traditional willow knife

◀**Myriad uses of willow, for furniture and screens as well as familiar baskets; inset, peeled 'white' and 'buff' willow ready for soaking**

Photos Hugh Mayfield

From the base grows the basket; crossed rods held in place with a foot, top left, as weaving starts in a circular pattern. Once the required diameter is reached, left, side rods are inserted, bent upright and held in place with a metal hoop as the sides are woven, above

are cut to within 6-8in of the ground to allow speedy regrowth the following season. Harvesting is usually annual, but some stems intended for more robust work are left for up to three years to thicken. The cut stems are bundled into 'bolts' and transported back to the workshops for sorting into lengths. A tractor with trailer attached is the usual conveyance, but John's cavernous estate car, which he backs into the marshes with alarming dash, is equally effective.

'White willow' is prepared when the stems are still sappy by immediate bark-stripping; this can be postponed until May by standing the bolts upright in wet hedge-bottoms or by frequent manual soaking. 'Buff willow', an attractive cinnamon-coloured alternative, results from boiling stems in hot water for three or four hours in a 10ft steel bath, raised above a brick wood-burning hearth. Boiling dissolves bark pigment, aids easy peeling and colours the stems. Some unskinned 'brown willow' is used just for its rustic appearance.

Before manufacture begins, often months after harvest, stem pliability is restored to all three types of willow by soaking in a water-filled vessel that looks like a horse-trough. White and buff willow are soaked up for up to four hours; the more impervious brown type is steeped for several days.

Baskets and a range of wicker goods are crafted in the ancient upper room of the former family cottage. Tools are traditional and simple: a knife and shears for cutting and trimming rods to length; a flat board and spike to hold and turn the work in place; a flat weave-compacting hammer; a pricking knife which delicately scores the rod to make it pliable; a bodkin, and a measuring stick. John's only concession to comfort is a tiny work stool.

BASE MAKING IS THE FIRST STEP in basketry. The radius of the base is made with sets of rods crossed at right angles and unceremoniously held in place on the stool with a foot. Weaving in a circular pattern, further rods are pulled alternatively over and under the radials — which are pushed apart to form spokes — until the required diameter is reached. The ends are trimmed and the base is pierced at its centre with a bodkin, and pushed on to the spike. The ends of thicker rods, which will form the uprights, are sharpened and rammed, at 1in-1½in spacings, horizontally into the rim. Once all the uprights are in place, each is scored where it enters the rim with the pricking knife, which enables the rods to be bent through 90° without splitting. The rods are bent upwards and held in place with a metal hoop and weaving of the basket sides can start.

Intended use and regional style have an influence on the choice of willow and weave. John uses the techniques of 'randing', 'slewing' and 'whaling'; ancient nefarious-sounding names that still arouse the suspicion of the village bobby. Randing is the simple process of weaving with single rods; slewing describes the use of three or four rods together, whilst whaling is alternate weaving of sets of three thick rods, then three thin rods, often in contrasting types of willow.

Perched on his stool with his legs holding the spiked board, John works quickly, alternately weaving, and tapping down the rods with his flat hammer. When the basket is the right height, John trims the ends and adds thick braided rims and handles. The whole process takes up to two hours, depending on size, and then the baskets are finished with two or three coats of clear varnish.

Basket manufacture is now very much on

a small scale compared to pre-plastic days. John's other products — plant holders, screens, picnic hampers and fencing — are all based on basket-making techniques and keep his business viable. Another development crucial to his survival has been the expansion into cane-furniture making. Currently in vogue for the garden and the home, this furniture relies on imported canes (botanically either grasses or palms) from Malaysia and Indonesia. Three types of solid cane are bought in 50kg bundles of varying lengths. Strong Manau and Tahiti varieties are used for furniture whilst the more flexible Kaboo is used for basketry, and when split, as 'lapping' material for joints.

The frameworks for chairs and settees are made by bending the cane to shape in the vice (pre-steaming above the hot bath, or fanning with a hot-air gun or blow-lamp on the beds, is essential for elasticity). The cane loses shape within seconds if it isn't restrained in purpose-made formers, where it stays for 24 hours to assume its permanent shape.

Dousing with cold water speeds the process. The frames are fixed with heavy-duty 3in staples, fired from a compressed-air staple-gun — a rare concession to high-tech. The joints are bound tight with split Kaboo cane which gives added strength and improves the appearance. After varnishing, the furniture is fitted with loose cushions bought from a local manufacturer.

John's commitment to the ancient craft withstood the economic recession in Ulleskelf. Now with the increase in heritage-hungry tourists, particularly from nearby York, and a growing demand for practical wickerwork, he is proving that traditional basket-making can once more be a profitable business. ∎

DISTRESSING NEWS

Is distressing just another form of faking? Some furniture restorers argue that it is, and that there's no distinction. But the word 'faking' has rather disturbing overtones, and to me, they're two quite different things.

In wood-finishing jargon, distressing is a method of simulating wear and tear and age on woodwork, whether it be furniture, panelwork, beams, or a piece of joinery. As the work's done on both the substrate and the finish, they must be compatible. Repairing an antique piece of furniture, for example, involves taking great care to choose a compatible piece of wood, matching the running grain area, distressing the new wood to match the surrounding section, and finally polishing and carrying out any distressing to the surface coating to match the rest of the piece. With the passage of time, the 'new' repair ages and blends to become part of that furniture.

A fake job, on the other hand, might mean gluing on any old piece of wood, which would be alien to the whole effect and stand out like a rape seed flower in a cornfield. Faking can also be any repair to a piece of furniture or joinery carried out using a plastic filling, graining and tinting over.

For distressing furniture, you can use various simple objects to simulate age. A lump of loose chain can be hammered on to the substrate surface, or a piece of old brick or stone rubbed up and down on it. The danger here is to overdo the markings, and an over-distressed surface is just as bad as an under-distressed one: try to get a happy medium. Some restorers use very strong acids to burn in and simulate age to wood. Most of us develop our own special methods of distressing.

Modern reproduction furniture is sometimes marketed as 'distressed finished', which can be used to hide bad workmanship or to satisfy current market trends. This finish consists of applying dark stains or pigments to the corners of carving or mouldings; or 'splattering', using an attachment on a spray gun such as the Devilbiss Gravity Feed. This applies a controlled splatter of spots of various colours, which can be pleasing, but again, should not be over-done. There's also the instant distressed finish, like the 'take-away beams' obtainable from large DIY stores, which are plastic and simply require a few panel pins to fix. The problem is, their too-even colour gives them away.

The tools you'll need for distressing are very basic: no machinery, just hand-tools. I've had my well-worn set for over 30 years, and they're still going strong. For larger distressing work – to items such as planks, beams and large joinery work – rasps and adzes can be used.

New repairs to old furniture can stand out like a sore thumb if the timbers don't match. Noel Leach shows you how to simulate wear and tear and age on wood, and describes how he restored one crumbling piece to its former beauty

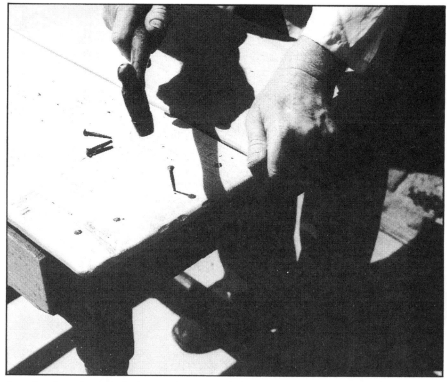

Securing the oak top to the base, using iron nails for authenticity; pre-drilled holes prevent splitting

To be successful in distressing wood, you must have a keen eye for detail, or better still, some artistic training. Perfection in this kind of work takes many years of observing and working with old furniture. I've seen furniture turned out from well-equipped workshops with just two cuts by a Stanley knife and a few marks from a hammer to pass as distressing; it would have been better if they'd left well alone.

To distress new wood, all sharp corners are rounded off, to remove machine markings such as from saw and plane blades. A curved carving chisel or gouge is an excellent tool for this purpose. Woodworm holes can be simulated by using a ¹⁄₁₆in drill to bore clusters of holes. Shakes and splits can be cut in along the grain, using a very narrow chisel or knife. Burn marks on edges can be simulated with a hot poker, while ink stains can be produced – yes– by using ink!

I recently had a brief to restore a mid-

17th-century side-table in oak, brought in pieces into my workshop by a client. What a sorry sight it was! I've had many a piece of furniture brought to me in tea-chests, boxes, carrier bags, even a wheelbarrow; this piece I saw for the first time in the back of my client's car boot. I must confess my heart sank at the sight and state of it, but one has to have vision.

The first thing I do with old furniture is to apply an anti-woodworm fluid to all the pieces and allow them to dry, before bringing them into the workshop for observation. The legs of this piece weren't too bad, with very little woodworm, but one of the rails had so much infestation that I needed to make a copy and refit. The drawer, though in pieces, only required refitting together, and I had to turn a new knob. But the top was another story: made in two thin planks, it was so infested with worm that it crumbled in my fingers. I'd have to make a new one.

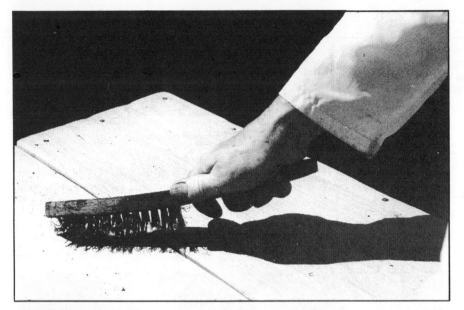

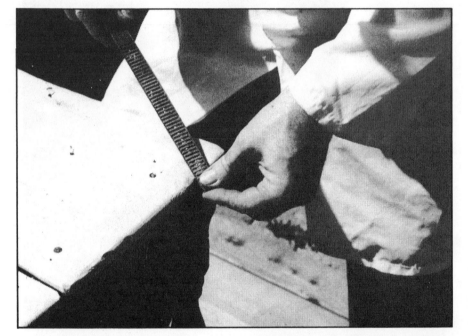

a 9in crack. The whole surface was then very carefully chiselled, using a carving chisel with and across the grain; this effect gave the whole surface a nice uneven texture.

I sanded the surface using 80-grade aluminium oxide abrasive papers with the grain, and dusted it off. Next, using a small ball pein hammer, I indented the whole surface, taking care not to overdo this treatment. Further distressing with a gouge chisel completed the work to the table top, and I was quite satisfied with the result.

I now re-sanded, using 150-grade aluminium oxide papers and making sure all the rasp marks were removed. Finally, I drilled a few simulated woodworm flight holes, just for general effect.'

This was the time to check over the whole piece. I found I had not distressed the new knob I'd turned, so I did this, plus a little extra work to one of the new rails. All was now ready for re-finishing.

For this, I decided to use a chemical stain which would simulate age better than any other type. A chemical stain is permanent, and when applied to wood causes a reaction within the chemical structure of the fibres, producing a change of colour. Oak contains large amounts of tannic acid and reacts with certain chemicals. One of these, mild acetic acid or white vinegar, can be combined with iron filings which have been soaked for a few hours, and the resultant fluid (upon dilution) used to produce a weathered grey effect. To simulate the effect of ageing iron nails on oak, touch in a strong solution of this mixture around the nails.

Scrubbing out the soft fibres in the oak grain with a wire brush (left, top); using a rasp to round off harsh edges of the new boards (left); cutting simulated splits or cracks with a 1¹⁄₁₆in chisel (below)

I repaired the frame of the table, fitted a new rail, and then set to work cutting out two new planks of English oak. This wood was sawn, not planed, and I removed all saw-marks with a carving chisel to the underside, removing the sharp edges on the edge joint at the same time. I also drilled holes in the oak to take the iron nails. Owing to this period of furniture, nails were used rather than screws, and drilling the holes prevented splitting. The top was now secured, and at last the table was stable.

I scrubbed the new oak to remove all the soft fibre in the grain, using a wire brush. Then I stripped the whole frame and drawer to bare wood with a chemical stripper, removing all the old varnish and paint of past decades.

Now I had to carry out work on the top section, as the new oak stood out alien to the framework. Using a rasp, I rounded the sharp corners of the edges as unevenly as possible. I decided to simulate a crack on one plank, so with a very thin chisel, I cut in

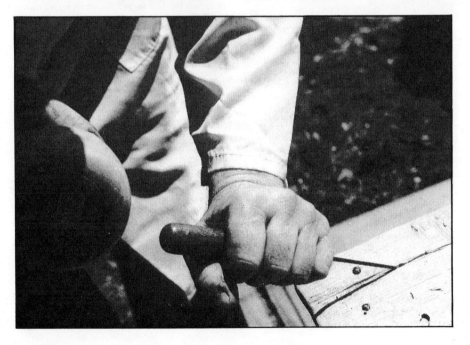

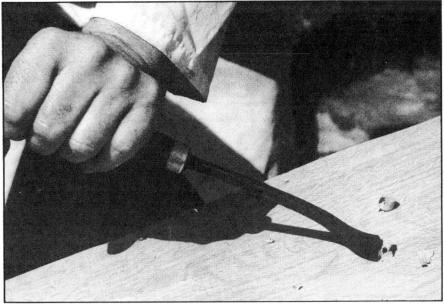

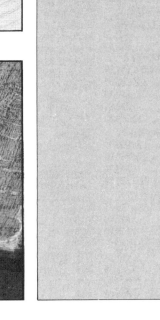

Another distressing technique (left) is to cut with and across the grain, using a carving chisel. Touching in and around the iron nails (left, below) with a chemical stain reacts with the oak's natural tannic acid to produce an ageing effect

Right: indenting the flat surface of the top with a ball pein hammer must be done with care and restraint

Before polishing, I applied by pad a weak solution of a mixed solvent stain to the whole table until I got a colour I was happy with. When the stain was dry, I applied a thin coating by mop of a shellac sealer. Then I sanded the whole thing using 320 Lubrisil abrasive paper, and dusted off.

Now came the time for elbow-grease: I applied a good-quality coloured wax polish with the help of 0000 steel wool and hessian. This always takes time, and what I generally do is spend half-an-hour a day waxing a piece of furniture, then flat down the following day, re-waxing until I have a fine patina. Finally, the table stood fully restored in all its glory – mission accomplished.

The joy of seeing a piece of furniture fully restored to its original beauty is something I can't describe. When my client took it away – delighted, to say the least – a little piece of me went with it. ∎

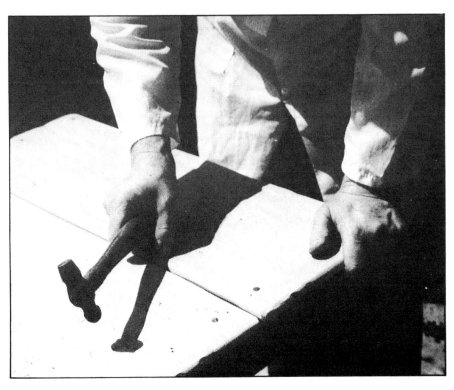

Wheelspin

● **Above left,** *the 'flyer drag' spinning wheel before and,* **right,** *after restoration*

Spinning old and new — we look at two variations on the endless theme of spinning wheels. First, Frank Lapworth explains how he restored the form and function of a mid-European 19th century model

When some friends of mine bought an old spinning wheel in very poor condition about a year ago, I was asked to have a look at it because of my interest in spinning. (My wife and I are both fanatical spinners, and we give demonstrations at craft fairs and lectures to local groups and colleges.)

As soon as I saw the wheel I offered to restore it. It is of the 'flyer drag' or 'bobbin lead' type, where the bobbin is driven continually by the drive-band round the wheel. The flyer — the U-shaped piece through the centre of which wool is twisted, and then distributed along the bobbin by the hooks — is dragged round by the yarn itself as it is wound on to the bobbin. Both bobbin and flyer have to turn of course, but at different rates. The twist of the yarn — loose or tight — is controlled by a leather strap which acts as a brake on the flyer's rotation; the drag on the flyer is controlled by turning a knob to adjust tension on the

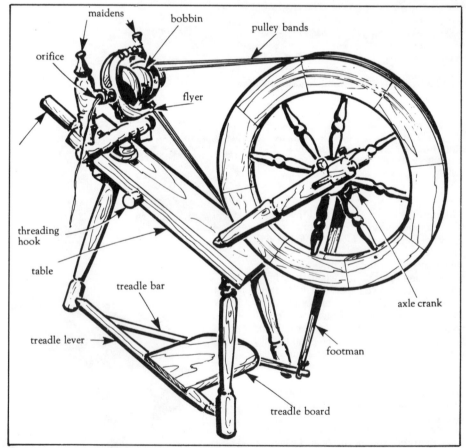

● **Above:** *Naming of parts. The wheel imparts twist to a supply of fibre fed through the orifice, turning it into yarn which is wound on to the bobbin. From Woodworker, Jan 85*

108

Wheelspin

strap, tightening or slackening it.

The overall design of the wheel is typical of the kind used in southern Germany, Austria, and the Tyrol, and my ideas about its origins were verified by some German printed on the underside of the treadle. It's impossible to read clearly, but the word Wien (Vienna) is just legible, a hint at the address of the maker. One can tell the wheel had been used long and hard from the wear in the parts of the mechanism — notably the flyer and wheel-bearings, and particularly where the brake-band goes over the flyer. There were also minute grooves worn in the flyer-hooks, which suggest it was probably used for spinning flax. If it had been used for wool, the grooves would have been larger. It's difficult to tell, but the sort of use it had obviously had and the way it was made would date it at between 1830 and 1850.

It's made from a variety of woods. The legs, uprights, the crosshead 'mother-of-all' on which the flyer assembly is mounted, the maidens — turned pieces that project from the mother-of-all to carry the flyer itself — and drive-band tensioner are all walnut or some similar hardwood. The flyer also has a walnut boss, into which oak arms of the 'U' are dovetailed. The rest of the wheel is of a close-grained softwood, probably pine, and it's all stained a dark walnut-brown.

When I first saw it, the wheel was in generally pretty poor shape, although the parts were almost 100% original, and I could see where it had been repaired over the years to keep it going. Repaired not restored — a confirmation of my idea that it was a worker's wheel and not a piece of decorative furniture. It had also suffered from the ravages of woodworm, which had damaged every part. The wheel itself was well eaten away, the surface particularly so.

Preparation

First I took the spinning wheel apart and thoroughly cleaned it with white spirit to rid it of years of accumulated grime and grease. This also gave me a chance to inspect it more closely and see what needed to be done.

Although there was now no evidence of active woodworm, I treated all the timber several times with Cuprinol woodworm killer, and injected the flight-holes with the fluid. I reamed out the flight-holes to a slight taper with a Swiss needle-file, sanded hardwood cocktail-sticks to fit the taper, and glued and tapped them into place. Then I cut the ends off slightly proud of the surface, and when the glue had set sanded them flush to match the contours of the wood.

The job

Restoration proper could now begin. Here is a list of the things that were wrong with it and what I did, in the order I dealt with them.

The footman — the driving member which connects the treadle to the cranked axle of the driving bar — was split at the upper end, and on the rear side (the side away from you

● *Left, the spinning head showing worm-damaged flyer and extinct brake-band*

● *Right, the wheel, badly pock-marked, awaits cocktail-stick treatment*

as you sit and spin) a piece of the timber had decayed away next to the crank slot. The split at the top had been repaired by driving an iron staple into the top end to bridge the split and hold the two halves together. This driving member is also sometimes called the 'pitman'.

I removed the staple and glued the split together. The decaying timber at the rear was cut away, and I cut a piece of mahogany to fit and glued it into place.

The wheel, which is made in two asymmetrical halves, had also been repaired with staples, four in all, to hold the joints together; the side of the rim was badly worm-eaten across its surface, and there were deep, irregular channels in the wood. The metal crank-arm was bent and out of line with the spindle.

I straightened the crank arm and removed the staples, whereupon the wheel sprang apart at the joints. In order to make it fit together again, I had to slightly trim the ends of two of the spokes in the shorter piece of the wheel. Only then would it go together properly. I repaired the surface damage by making some walnut wood-dust, mixing it with a little PVA glue and rubbing this paste into the damaged area. When it was thoroughly dry I sanded it smooth. There was also a decorative short finial missing from the inside edge of the wheel-rim, so I turned one up to match and fitted it.

The flyer arms, which are compound-dovetailed into the boss, were loose, and the hole in the rear maiden (towards the footman and crank) that carries the flyer spindle or 'quill' was badly worn. I don't think the leather brake-band and tensioning knob were original; the brake-band itself was fixed to the maiden with a tin tack!

I reglued the flyer arms back into the boss, and made a new tensioning-knob and shaft. I made a new brake-band, and secured it with a buttonhole fixing over the knob at the outer end of the maiden. The spindle bearing in the rear maiden was comparatively simple to plug and re-drill.

The front upright was cracked and in danger of coming apart; the **stool** or **saddle**, the flat 'base' which carries the legs and wheel uprights, was cracked across the centre, and the legs were loose.

I glued and cramped the upright together, and filled other cracks which wouldn't cramp up tight with pieces of walnut, which I stained to match as near as possible. I reglued the stool and filled the wood where necessary, but it was impossible to remove the legs for re-pegging because nails had been driven in to hold them. To get those nails out might have done more damage than I wanted to risk — I had no wish to turn up new legs, or get into boring out the old wood for new spigots. The answer was to re-peg the legs from underneath, instead of through the sides of the stool where it had been done originally.

Finally I stained over the whole spinning wheel with walnut stain, and repolished it with clear Briwax. I replaced the drive-band, as the one that came with the wheel was too thick to get sensitive tension adjustments, and put a leather thong in place of the piece of string which attached the treadle to the footman.

To complete the outfit and make it into a practical spinning wheel, I made a threading-hook, a 'Lazy Kate' bobbin rack, and two spare bobbins. I have tried it — it works fine, within the limitations of the design — and my friends were delighted! ∎

The flat spin

Roger Sear's Kingston spinning wheels look traditional, but they boast some subtle modifications. Here's how to make one — with spinning tips included!

The traditional image conjured by the words 'spinning wheel' is a charming old lady in voluminous clothes sitting outside a rose-entwined cottage behind some romantic contraption. The image persists, but it's nostalgic romance, not fact.

The old-time spinner lived on the lower breadline; part of a tenuous worker chain in which a break could spell disaster for many. The shepherd — the supplier — was the first in line, followed by the comber who prepared the fleece by lashing it through heated combs to enable the spinner to make the fine worsted yarn for the weaver's loom. Each link in this chain had to hold. As many as nine or 10 spinners could just manage to keep one weaver supplied with yarn, but improvements to looms like the flying shuttle speeded weaving up more and more, and hard-pressed spinners simply couldn't keep up. Despite the extra capacity of the 'Great wheel', or 'Walking wheel', it was not until the 'Flyer wheel' was introduced in the 15th century that spinning was speeded up, and until the 18th-century invention of the spinning jenny, the flyer was the only wheel that gave the weaver enough yarn in enough time.

The two major types of wheel that evolved are the Saxony with a sloping bed, and the upright Hebridean or Shetland wheel. Most serious spinners who spin the gossamer-fine yarns favour the Saxony, more stable than the Shetland which was used where space was really at a premium.

My first introduction to spinning came in 1923 when I was five. One of my duties was to rotate a 48in great wheel for my lace-maker great-aunt. Years later I still retained an interest in spinning, but nowhere could I find the wheel that I really wanted, so I resolved to make one. I went the rounds of museums with steel tape and camera, and visited hundreds of hand spinners, many of whom expressed decided views on the shortcomings of available wheels. Poor adjustment, heavy action, a tiring treadle action and too-low gear ratios were the main faults they listed. Though they didn't regard the appearance of the machine as important, they all thought a wheel should look fairly traditional. Most preferred the Saxony to the Shetland, the main reason being stability. All wanted doubled-band systems (where one belt round the large driving wheel runs both the bobbin and the flyer) and a standard flyer system as distinct from overhung types. An improved belt-tension system rated very highly amongst desirable improvements.

● **Above:** a Saxony wheel. Roger himself has tried and tested many variations, as you can see from the box-mounted version **right**

I was surprised at so much criticism, yet realised as a spinner that I had never really been happy with the antiquated, coarse, wooden-threaded sliding block system for adjusting the driving-belt tension. The obvious answer was a hinged block (damsel) that would allow very sensitive adjustment with a 26tpi screwdown wheel; this solved the problem most effectively. Fig. 1 and the photo above right illustrate the idea, and confirm my motto in the workshop — KISS (keep it simple, stupid!).

The heavy action necessitated much research. It seemed that friction had to be reduced and the stroke of the crank connecting treadle to wheel should be modified. I tried an adjustable crank out on a number of skilled spinners, who all set it up within $\frac{1}{16}$in of each other, so that was another to cross off the list. A 3in stroke, $1\frac{1}{2}$in cranking has proved ideal, and operator fatigue is almost eliminated.

A $\frac{1}{4}$in axle diameter means the bearings can be made of bronze, Oilite, PTFE or even epoxy resin. I know these materials aren't traditional, but b . . . . . r tradition — I want to spin, not struggle. The axle will bend cold if you use mild steel.

Now came the real crunch — speed. Most spinners treadle at about the speed of a Viennese waltz, and to obtain acceptable spinning speed meant a wheel to flyer-pulley ratio of about 7 or 8:1. To get the

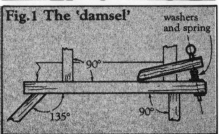

Fig.1 The 'damsel'   washers and spring

90°

135°   90°

belt in contact on 40% of the whorl that drives the flyer (whorl = pulley), you would need a driving wheel with a minimum diameter of 26in, which would allow a flyer whorl of 3in diameter, ample for controlled slip. The extremely critical bobbin whorl-to-flyer whorl ratio *must* be 13:19 at the circumference measured at the

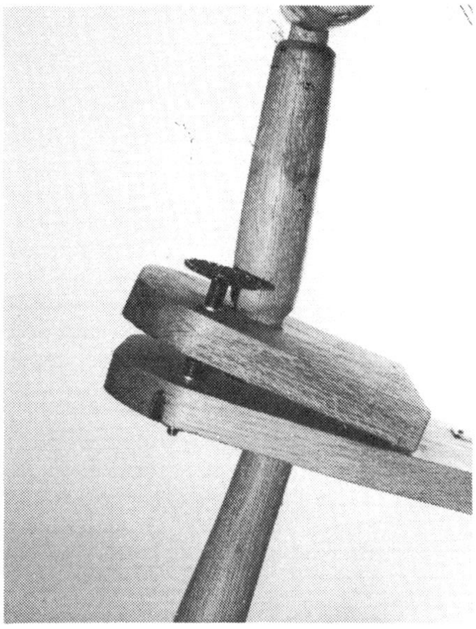

● *The hinged block or 'damsel' allows adjustment of the drive-belt tension with a sprung threaded bar*

bottom of the V-groove, a steep, deep 'V' of about 1/4in. I have found these dimensions give the best results, but many will say 'but my wheel spins OK.' Well, it might, and Bleriot's plane flew. So does Concorde!

Making a wheel

First you need to set out the rim shape; a quarter segment will do for a felloe mould. For a 26in wheel, a 26in external and 20in internal diameter will do. Cut four segments from 1 1/4in material; leave about 1/4in waste on the outside, but cut internal as finely as possible. Form the circle and shoot the ends of the felloes to fit and either tongue or dowel them together. Try a dry run with blocks nailed on a board and wedges to act as cramps. When the joints satisfy you, glue them up and put aside flat to set.

Now forget the rim while you cut a 7in diameter disc from the same stuff as the felloes and clean it up. This is the hub or nave. Centralise the hub in the rim and measure the spoke length between hub and rim. Now add 1in to this length to get the full length of your spokes. Decide how many spokes you wish to have — 12 or 16 is the best number — and cut and turn them; but 1in of each end must be parallel turned to 1/2in diameter, and I mean dead 1/2in! Finish the spokes off at this stage or prepare to swear later!

Clean up the inside — only the inside — of the rim with a flap-wheel. With dividers or a large protractor, set out the spoke positions round the inside of the rim and drill a 1/4in-diameter hole 1in deep at each spot. Lay the rim on a flat board and position the hub spot on, then strike a line from each spoke point on the rim to the centre-point of the hub. Mark these lines over to the edge of the hub and drill a 1/2in hole 1 1/4in deep at each point. Dry-fit the spokes, and check when they're pressed right home that you have a 3/8in minimum gap at the rim end. Now drill the rim end of each spoke and insert a 1/4in dowel protruding 5/16in. By now you will have tumbled the method! Squirt glue into the hub holes and insert the spokes. Lay the spoke/hub assembly inside the rim, spot-glue the dowel ends and slide them home into the rim, ensuring that both rim and hub are cramped down to avoid twisting. The wheel is now assembled and, after wiping off any surplus glue, it should be left to dry.

When the glue has set, drill a 1/4in hole at the hub centre for the axle, lay the wheel flat on a scrap board and drive a 4in nail through the axle hole. Leave 1in standing up, and cut off the head. With this as a centre, use a trammel to strike the outer circumference of the rim, then bandsaw off and clean up the whole wheel. With a half-round cutter in the router, form the belt groove, working from both sides, and clean it up. The flat of the rim can now be carved, inlaid or just polished — the choice is yours.

If you don't work metal on your lathe, you'll have to find someone to make two flanged collars from brass or alloy as shown in fig. 2. Form the axle as in fig. 3 from 1/4in bright mild steel. Screw the collar on to the wheel and cut a 3in-diameter disc from matching timber about 3/8in thick with a 1/4in central hole. Set the axle vertically in the vice and slide on the wheel, followed by the disc. Fix the disc to get the wheel true, or at least within 1/8in. That's the wheel finished; now for the rest.

Fig.2 Drive collars

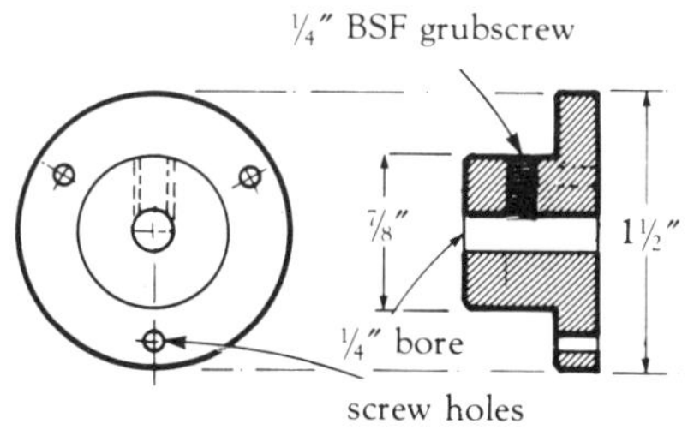
1/4" BSF grubscrew
7/8"
1 1/2"
1/4" bore
screw holes

brass or aluminium

The structure

The next stage is the saddle, or base, and the legs, or columns. For the saddle you need 26in of 7x1 1/4, cut to the shape shown in fig. 4 and cleaned up. Put the saddle aside and concentrate on the three legs which should be around 1 1/2in square, two 14in long and one 20in long. Rough-turn these to 1in diameter along 2in on one end, then bore 1in-diameter holes in the saddle as shown and fit the legs. When the legs have been tried in position and trimmed to a firm stand, turn them to any shape that pleases you but leave the bottom 2in fairly plain. You'll see why later on. With the legs now ready to be fitted, make a saw-cut about 1in vertically down in the top end of each leg. Glue the legs in with the sawcut *across* the saddle and wedge them home.

Use 1 1/2in stock for the columns holding the wheel, about 20in long and rough-turned with the same 1in parallel portion as the legs. Bore the 1in holes in the saddle as shown in fig. 4, dry fit the columns and offer up the wheel. Allow the rim to run about 1in clear above the saddle and mark off the axle holes. Carefully drill a 1/4in hole at your marks and try the axle, checking it's true with the saddle and square across. Turn the two columns to your choice of shape, then screw two threaded 1/4in-bore lampholder bushes in on the inner faces for bearings. Flush off the larger portion. The columns are fitted like the legs, but glue them in with the axle slid into position for true running.

Fig.4 The saddle

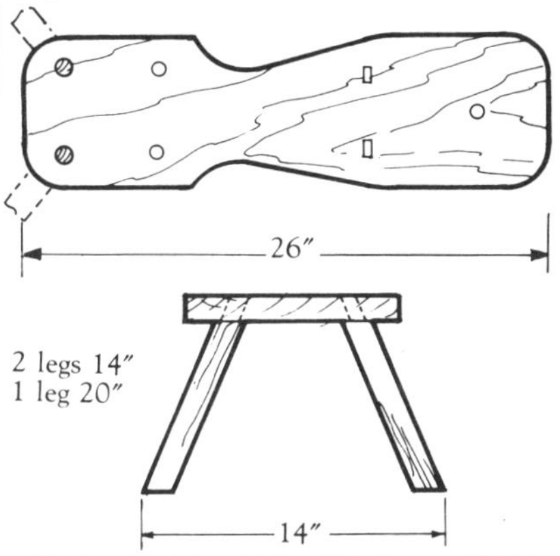
26"
2 legs 14"
1 leg 20"
14"

Fig.3 The axle

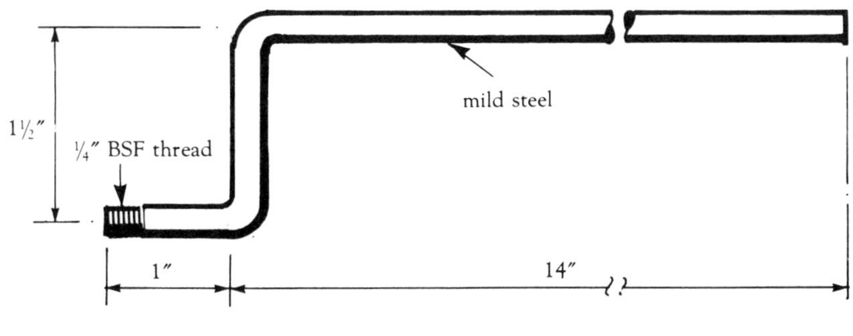
mild steel
1 1/2"
1/4" BSF thread
1"
14"

The flat spin

The damsel

The damsel block is the next task. Cut it out as shown in the photo and fig. 1, then let in the butts and screw it into position. Drill a ⅜in hole for the adjuster, which you can make from ¼in BSF studding. Turn a 2in-diameter knob, and set a ¼in nut in on the underside with Araldite. Screw in the studding, with Loctite or Araldite on the thread, and then thread it through the hole with washers and a spring between the damsel block and the saddle. Solder a nut on to a piece of brass and fit it underneath the saddle to allow the damsel a degree of controlled tilt.

The spinning mechanisms

Now the complication really starts! 'Mother-of-all' is the name given to the T-shaped contraption that actually carries the spinning mechanism. It is made of two 1½in cylinders, one with a 1in spigot turned on one end and a ¾in spigot on the other. It's about 12in overall length. The 1in end of this lower cylinder fits vertically into the damsel and is glued and wedged. Next comes the crossbar, the other cylinder about 15in long. Set the wheel up in its bearings and rest the crossbar on the ¾in turned end of the vertical cylinder, about two-thirds of the length to the driving side. Sight the belt groove, mark the feed-line point on the crossbar about 2in from the back (the connecting-rod side) and drill a ¾in vertical hole right through the crossbar at the point where the crossbar and lower cylinder meet. Now fit the crossbar on dry and mark the rope line position. Measure back from this point 2in and drill a vertical ½in-diameter hole. Measure 8in forward from the centre of this hole, and drill another. These two holes will carry the maidens which carry the flyer 'quill'. You will need two pieces 1¼in square and about 7in long for the maidens; turn these to your fancy, the bottom 1½in further reduced to ½in to be a fairly tight push-fit in the holes on the crossbar (to be known as the mother-of-all from now on).

Next you need two pieces of ¼in-thick leather, 2x1in, for the bearings which fit into mortises cut 4in above the turned shoulders of the maidens that bear against the mother-of-all. These will look like little flags when glued and pinned into position.

Get a metalworking friend to make up the quill from fig. 5, and you can be getting on with the treadle section. With all your work set up, stand on one side of the machine with the wheel on your right — to be known as the 'driving side' from now on. Mark off and drill a ¼in hole through the two driving-side legs 2in above the floor. These holes must be aligned, as they carry the pivot-pins for the treadle crossbar. Now cut a piece of 1in square stock to fit between the two legs, and drive a 4in nail through the leg and into the crossbar at each end. Cut off the nail heads and you have your pivots.

The footplate is ⅜in thick, 5 or 6in wide and long enough to project 1in over the crossbar on the driving side. It reaches on the other side to a point exactly below the crank point. The footplate may be shaped as you wish but should almost form a point at the crank end. Drill a ¼in-diameter hole near this point.

The connecting rod or 'pitman' should be ¾x¼in section with a ¼in hole drilled at the bottom for the thong which laces it to the footplate. The length of rod may be determined after a trial run. Pack underneath the footplate to bring it up to dead level with the floor and, with the crank at the bottom of its stroke, mark and then drill the hole at the top of the rod to receive the crank. Tighten the grubscrew on the collar to hold the axle to the driving wheel, and try it for running. Sod's Law will undoubtedly apply at this stage, and the wheel will have a heavy spot, but this will be to your advantage later on, so worry not and don't try to adjust the lateral movement of the wheel between its columns at this stage.

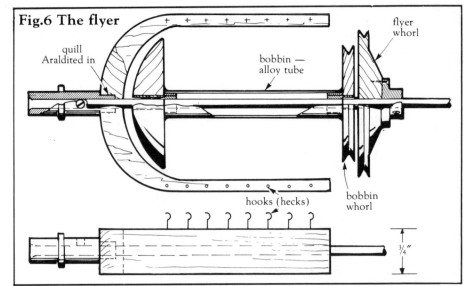

Fig.6 The flyer — flyer whorl; quill Araldited in; bobbin — alloy tube; bobbin whorl; hooks (hecks)

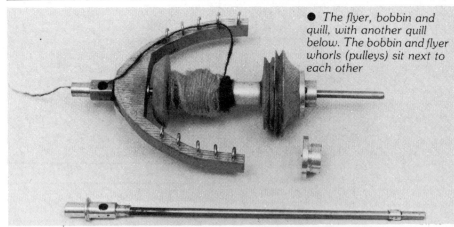

● The flyer, bobbin and quill, with another quill below. The bobbin and flyer whorls (pulleys) sit next to each other

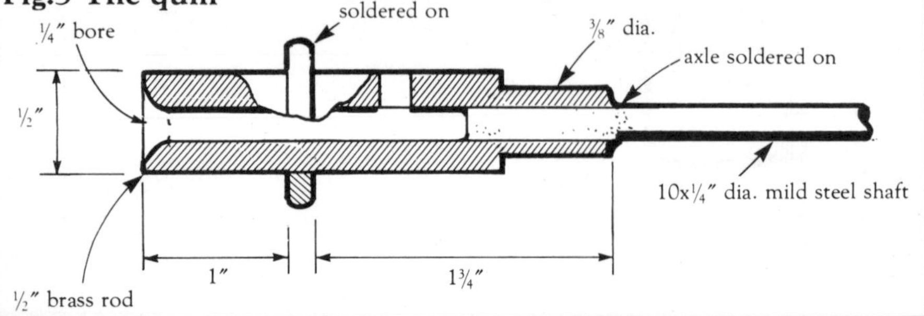

The flyer/bobbin

The flyer/bobbin assembly is rather complicated, so if I seem pedantic please bear with me. To begin with you will need:
● Three discs of 3in diameter, 1¼in thick with a ¼in central hole.
● 7in of 5x1in hardwood.
● 7 or 8in of ¾in-diameter aluminium tubing (try a piece of curtain rod for this).
● 15 small screw-hooks ⅜in long.
● A spool of medium whipping twine (get it from a yacht chandler).

Fig.5 The quill — ¼" bore; ½"; ½" brass rod; 1"; 1¾"; brass washer soldered on; ⅜" dia.; axle soldered on; 10x¼" dia. mild steel shaft

- A short length of ¼in studding.
- Two nuts with washers to suit.

The flyer itself is U-shaped with the bottom (curved) portion 1in across, blending into the ⅜in sides fairly rapidly. Clean it up and remove the arrises. Now hold the flyer in the vice and drill a ¼in hole centrally through the 1in end. Slide the flyer along the quill shaft so that it resembles a trident, check it for truth, remove it and counterbore for the ⅜in quill section. Glue it on with Araldite so that when laid flat the quill hole faces upwards.

Fit a Jacob's chuck on the lathe and thread one of the 3in discs on the piece of studding as a mandrel. Turn one face to fit the loop of the flyer when slid on the quill shaft, making sure you have a clearance of ¹⁄₁₆in. Replace the disc on the mandrel with the curved side to the chuck, and turn a spigot to fit the aluminium tube about ⅝in long. Sand and remove.

Turn the second disc with a similar spigot but just leave a ⅜in section untouched on the edge. This will be turned later.

Take the third disc, fit the flanged collar like the one on the driving wheel, mount it on the mandrel and tighten the grubscrew in the collar. Just clean up the diameter, and turn a sweep up on the collar side to leave a ⅜in flat portion. Now sink a ¼x¼in V-groove in which to run the cord drive, and run a length of *soft* wire round the base of the V-groove to measure the *exact* circumference. Divide this measurement on your calculator by 19 and multiply the result by 13. Cut this new length to give you the circumference of the V-groove bottom on the second disc. Tricky, but reduce it slowly until it comes right.

Drill a ½in hole in the leather bearing on the driving side, insert the quill up to the flange, sight the quill with the main axle and mark and drill a ¼in hole in the other leather.

Now comes the moment of truth! Thread the discs on to the quill with the spigots facing each other and the collared pulley (whorl) flat to the no.2 disc. Now ease the big driver over to the back and slide the pulleys along the quill to run fair to the wheel groove. Lock the grubscrew and set the loose pulley about ¹⁄₁₆in away; caliper the distance between the faces of the spigoted pulley and the feed end of the bobbin. Cut the aluminium tube to this length and Araldite it on to the spigots to make the bobbin. When it's set, ease it to a light running fit. You will only need one bobbin with the Kingston system.

Slightly oil the quill spindle and slide the bobbin on. Check for a very easy fit, then feed the flyer whorl on so the bobbin turns freely. Lock the flyer whorl grubscrew and fit the assembly in the two leather maiden bearings (the horizontal mother-of-all can still turn on its ¾in spigot) and sight the V-grooves with the groove on the driver. A spacer may be needed at the back.

Set the damsel to half position and tie one end of the whipping-twine belt to a maiden. Pass it round the driver and over the bobbin whorl and round the driver once more. Tie

a slip knot (tight) so the same belt drives both bobbin and flyer whorls, pull just tight, lock up the knot and carefully seal it with a match. If the belt fouls the ends of the flyer, cut back the arms to clear it. Try the run of the wheel, turning it anti-clockwise from the driving side: adjust side 'float' in the driver with packing, and watch the bottom run of the belt. Swing the mother-of-all to get a fair feed with both lines. Oil the leathers and run the wheel for a while. When it runs smoothly and the belt is running fair, put a screw through the ¾in spigot to lock it.

Now make a pencil mark on the flyer (the quill-hole side) just on the aluminium side of the bobbin end, remove the flyer assembly and strip off the whorls and bobbin. Hold the flyer arms in the vice and, from the pencil mark (quill-hole side of flyer) screw in the small hooks. These are known as 'hecks'; you will need to space seven equally along each arm of the flyer to distribute the yarn along the bobbin. Remember to screw them in on the same side of both arms and open to the outside face. Now reassemble and test.

Treadle the wheel over and adjust the belt tension so that it just spins the flyer, but when the flyer is held with a finger touch the bobbin spins and the belt slips on the flyer whorl. Now cut off the spare axle, leaving 2in projecting to carry the hanker. Fig. 6 shows the hanker, so make it as you will need it. Push the hanker on the axle and screw a heck into the mother-of-all to give a fair lead to the yarn, and you are ready to spin.

Fig.7 The hanker

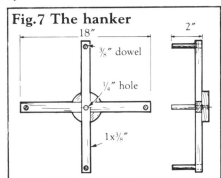

I haven't attempted to tell you any turning patterns, as you're probably a better turner than I am — you couldn't be worse. My wish was just to tell you how I build my own wheels, and they are perfect spinners. My lathe is an 1886 Britannia screwcutter swinging an 8in chuck, and by reversing the gear train and hand-turning the lead screw with a router clamped to the compound slide, I can cut a multiple-start spiral of one turn in 4in — so I have fun!

Happy spinning! ∎

Spinning on a Kingston system Wheel

You will need fleece to use your wheel, preferably carded. This can usually be obtained from a local craft shop or one of the specialist suppliers. Fleece with a reasonably long staple (fibre length) is needed, and we would suggest Romney Marsh or Cheviot to start off with.

Tie a 2ft length of commercial yarn on to the bobbin and thread it round a hook, through the hole in the top of the quill, and out through the aperture (a bent hairpin works well). Now check the drive belt is just tight enough to spin the bobbin whilst the flyer is held with one finger. The belt must be able to slip on the flyer whorl. Hold the end of this leader about 6in from the quill between thumb and forefinger of the right hand, the rest in the left about 4in back. Now start to treadle the wheel anti-clockwise, and the yarn in front of the right hand will start to store twist. The yarn will be drawn in and on to the bobbin, but keep the pinch on and move your hands towards the wheel. But slide the left hand back about 6in and *slide* the right pinch back to the left . . . the twist will follow it, but it *mustn't* be allowed to pass the pinch . . . feed both hands forward to allow wind-on, and repeat the operation till it gets easy, then unwind and do it again . . . and again . . . and again.

When you have mastered the wind-on (tighten the belt to increase pull if it's not enough), pull out from your fleece a small handful and make a 'roving'; a sausage about a finger's diameter. With about 12in of leader out, hold a *few* wool fibres against the leader in the right hand and pinch the rest gently in the left about 3in back . . . Start the wheel and the leader will grip the wool, so then slide the right hand back towards the left, moving the left hand back, which allows a few fibres to slide through. *Both* hands move forward in unison to allow wind-on. The yarn will form in front of the right hand and wind on, the thickness being controlled by the amount fed through from the left. Practice but don't worry if it's a bit lumpy; this is why I said practice. As the bobbin fills, move the yarn along to the next hook till the bobbin fills that. When the bobbin is full, lift the belt from the bobbin whorl over on to the flyer whorl, put the hanker on the axle and wind off. Tie off the hank with tape, remove it from the hanker and wash it with detergent; rinse it and hang it up with a heavy weight on it to dry. When it's dry, ball up and make another hank; same treatment. The yarn must be plied for knitting, so place both balls in a bowl and tie both ends to a leader as if you were spinning. Tighten the belt a little and treadle the wheel *clockwise*, holding the twin yarns between your fingers . . . it will ply and wind on fast. You can do it . . . now practice!

Happy returns

● *The flight not of the humble bee, but of the boomerang – WOODWORKER style*

No-one to frisbee with in the still summer evenings? Or perhaps you fancy knocking off the odd kangaroo. Rik Middleton has been developing the art of making and flying boomerangs, and presents his findings

The boomerang is probably one of the world's oldest wooden toys. But it originated as a weapon of war and hunting — not a plaything. The killing boomerang is too heavy to return, and who would want it to? I like to think the return-boomerang came into being by accident when a father made a harmless lightweight model of his favourite weapon for his son to play with; but I wonder whether the son ever got to play with it after its unusual homing behaviour had been discovered.

Australian aboriginal men have used return-boomerangs as toys and in flying competitions since the early ages. These boomerangs can bring down a few flocking birds, but they bounce off kangaroos.

The hunting boomerang of the Australian aborigine (and incidentally the Ancient Egyptian) was a stick sharpened at the leading edge of its flat blade, with shaped extremities and a distinct bend in the middle. This bend meant it could be thrown, spinning without falling about its long axis. The axis of spin was at right angles to the blades and when the weapon was thrown forward, spinning in a horizontal plane, curvature and twists in the structure gave it lift to counteract its weight; so it could fly at a fairly constant height for a considerable distance.

Australian aboriginals are said to have decapitated kangaroos at a range of around 100yds — if you imagine 5lb of well-sharpened hardwood doing 60mph and 200rpm you can see how. In the genuine aboriginal boomerang the bend is the

● *A 8oz 'war' boomerang with an easy 125yd range. Can you throw half-a-pound of ply 125 yards?*

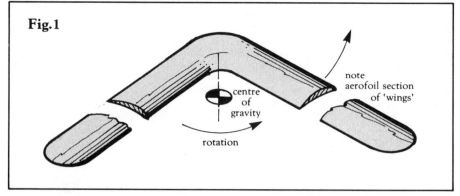

Fig. 1

centre of gravity

note aerofoil section of 'wings'

rotation

natural branch point of a tree. I've never got round to trying this, I just use plywood.

Standard exterior grade plywood isn't strong enough to take the knocks. Birch ply is suitable — seven-layered ⅜in is about right — but best of all is the type with dark red-brown glue layers. The stuff with colourless glue isn't as strong or convenient

during construction.

A boomerang is basically a propeller with two or more blades, which are aerofoil sections with a small positive uptilt or 'angle of attack'. When it's thrown forward with spin, both aerofoils meet the air front-edge first. The traditional boomerang (fig. 1) is therefore a low-attack-angle propeller, with one blade missing, but this doesn't affect flight or return; a large model-aircraft propeller with three blades will return if it's thrown correctly.

The return effect is caused by the gyroscopic properties imparted by the spin. Forward motion, along with the spin, means that one wing (the one going forward at any given moment) has a higher airspeed than the one going backwards. This makes the entire gyroscopically-spinning projectile move in a strangely distorted manner known as 'precession'.

Precession will take place if you take a bike wheel in two hands, by the ends of its spindle, and spin it hard. Now try to push it into a horizontal position so your right hand is above your left. It'll move all right, but definitely not where you're telling it to. A very weird experience when you try it for the first time.

Enough of the physics; quite simply, when a boomerang is thrown correctly it flies a gradually decreasing spiral path. The trick is to adjust the throw so the end of the first spiral occurs at ground level and the boomerang falls at your feet or, when you're more ambitious, at a catchable height.

Making a boomerang

I cut my boomerangs out of $\frac{3}{8}$in ply with a jigsaw. The blades have to be shaped to low-angle aerofoils like aircraft wings. Draw a large seven-layer sandwich in the proportions of your wing (2in wide is recommended). Draw your own idea of an aerofoil section on it and project the points where your section meets the glue lines in the plywood up to the surface. Connect these all to a single point above the section and find the level where this makes the whole section 2in wide. Measure off where the glue lines should come and you have drawn a contour map of your aerofoil (fig. 2).

I use a Cintride coarse disc to remove material down to the approximate shape. This rips stuff off very brutally and you might find that a rasp or Surform, or even a spokeshave, allows more control and time for your first considered actions. The convex surface of a Cintride is ideal for the slightly concave aerofoil underside. You can easily judge the shape you're creating with the recommended plywood type, as the glue lines stand out clearly like countours on a map.

The shape you cut out can vary enormously. But from past good (and bad) results I've learnt that the wings should be about 2in wide and 9-12in long. The optimal internal angle at 12in long is about 120° or just under; this comes down to roughly 90° at 9in long. Too large an internal angle gives the boomerang a rapid rate of sink, and it inevitably hits the ground before completing one spiral path. My best traditional-style boomerang has 12in blades with an internal angle of 115°, weighs 4½oz (125g) and is 7mm thick at the thickest point. This returns easily in still air, but heavier models and those with shorter

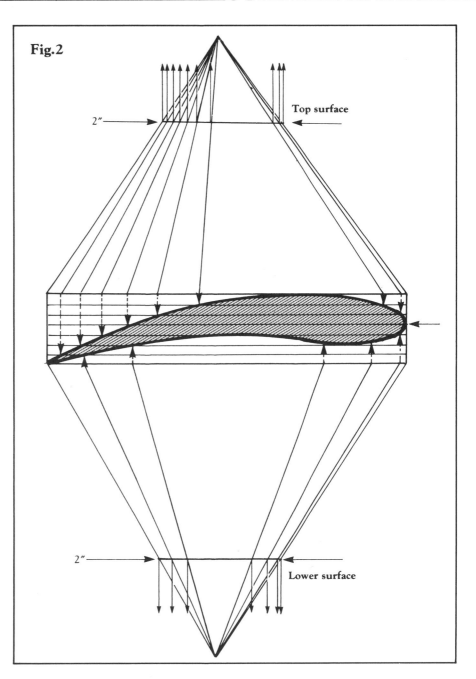

Fig.2

Top surface

2″

Lower surface

2″

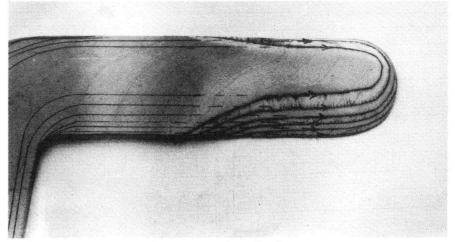

● *Cutting the profile; check it corresponds to the drawn contours*

wings will only return wind-assisted or with more throwing power. Three- and four-armed boomerangs return even more easily and are recommended for children.

When you've shaped and sanded the boomerang to a smooth and regular contour, treat it against water penetration and abrasion — I have used polyurethane, but two-part plastic coating is better. My earliest models had a smeared-on coating of Araldite, thickest on the exposed points — it must have been cheaper then.

Throwing it

You really need 100yds clear in all directions for safety. Never throw in a high wind; and I strongly recommend that you wait for flat calm conditions at least until you've gained a few hours 'flying time'. If there is a slight breeze it must be coming in directly from your left.

Grip the boomerang firmly in your right hand. You need to throw it hard and spin it fast with a wrist movement. It should pass your head nearly vertical for a first try.

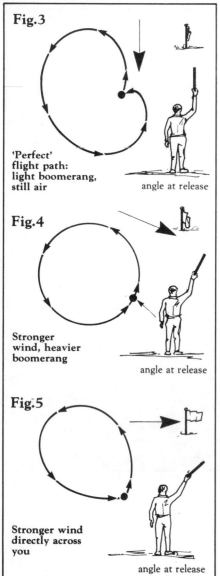

Fig.3

'Perfect' flight path: light boomerang, still air

angle at release

Fig.4

Stronger wind, heavier boomerang

angle at release

Fig.5

Stronger wind directly across you

angle at release

Throw it at an imaginary point 20yds in front of you, head-height. It will bank away left. If it climbs and accelerates towards you from a great height, you didn't have it near enough to vertical. If it banks left but drifts down to hit the ground away to your left, you should lay it over further from the vertical as you throw, and/or throw it harder. If it keeps hitting the ground to your left, the internal angle is too large.

A word for the left-handed among you. Left-handed boomerangs are mirror images of right-handed ones so you probably won't be able to throw those illustrated. Go through this article and transpose every 'left' into a 'right', and vice-versa, and view all diagrams through a mirror.

Variations of flight-path are possible. What I call a 'perfect' flight-path is when the boomerang banks left and maintains a constant height as it goes round behind you and comes in at you from about 45° front-right. This usually only works with a light but long-wing boomerang in still air (fig. 3).

If there is some wind, this flight-path gets distorted downwind and you'll have a long walk if you try to get a full throw. Wind from the left needs an 'incomplete' flight-path so the wind foreshortens the first half of the spiral path and carries it back to you. You'll need lighter throws, further off the vertical for light long-wing types. Shorter and heavier boomerangs are easier to control in this situation (figs 4 and 5).

Remember that although the boomerang only weighs 4oz or so, the advancing wing-tip of a boomerang can have a ground speed in excess of 100mph. I don't recommend trying to catch it until you have had many hours of flying time, and even then wear a glove. Remember also your responsibility to local property and the spectators you're likely to attract. If a crowd of children gathers around your heels, the only safe thing is to pack up and go home. In some parks you may fall foul of model aircraft bye-laws; please check. WOODWORKER and I can accept no responsibility for damage caused by your boomerangs!

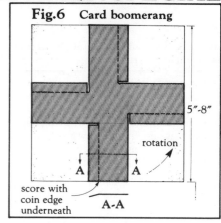

Fig.6 Card boomerang

5"-8"

rotation

A   A

score with coin edge underneath

A-A

The indoor model

This is made from card; the sort used for exercise book covers is ideal. Paper plates are a good alternative. Cut a square as shown (fig. 6) and then mark and cut the cruciform shape. This model relies for lift on ailerons (hinged flaps), scored with a coin edge and turned down.

Throw from thumb and forefinger, giving lots of spin from the vertical plane.

Experimental models

Distribution of weight can markedly influence the flight-path of a boomerang. You can re-distribute weight by drilling a series of $3/8$ or $1/2$in holes through the wing. This makes the boomerang a bit less robust, but you could make the wings a little thicker in the first place. Weight the holes with fishing lead weights and seal up the top and bottom smoothly with wide sticky tape. Try moving the weights from the centre to the two wing ends, and watch the flight-path change.

I've failed to come up with a design for a joint at the junction of the wings which would allow the internal wing-angle to be changed from one throw to the next — and withstand the considerable torque stress of the throwing movement. On safety grounds, I've rejected anything that uses wing-nuts. A challenge for WOODWORKER joint specialists? ∎

● *A three-arm model. The ends were left uncut then shaved off for wingtip weight adjustments*

Wooden thoroughbreds

Anthony Dew is an ex-merchant seaman spreading the rocking-horse message from a converted abattoir. Leonard Markham sought him out

The rocking horse is making a comeback. Once firm family favourites, bowing more recently to the fashion for electronic family playthings, these traditional and attractive toys are re-emerging — largely because of the work of craftspeople like Anthony Dew.

Anthony was originally a merchant seaman, but his fast-developing international reputation for thoroughbreds in wood has grown from the time when he started making rocking horses after taking a carving and sculpture course. Several commissions followed and business flourished, allowing Anthony to develop his rocking-horse passion full time. Two years ago he move to a former abattoir and butcher's shop in Holme-on-Spalding Moor, and set to on his own conversions and extensions; now he has fully-equipped workshops and an eye-catching retail outlet — a popular tourist attraction.

Anthony sells self-assembly kits and accessories as well as completed horses, and has also written a book for home horse makers, *Making Rocking Horses*, which carries full constructional details and scale drawings.

Although hobby horses and simple plywood kits are a commercial essential of his business, the manufacture of fully-carved traditional rocking horses is Anthony's chief delight. He makes three sizes of horse to suit individual requirements, all displaying the impeccable pedigree of an acknowledged craftsman's precision and excellence.

Selecting the timber for horse heads and bodies, Anthony looks for stability and sympathy to the chisel. Yellow pine has always been ideal, but increasing rareness and price have pushed him towards Malayan jelutong. It has the visual drawback of surface latex ducts, but such blemishes can always be filled and hidden with paint. Anthony crafts high-prestige steeds from the finest Brazilian mahogany, finished to enhance the inherent richness of grain and colour which particularly appeal to adult buyers. Ash is chosen for horse legs because of its resilience to shock and stress; Anthony prefers Douglas fir for stands. All the timber is bought kiln-dried.

Constructionally, each horse consists of 12 main pieces: head, neck and legs sections, upper and lower body-blocks, and two sets of middle side-blocks enclosing an inner cavity. Equestrian features and musculature are carved from eye- and ear-pieces, and neck and leg muscle-blocks.

● *A champion mahogany steed in Anthony's display area, ready for the nursery*

photos Hugh Mayfield

Using patterns for each size of horse, Anthony scribes each piece on timber of the right type and thickness before cutting it on a heavy-duty bandsaw. He keeps 'horns' on both the neck section and the upper body-block to assist cramping. He creates a degree of animation by cutting the head section ½in over-size and bevelling its joint-face before gluing the head to the neck; the resulting angle of the head produces an impression of life. After roughing the surfaces to be jointed, Anthony spreads Cascamite glue and cramps the head and neck sections together using the neck cramping-horn and the horse's forehead, protected by an offcut. Two headless 1in panel pins, tapped into the area to be joined, help gluing and prevent slipping when the cramp is tightened.

When the glue is dry the ears of the horse are roughly separated with a coping saw and the facial cuts outlined in pencil. Then the delicate process of evolving the features — unique to every horse — can begin. Anthony uses a variety of chisels and gouges; he urges those with limited carving experience to avoid disaster by practising with clay or Plasticene models.

After gluing the neck muscle-blocks into position, the carved head and neck is fixed to the upper body-block. The surfaces are glued and joint strength is augmented by tapping ½in glued pegs into ½in holes,

drilled from the underside of the upper body-block.

Mortise joints were preferred by many old rocking-horse makers to fix the legs, but Anthony uses glued and dowelled butt-joints, strong and simple to construct. The lower ends of the legs are carved before fixing, then the splays of the upper legs are marked on the lower body-block, and their housings cut. The legs are glued and cramped into position, with nails to assist cramping (unsightly nail-holes will be hidden by the muscle-blocks). After joining, two ½in holes are drilled through each leg into the lower body-block, and glued dowels tapped in as before. The leg muscle-blocks are glued at the top of each leg, their tops planed flush with the top of the lower body-block when they're dry. The four middle blocks are glued and dowelled to the lower body-block, and finally the head and upper body-block are fixed the same way. Then the carving of the body begins.

Equine contours are sculpted with, in sequence, a draw-knife, progressively smaller sizes of gouge, and a spokeshave. A power sander completes the shaping. Among the numerous and varied tools of the rocking-horse maker's multi-faceted trade — Anthony is carver, joiner, gessoer, leather worker and blacksmith all in one — the carver's chops take an essential role. Their narrow jaws, which hold almost any shape at almost any angle, are ideally suited to the carving and shaping processes. The construction stages finish with fitting the saddle block, cutting a groove for the mane, and drilling the tail-hole. Two cross-struts are fixed to the hooves for mounting on the stand.

Then the surface of the horse must be covered with gesso, a mixture of whiting and animal glue derived from rendered-down rabbit skins. It is worked while it's hot to a thin, smooth cream, which is brushed on to the horse in successive coats for a blemish-free painting surface. The traditional dappled grey finish requires several coats of undercoat and up to three coats of gloss; the surface is then dabbed with a paint-dipped latex rubber pad, held in a cover of mutton-cloth. A pattern of roughly circular dappling is extended to head, neck and body until Anthony gets the desired random effect; hooves, eyelashes and eye-rims are painted in a matching colour. After the genuine horse-hair mane and tail have been fitted, glass eyes are installed, ear, nose and mouth cavities are picked out in red paint, and finally a coat of shellac varnish seals the surface.

Anthony uses only tried and tested techniques and materials to create something that is both an item of fantasy for a thousand headlong rides, and a piece of furniture of enduring appeal. Such thoroughbreds deserve only the best accoutrements — only finest-quality tack is used to ready the horse for its final mounting.

The frames are of two types, the well-known bow rocker, and the increasingly preferred swing-iron. The swing-iron frame, patented in 1880, requires less room

than its rival, but the chief appeal to parents is that it's inherently safer — for both rider and spectator!

The douglas fir swing-iron stand consists of a top rail from which the brass swing-irons hang; a long bottom rail; cross-pieces for stability, and two lathe-turned stand-posts. Once the hoof cross-struts are fitted, the horse is ready for the nursery.

It's a fortunate child indeed who receives one of Anthony's incomparable steeds (they cost several hundred pounds), but

many connoisseurs of quality from as far away as Saudia Arabia and the US have willingly paid the price. Less wealthy admirers may only dream of ownership, but Anthony's book is there to encourage even those with modest wood-working skills to build these treasured toys. ■

● The drawings are reproduced with Anthoy Dew's permission from his book *Making Rocking Horses*, published by David & Charles at £7.95.

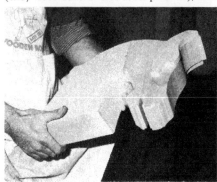

● *Head and neck, glued ready for carving; note the grain directions*

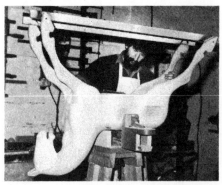

● *Hand finishing, the horse held in the carver's chops*

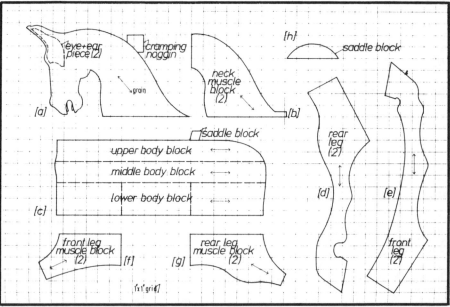

● *Anthony marks out a head from a template*

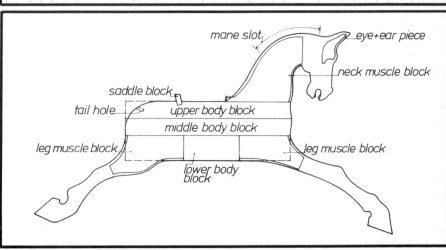

SASH SECRETS ONE

Alec Limon describes the traditional method of making a double-hung sash window

Preserving the original architectural style is important when refurbishing property and this often means that you produce special joinery. Modern double-hung sash windows use a spring system set into the sash stile instead of the old-fashioned weights to counterbalance the sash. This means that the standard double-hung sash frame does not have the large box-stiles like the older windows: you could make a dummy box, of course, to fill in the existing reveal, but why not make the replacement window similar to the original in all respects, including sash weights, pulleys and cords.

Materials

Making a box-section window frame is an interesting exercise, but all the different timber shapes may not be obtainable from your merchant and you may well have to produce some of the mouldings yourself. For instance, you may not be able to find pulley stile, but it would not be hard to make as it simply needs both edges rebated to produce a tongue on opposite corners. Naturally, a hardwood sill would be ideal, but most of the old frames were made from softwood throughout and it has proved to be very long lasting: today you can use softwood treated with preservative for extra durability.

Both the internal and external cheeks of the frame are made from square-edged boards, but the external cheek can have a chamfer or a small moulding run on its outer corner. The square edge of the internal cheek carries a staff bead (in some catalogues this is called a stop bead). Fortunately, sash stile, top and bottom-rail mouldings are still made in the traditional ovalo pattern and in sizes 50×50mm sash stile and 50×100mm bottom rail as well as 38×50mm sash stile and 38×100mm or 38×

75mm bottom rail. Sash bar in 50×25mm and 38×25mm is also still obtainable, if the sash is to be glazed in small squares. Meeting rail is either 57×38mm or 44×32mm. Parting bead is 25×13mm. Sills are usually 75mm thick and from 125mm to 175mm wide. The bottom edge of the bottom rail will have to be bevelled to match the weathered rebate of the sill. Some of the old windows had the bottom rail of the lower sash rebated to match the sill and sometimes the bottom staff bead would be moulded on to a board two or three inches wide to provide a draught and water stop.

Grooves are needed in the side cheeks to take the tongues of the pulley stile, and the internal cheeks also need a groove to take the tongue of the internal wooden lining. Traditionally, reveals were not usually plastered as they so often are today. The sill, of course, has a groove for the tongue of the window board.

It makes sense to look carefully at the window you are replacing and to copy it as far as possible.

Constructing the frame

When making this type of window, where it is essential that the sashes will meet exactly when closed, it is best to start by making a setting-out rod: this is a piece of plywood or planed timber on which a full-size vertical section and a full-size horizontal section can be drawn out, enabling exact measurements to be taken and the various members marked out by laying them on the setting-out rod. In this way the exact positions and sizes of the mortise and tenons, the grooves and other joints are determined.

Cut a housing in the sill (fig. 2) to take the pulley stile and a wedge; slightly angle the side of the housing to match the angle of the wedge. Cut away the sill ends to take the side cheeks. If the external cheek is square-edged it can run through, but if there is a moulding on the outer edge you'll have to cut the end of the cheek so that the moulding stops on the top of the sill; the cut-out on the end of the sill will, of course, have to be that much smaller.

Before you can fix the pulley

stile you'll have to fit the pulleys about 100mm from the top of the stile. You also need to make an access to get at the weights for cording and repairs: this is called a pocket and its size and position depends on the size of the weights, which in turn depends on the size and therefore the weight of the glazed sash. Generally, the pocket is from 225mm to 300mm in length and the top of the pocket is around 450mm above the sill. It must be possible to get the top of the weight out of the pocket, so it is better to be a little too high than too low, which would make it impossible to withdraw the weight. The width of the pocket is from the edge of the stile to the centre of the groove for the parting bead. In the days when these sashes were installed as the normal window, the pockets were cut with a wide thin chisel (called a pocketing chisel), but you probably won't find one anywhere today. The pocket was cut in with the chisel from each side of the pulley stile making it slightly smaller on the inside than the outside. A sharp blow with a hammer or mallet would then break out the pocket leaving a slight step or rebate which would prevent the loose piece falling into the hollow box. Without this thin chisel you'll have to make do by simply cutting the ends of the pocket at an angle and screwing it at the top and the bottom. The old pockets were cut at a V-angle from the outside at the top so that the end of the pocket was trapped and only needed screwing at the bottom.

Glue and wedge the pulley stile into the sill housing, and house the head of the frame, which is made from pulley stile, to take the stile and nail into place. The side cheeks are simply nailed into place. The sides run right through and the head pieces are fitted between them. The cheeks at the head are supported by gluing and pinning triangular strips along the inside. The head of the frame is as long as the sill and from its underside, inside the box, a parting slip is suspended to keep the weights separate: without this thin strip one weight could easily come to rest on the top of the other and without the weight's balancing influence the sash would jam.

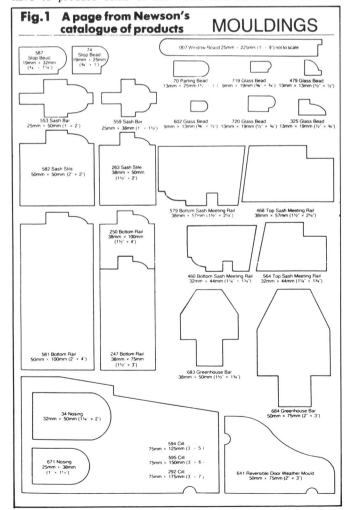

Fig.1 A page from Newson's catalogue of products MOULDINGS

587 Stop Bead 19mm × 32mm (¾ · 1¼)

74 Stop Bead 19mm × 25mm (¾ · 1)

007 Window Board 25mm - 225mm (1 · 9) not to scale

70 Parting Bead 13mm × 25mm (½ · 1)

719 Glass Bead 9mm × 19mm (⅜ · ¾)

479 Glass Bead 13mm × 13mm (½ · ½)

553 Sash Bar 25mm × 50mm (1 · 2)

559 Sash Bar 25mm × 38mm (1 · 1½)

602 Glass Bead 9mm × 13mm (⅜ · ½)

720 Glass Bead 13mm × 19mm (½ · ¾)

325 Glass Bead 13mm × 19mm (½ · ¾)

582 Sash Stile 50mm × 50mm (2 · 2)

263 Sash Stile 38mm × 50mm (1½ · 2)

579 Bottom Sash Meeting Rail 38mm × 57mm (1½ · 2¼)

468 Top Sash Meeting Rail 38mm × 57mm (1½ · 2¼)

250 Bottom Rail 38mm × 100mm (1½ · 4)

460 Bottom Sash Meeting Rail 32mm × 44mm (1¼ · 1¾)

564 Top Sash Meeting Rail 32mm × 44mm (1¼ · 1¾)

581 Bottom Rail 50mm × 100mm (2 · 4)

247 Bottom Rail 38mm × 75mm (1½ · 3)

683 Greenhouse Bar 38mm × 50mm (1½ · 1¾)

684 Greenhouse Bar 50mm × 75mm (2 · 3)

34 Nosing 32mm × 50mm (1¼ · 2)

594 Cill 75mm × 125mm (3 · 5)

595 Cill 75mm × 150mm (3 · 6)

671 Nosing 25mm × 38mm (1 · 1½)

292 Cill 75mm × 175mm (3 · 7)

641 Reversible Door Weather Mould 50mm × 75mm (2 · 3)

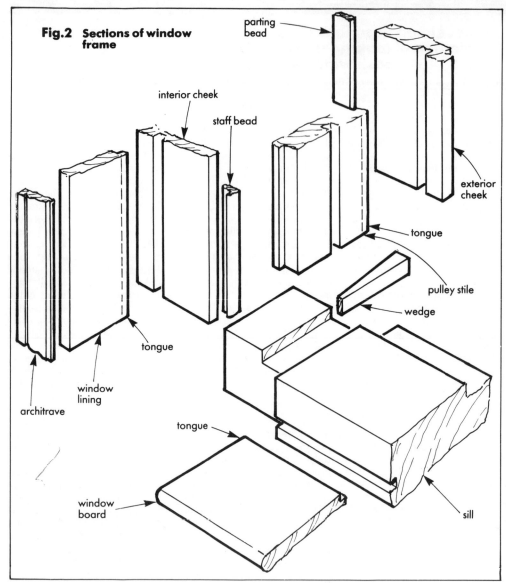

Fig.2   Sections of window frame

parting bead

interior cheek

staff bead

exterior cheek

tongue

pulley stile

wedge

tongue

architrave

window lining

tongue

window board

sill

Making the sashes

If the frame has been carefully made to the exact sizes given on the setting-out rod, then the sashes can be set out from the rod with confidence, knowing that they will fit correctly when they are closed. It is usual to make a fancy horn at the bottom of the top sash stiles and at the top of the bottom sash stiles (fig. 3): this not only improves the appearance of the sashes, it also enables the two meeting rails to have full-width tenons. The top rail of the top sash and the bottom rail of the bottom sash have haunched tenons. These sash stiles have to have a groove ploughed down the outer edges for the sash cords. The groove should run about three-quarters of the way down the sash.

If the sashes are to have glazing bars fitted, stub-tenon the ends into the stiles and rails: through-tenons would only be necessary in the case of very large sashes, when one or two of the middle glazing bars could be through-tenoned for extra strength. Where the glazing bars cross they can either be halved or little stub tenons can be made.

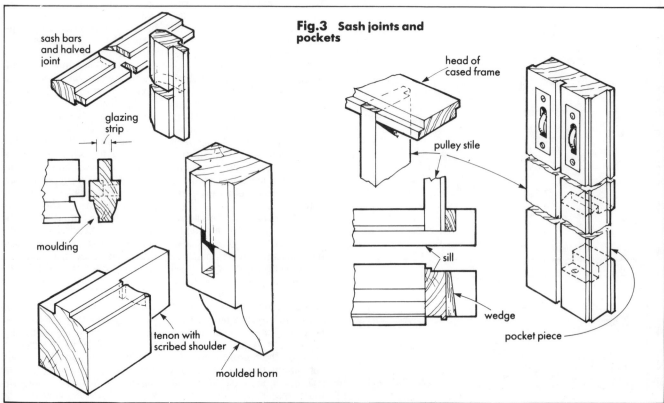

sash bars and halved joint

Fig.3   Sash joints and pockets

head of cased frame

glazing strip

pulley stile

moulding

sill

tenon with scribed shoulder

wedge

moulded horn

pocket piece

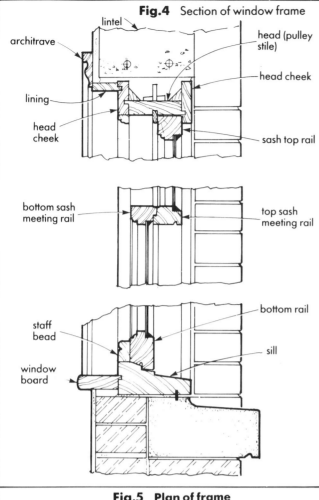

Fig.4 Section of window frame

- lintel
- architrave
- head (pulley stile)
- head cheek
- lining
- head cheek
- sash top rail
- bottom sash meeting rail
- top sash meeting rail
- staff bead
- bottom rail
- sill
- window board

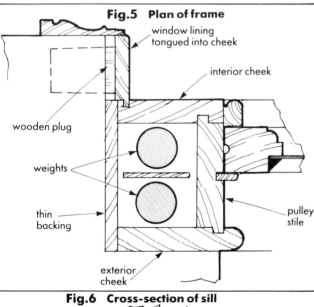

Fig.5 Plan of frame

- window lining tongued into cheek
- interior cheek
- wooden plug
- weights
- thin backing
- pulley stile
- exterior cheek

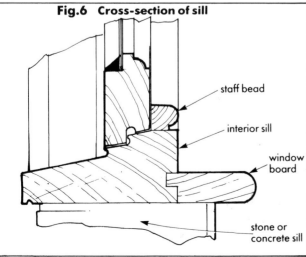

Fig.6 Cross-section of sill

- staff bead
- interior sill
- window board
- stone or concrete sill

After completing the sashes and glazing them, you need to weigh each sash and provide two cast iron weights for each: lead weights will only be needed if the sashes are very large and heavy. Being heavier than cast iron, the lead weights would be smaller.

Before installation, cover the back of the weight box with thin wood or plywood and cut the staff bead to fit around the inside of the frame.

Installation

After fixing in the brick reveal, you need to thread the sash cord around the pulleys. To do this, tie a piece of thin string with a small weight attached to the end of the sash cord: this is called a mouse. Pass the weight over the pulley and drop it into the box, retrieving it through the pocket and pulling the sash cord after it. Start by threading the cord over the pulley for the bottom, or inner sash; pull the cord out through the pocket across the window frame and over the other bottom sash pulley. Then pull it through the pocket again and over the top sash pulley at the opposite side of the window. From there the cord comes out through the pocket and over the last of the pulleys. Having threaded all the pulleys, firmly tie a weight to the cord and ease through the pocket and pull up to the top until it reaches the back of the pulley. Drive a small-headed nail through the cord into the face of the pulley stile to hold it in place, and cut the cord to length. Measure from the top of the sash to a point about 50mm short of the end of the groove in the sash; mark the sash and measure the same distance down from the top of the window frame and cut the cord off to that length. Tying another weight to the end of the cord, ease it through the pocket, pull it up to the pulley and nail the cord as before. Measure the sash, mark it, and take the same measurement from the top inside the frame, cutting off the cord and tacking it as before. Do the same with the bottom sash.

Hang the top sash first. Tack the cord into the groove using small round-head nails and making sure that they are angled so that the ends cannot touch the glass. As it is the top sash, when it is closed the weights will be at the bottom, but they must not touch the sill or the window won't stay closed; it will slide down until the weights are free again. To avoid this take the cord right to the bottom of the groove which effectively shortens the cord and holds the weights clear of the sill. The opposite is required when hanging the bottom sash: here the weights will be at the top when the window is closed, so to prevent them fouling the pulleys the cords are nailed well clear of the bottom of the groove thus lengthening them. None of the cords should be nailed near the top of the sash or the cord will not pass over the pulley properly. Four nails close to the end of the cord are all that are needed.

When the top sash is in place and the temporary nail has been removed from the cord, put the pocket cover in position and screw into place. Then tap the parting bead into its groove; this bead should not be nailed. If it is a snug fit it will stay in place; only old and damaged beads need to be nailed. When you've hung the bottom sash, nail the staff beads around the inside of the frame. Don't nail the side beads closer than about 150mm to the mitres or you could have difficulty later if they have to be removed to get the sash out for recording.

The final operation is to fit the wooden lining around the inside of the window. Plug the reveal and cut off the plugs in line with the back of the window lining. Fix the window board first and then the side linings. Ideally, the side linings are cut off to exact length and the head lining is either housed or simply nailed on to them before they are tapped into place as a single unit. If they are installed like this they will need fewer nails through them into the wall plugs (not so important with painted finishes, but with unpainted hardwood the less fixings through the face of the timber the better). When the linings are in place, fit an architrave around the window, tacking it to the edge of the lining and to the wall plugs. ∎

SASH SECRETS TWO

Rather than have a sash window drop, Stan Thomas explains how to re-cord one

The modern method of sashbalancing is of course by spring sash balance, with solid jambs as opposed to boxed. However, there are very many boxed windows still around, and these need re-cording from time to time; any obvious signs of wear, and they should be seen to immediately, for a falling top sash can cause serious finger injuries. It was always the custom to keep the panes of glass for both upper and lower sashes equal in size. But what some people omitted to do was to extend the bottom horns of the top sash, so that should it fall these would strike the sill and so prevent the guillotine action at the meeting rails.

To free the sashes, tap a 1in chisel in between the stop beads and frame, starting at the centre and working towards each end, to release the bead from the frame. Now return to the centre, and gently lever away the beads, working again towards each end, and identify for replacing. The bottom sash can now be removed. These stop beads will have nails – usually 1½in ovals – protruding: on no account should they be driven back as the effect on the paintwork would be disastrous. Instead pull them through with a pair of pincers.

With a corner of the chisel, break the paint seal both inside and outside, along the lengths of the parting beads (fig. 1). Now tap the chisel down into the bead groove, tight against the bead, and lever out the bead; but starting this time at either end. Again identify for replacing, and take out the top, or outer sash.

Removal of the pocket pieces is an easy matter, indeed, they sometimes fall away, but remember to identify. The weights are now accessible; if the window is double-hung, ie. both top and bottom sashes, there will be a parting lath, or wagtail, between the weights. Remove one weight, and simply pull the lath to one side for access to the other.

Having removed the weights, the correct lengths of cord must be marked on the frame. Turn a sash on its side, remove all traces of old cord and nails, and mark on the inside face the lower extremity of the cord, X in fig. 2. Repeat this on the other side, and on the other sash. Put the outer sash in place in the frame, in its fully-open position, ie. right down, and transfer the X mark on to the frame (fig. 3). Repeat this with the other sash – again with the sash down.

Open out a knot of sash cord, tie one end to something strong and give it a good pre-stretching. Now tie a knot at one end, and a sash mouse (fig. 4) to the other – a clove hitch if you are good at knots – and feed the mouse over the top, outer, pulley. A mouse is a strip of lead, about 4in long attached to twine. Fish out the mouse at the pocket, and pull the entire length of cord through until the knot reaches the pulley. Up now with the mouse, and through the opposite outer pulley, and again pull through all the cord (fig. 5). Now to the opposite side inner pulley, and finally to the remaining inner pulley (fig. 6).

There are two types of weight; one has to be tied – bowline if you can – over the

Fig.1 Prise off the parting beads with a chisel

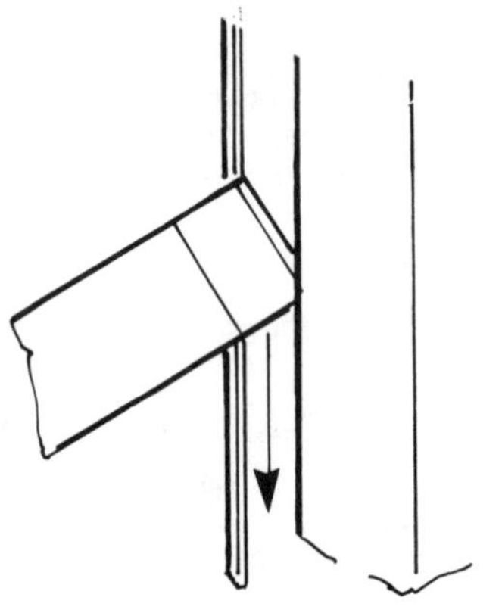

Fig.2 Mark X at the lower extremity of the cord

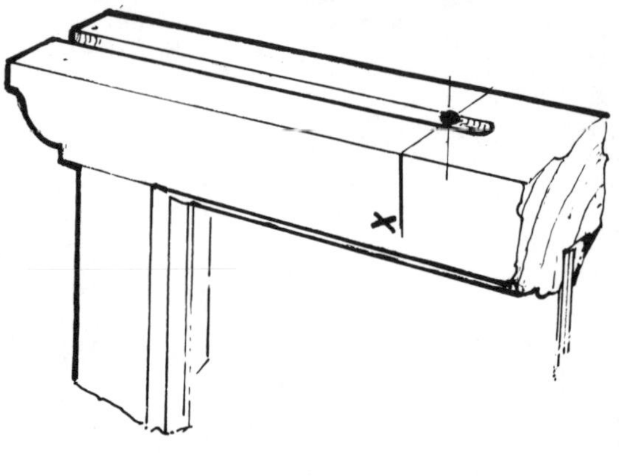

Fig.3 Marking end of cord on window frame

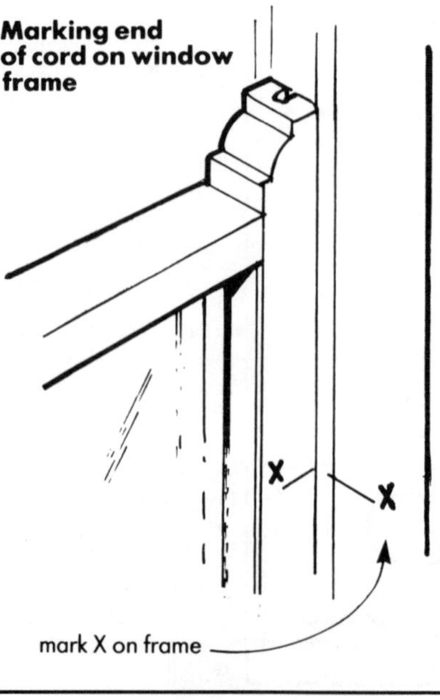

mark X on frame

Fig.4 A sash mouse

top, while the other has an eye hole for a simple half-hitch. It is important that they are properly tied, otherwise they will not hang plumb (fig. 7 A and B).

Tie a weight to the free end of the cord (fig. 6), and pull this until the weight rises up to the back of the pulley. Tap a 1in wire (round-head) through the cord and into the frame, near the pulley. Pick up mark X on the cord, and cut 1in longer to prevent the weight from clashing against the pulley when the window is opened fully. Do this four times (fig. 8).

It is now simply a matter of fixing the cords into their sash grooves (to mark X) with about six 1in wires per cord, using a cross-pein hammer for driving the nails down into the grooves. Be careful however, that the nails don't come too near the top, or the cord won't go over the pulley; and most important, that the sash isn't corded inside out, with putty on the inside – I've done that!

Cord the outer sash, and place in position; down of course. Replace the pocket pieces and the parting beads, then the inner sash and stop beads. Finally, remove the four nails that temporarily held the cords while they were being fixed to their sashes.

This, of course, is an ordinary double-hung window. But there are variations. In fig. 9 the two side jambs are boxed, but the centre is solid mullioned. In this case the sashes are hung 'one-up-one-down' (1 and 2 in fig. 9 looking from the inside). The left-hand cord of sash 1 goes in the normal manner, up over the pulley. But the right-hand cord would pass along under the head of the frame, hidden by a screwed cover-strip (fig. 10A). The right-hand cord of sash 2 is normal, while the left-hand passes along the head of the adjacent fixed sash (fig. 10B).

In a Venetian frame with solid mullions (fig. 11), the smaller, side sashes are fixed, while the cords for the two centre sashes go over the top. This task may seem daunting, and even re-cording ordinary sashes may be approached with some caution, but if the procedure is followed carefully the job is satisfyingly simple. ∎

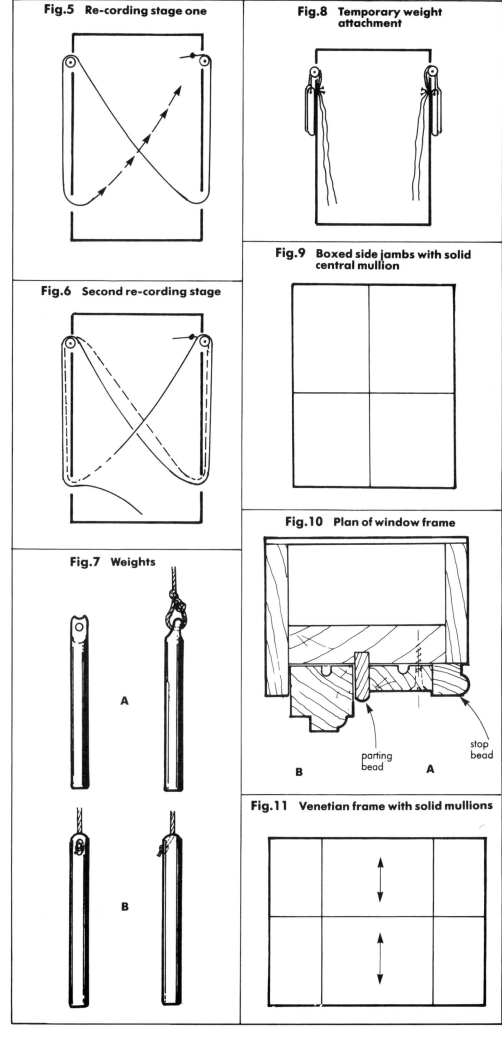

Fig.5 Re-cording stage one

Fig.6 Second re-cording stage

Fig.7 Weights

Fig.8 Temporary weight attachment

Fig.9 Boxed side jambs with solid central mullion

Fig.10 Plan of window frame

parting bead

stop bead

B

A

Fig.11 Venetian frame with solid mullions

WATER GATES

Leonard Markham visited a workshop that makes and repairs the lock gates on our canals and rivers

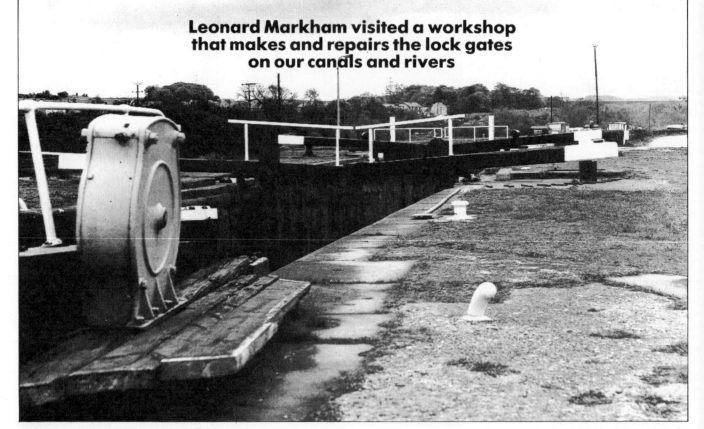

anals climb hills via the technology of the lock – essentially an aquatic lift controlled by sluiced head and tail gates. Invented by the Chinese in around 350 AD, the lock evolved independently in Europe, with the first record of hinged gates attributed to Leonardo da Vinci in 1497. The first major canal in the British Isles, the 15-lock Newry Navigation in County Down, opened in 1744, and was the forerunner of several thousand miles of waterways dug between the late 18th and early 19th centuries.

After decades of decline, canal restora-tion is on the increase, spurred principally by conservationist and leisure interests. Much of the work on repairing and replacing lock gates in the UK is undertaken by British Waterways, whose Stanley Ferry repair yard in west Yorkshire is one of four such establishments in the country. Situated near the famous Stanley Ferry aqueduct, a grecian-porticoed construction of 1839 on the Aire and Calder Navigation, the yard makes gates for all British Waterways regions, offering a service to both public and private sectors. Yard manager Malcolm Evison, a trained marine engineer and once a chief engineer in the Shell tanker fleet, gave me a technical tour.

Lock chamber levels are controlled by either single or paired, usually mitred gates; dimensions and designs vary accord-ing to canal widths, constructional con-straints, aesthetic and, in some cases, 'listed building' requirements. Fabrication is generally in unseasoned timber or steel, depending on local requirements, although advocates of timber point to its superior resilience and impact elasticity. For many years now the favourite timber for lock gates and inland canals has been English

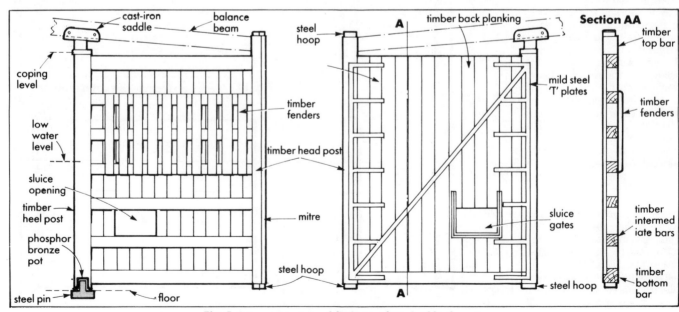

Fig. 1 Components and fittings of typical lock gates

oak, pre-cut to length and delivered wet.

British Waterway's demanding specification insists on home-grown, light-coloured, winter-felled timber, free from large, loose or dead knots, shakes, sapwood and waney edges. All baulk timber must be cut from the heart of the log. Despite these stringent requirements and the unusually large volumes and dimensions of timber needed, there are no supply problems.

For lock gates that are installed in brackish or sea-water conditions imported greenheart timber, which is exceptionally water-tolerant, is usually specified. This is a relatively straight-grained material, however, and tends to split along its entire length, resulting in constructional wastage and in-situ impact damage. It's also unpopular with woodworkers, as it's difficult to work and liable to crack, with splinters often becoming septic.

Rectangular lock gate frameworks, using members 9-14in thick, consist of vertical heads, pivotal heels and horizontal bars. Mortise-and-tenon joints, linseed-oiled and fixed with ramin dowels, are used throughout. Accurate cutting and in-situ swelling ensure strong jointing. Where customers prefer, this strength can be increased by using a special cement supplied by BIP Chemicals.

For many years, sluice doors – 'paddles' in canal terms – were also made in wood. Today, the Stanley Ferry yard uses a more robust, specially manufactured plastic sluice, housed above the bottom bar. The sluice can be either manually or power operated. The whole framework of the gate is strengthened by rebated and spiked 'L' and 'T' angle-plates made in mild steel. Head and heel ends are adzed to take the hoops. These prevent splitting and minimise wear.

Locked up: a typical set of lock gates, opposite, 'somewhere' in Britain, and, above, a pair of frames at the Stanley Ferry workshop

Lock makers: below left, routing rebates to take the 'T' and 'L' plates and, below right, cutting a tenon with a chainsaw

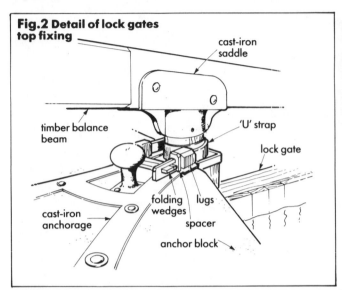

Fig.2 Detail of lock gates top fixing

cast-iron saddle
'U' strap
lock gate
timber balance beam
folding wedges
lugs
spacer
cast-iron anchorage
anchor block

Locking materials: oak planking to make gates watertight and galvanised nails made in the workshop

The hingeing mechanism at the sub erged end of the hollowed-out heel post is known as the pot, a phosphur-bronze recept-acle for the pivotal steel pin which is concreted into the door recess on the lock floor. At the other end, the heel is hinged to a mild steel or cast-iron frame set into the lock top. Clasping the heel post, a 'U' strap collar is fitted to anchorage lugs on the frame and wedged into position. Spacers between the wedges and the lugs allow for minor gate adjustments.

The recessed gate is operated by an angled fulcrum balance beam, fitted to a cast-iron saddle atop the heel post and jointed to the head. Gates are made watertight on the upstream side of the lock only, using 2-3in butt-jointed vertical oak planking, pre-drilled and fixed with 5in galvanised nails. Fitting refinements can include fenders, lock-top pedestrian planking and a variety of increasingly sophisticated mechanisms, including radio-controlled de-vices for operating sluice doors.

A set of gates, which are traditionally unfinished, normally lasts up to 40 years without replacement, although creosote or creosote-and-tar mixtures have sometimes been used as preservatives. To extend the life of its gates, perhaps to 75 years (they'll wait and see!), the Stanley workshop has begun to apply Weatherseal, a recently available non-sealant, wood-breathable pre-servative, offering combined waterproofing and bacterial fungal inhibition.

To cope with the exceptionally large and heavy sections involved in gate manufacture, specialist heavy-duty machinery is used. A 30-ton capacity Avery overhead crane provides safe lifting. A 30in bandsaw is used to cut timber to length immediately after delivery. With its 30ft long bed, a modernised Pickles planing machine readily handles all lengths of timber up to 27in thick and 22in wide. A companion Pickles mor-tising machine takes up to a 2½in chisel. Tenoning, minor sawing, routing and fixing are done with portable hand-tools.

There are problems. Some of the largest gates cannot be delivered by road and, fittingly, these are water-borne to their destination, from the canal basin that extends beyond the workshop doors. Others are 'knocked down' after manufacture and later re-erected on site.

An experienced and integrated workforce of carpenters, welders and fitters with a tradition going back over 130 years, the Stanley Ferry 'locksmiths' are proud of producing almost everything – even their own nails – in-house. After several lean years, they have recently completed their 35th set of gates in 12 months. A growing order book, hundreds of miles of still derelict canal, and a popular apprentice scheme point to a bright future.

In 1981, alongside the old and now redundant aqueduct, a successor crossing was built by British Waterways – evidence of a steadily increasing optimism in the commercial viability of canals. With escal-ating road transport costs and growing congestion, the 'slow but sure' economics of canals can only have even wider appeal. ■

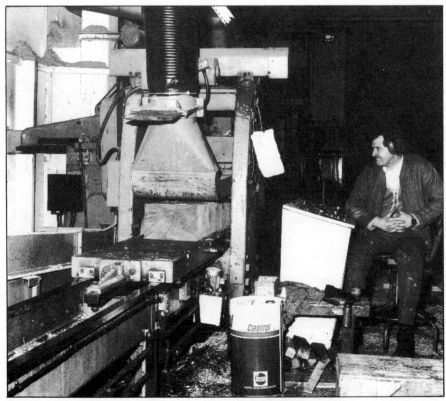

Locks away: the modernised Pickles planer can take planks up to 30ft long

ACKNOWLEDGEMENTS

The Publishers would like to thank the following for the inclusion of their articles in this book.

Wooden wonder	Stuart Howe	May	1986
Trouble-free curving	Stan Thomas	July	1987
The craft of cabinetmaking	David Savage	February	1986
The craft of cabinetmaking	David Savage	March	1986
The craft of cabinetmaking	David Savage	February	1987
Scarfing it	Malcolm Wintle	November	1986
Where scribe and mitre meet	Stan Thomas	September	1988
A cottage door	Bob Grant	January	1983
Miniature marvels	Michael Terry	December	1987
The building contractor	Tony Sattin	January	1986
Clever cleaner	Don Solman	June	1987
Smoke your own	John Turner	December	1986
Not so dusty?	Dr Bob Clewlow	February	1986
A coffee table	Bob Grant	January	1983
Times past, times present, times future	John Helmsley	May	1988
Reflections on a bench	Alan Peters	March	1983
Furniture or fantasy	Philip Monaghan	February	1990
Into shape	Mark Kenning	August	1989
Power planting	Ivan Phillips	July	1989
Hanging around	Jim Robinson	September	1988
Back numbers	Dr Waring Robinson	August	1988
A seat in the sun	Peter Anstey	April	1988
The great craftsman	Alan Peters & John Helmsley	March	1988
Computer consolation	Bob Grant	October	1987
Three-quarter times table	Jim Robinson	August	1989
Brolly folly	Tim Kidman	January	1987
Upstanding	Mike Rate	February	1990
Doubled up	Leslie Stuttle	September	1986
Table-top seat	Vic Taylor	March	1986
Crossing the bar	Jim Corcoran	February	1986
Hand-made and handsome	Mark Ripley	February	1986
The quiet American	Aidan Walker	January	1986
The Morris men	Max Burrough	January	1986
The watertight case	A & G Bridgewater	May	1986
Past defence	Peter Howlett	September	1986
Timber support	Brian Boothby	August	1988
Wicker's world	Leonard Markham	November	1987
Distressing news	Noel Leach	June	1989
Wheelspin	Frank Lapworth	July	1986
The flat spin	Roger Sear	July	1986
Happy returns	Rik Middleton	July	1987
Wooden thoroughbreds	Leonard Markham	May	1986
Sash secrets one	Alec Limon	May	1989
Sash secrets two	Stan Thomas	May	1989
Water gates	Leonard Markham	June	1989